# America's Providential History

Including

*Biblical Principles of Education, Government, Politics, Economics, and Family Life*

## Mark A. Beliles & Stephen K. McDowell

*Providence Foundation*
*P.O. Box 6759*
*Charlottesville, Virginia 22906*

Published by the **Providence Foundation**, Charlottesville, Virginia.

First Printing, December 1989

. . . .

Eighth Printing, March 1996

*For information on purchasing additional copies of this book or learning more about the work of the Providence Foundation contact: Providence Foundation, P.O. Box 6759, Charlottesville, Virginia, 22906, Phone/Fax: (804) 978-4535.*

Printed in the United States of America

ISBN 1-887456-00-7

*We are grateful to Arnold Friberg for permission to use his painting 'The Prayer at Valley Forge"on our cover.*

Cover Painting

### The Prayer at Valley Forge

Valley Forge itself inspired this splendid masterpiece of patriotic art. Biblical painter Arnold Friberg has created a monumental and sacred scene, capturing what many Americans feel are the deep spiritual roots of our country. For further information about this painting contact: Urban Art Gallery, 309 Trolley Square, Salt Lake City, UT 84102, or call toll free, 1-800-745-3169.

# ACKNOWLEDGEMENTS

*Both of the authors were initially inspired to study and teach the material in this book through two sources: 1) the book The Light and the Glory by Peter Marshall and David Manuel and 2) the ministry and encouragement of Bob and Rose Weiner. Our ideas were then dramatically influenced by scholarly writings and loving personal training of Miss Rosalie Slater and the late Miss Verna Hall. Many other individuals have contributed to our development, and their writings are cited in this book. Mike Davis designed the layout, and we thank him for all the long hours and hard work which was invaluable. The word processing of David Smith, Sherry Bierley, Jane Michelle Kelly and Jackie Janitch is so appreciated as well. Our wives, Nancy Beliles and Beth McDowell, have contributed the greatest amount in our lives and work. Their names will not be found in the footnotes or credits of this book, but if you could read our hearts there you would find them above all other names except that of our Lord Jesus Christ.*

# America's Providential History

## Table of Contents

# Introduction

In *America's Providential History* we examine the history of America from a Christian perspective. Since God is the author of history and He is carrying out His plan in the earth through history, any view of the history of America, or any country, that ignores God is not true history. He is Sovereign over His creation and "His Story" in the earth, and is at work in significant, and seemingly insignificant, events to accomplish His purposes for mankind. This is a providential view of history and was held by the vast majority of those people who founded this nation.

While we do not look at all the events in America's birth and growth, we do highlight the Providence and purposes of God, and the faith of our founders. Understanding this will provide a proper framework in which other historical information can be properly placed.

We begin the history of America with Creation, and Adam and Eve, because if one does not understand God's plan and purpose for man from the beginning, he will not be able to understand how America fits into His overall plan. The history of America, or any country, cannot be studied as an isolated event.

We have designed the book to be easily studied and digested, yet we have included many excerpts from original sources (for example, numerous pages of Bradford's *History of Plymouth Plantation* and shorter excerpts of various sermons of the colonial clergy) to introduce modern Americans to the ideas, character, and literacy level of early Americans. Colonial Americans were educated far better by the home, church, and private sector than our youth today are by modern state schools, and at a fraction of the cost.

*America's Providential History* teaches more than just historical Christian facts. Biblical principles of education, law, government, and economics, the Christian idea of man and government, the Chain of Liberty moving westward -- in short a Biblical world-view -- are imparted through this book. While all of America's founders were not Christians (though a great majority were), almost every one had a Biblical world-view, even the non-Christians.

Most of our founders were Christians, but this does not mean they were without fault. Providential history does not mean "sinless" or "sugarcoated" history. Like the Bible, it introduces people God has used for His purposes, even though they had short-comings and sins not to be emulated. God is glorified even more when we see fallible, finite men used by Him. Since most modern secular texts tend to provide plenty of criticism of America's leaders (much of which is unfounded), our text has chosen to provide what you cannot find there in order to provide a balance. America's early leaders did sin, like all men, but their heart was to obey God. Today most of our leaders have a much different heart and mind.

Most Americans today, including most Christians, have a humanistic (man-centered) world-view. This is one great difference in early and present-day America and is a primary reason why our nation is experiencing great problems. Ideas have consequences. The internal beliefs and ideas of a people are expressed in their external actions. Today, we are experiencing the fruit of secularism. To see Godly change occur in America we must renew our minds to view the world from God's perspective as revealed in the Bible -- we must infuse the Faith of our Fathers into the life of our country.

In other words, we as Christians must learn what it means to disciple a nation. The study of America's history provides the best example of this, because colonial Christians discipled their nation. Part of the goal of the Providence Foundation, and our vision as its directors, is to accomplish this task. This book is one resource to assist in this endeavor (other books, resources, and seminars are listed in the back). We have not only worked to train Americans to think and act from a Biblical perspective, but also people from scores of other nations; after all, we are to make disciples of **all** the nations.

*Providence* is a word that signifies the Bible doctrine of the overruling power of God that governs in the affairs of men. The Providence Foundation is working to establish such an understanding in the hearts and minds of all people. We urge Pastors, Christian leaders, Christian schools, and home schoolers to use this book as a text for a regular class to help disciple people in a Biblical world-view. Many already do so.

The people of a free nation must have a foundation that will support liberty, for without it, that nation will surely fall. The great nineteenth century statesman and politician Daniel Webster declared:

> *"If we and our posterity shall be true to the Christian religion, if we and they shall live always in the fear of God and shall respect His Commandments,... we may have the highest hopes of the future fortunes of our country;... But if we and our posterity neglect religious instruction and authority, violate the rules of eternal justice, trifle with the injunctions of morality, and recklessly destroy the political constitution which holds us together, no man can tell how sudden a catastrophe may overwhelm us that shall bury all our glory in profound obscurity."*

To bring God's liberty to the nations and secure their future fortunes is the goal of the Providence Foundation. We start Chapter One with a quote by Benjamin Franklin: *"He who shall introduce into public affairs the principles of primitive Christianity shall change the face of the world."* We are working in this way to change the face of America and the world.

---

## Chapter 1

---

# God's Plan for the Nations

*"He who shall introduce into public affairs the principles of primitive Christianity will change the face of the world."*[1]
*-Benjamin Franklin*

The goal of *America's Providential History* is to equip Christians to be able to introduce Biblical principles into the public affairs of America, and every nation in the world, and in so doing bring Godly change throughout the world. We will be learning how to establish a Biblical form (and power) of government in America and we will see how our present governmental structures must be changed. Since the principles we will be learning are valid in every society and in any time in history, they will be able to be applied throughout the world and not just in America. As we learn to operate nations on Biblical principles, we will be bringing liberty to the nations of the world and hence fulfilling part of God's plan for the nations.

### The Need for World Reformation

The Bible reveals to us that the world longs for liberation. Romans 8:19,21 says that "... creation eagerly waits for the revealing of the sons of God... because creation itself also will be delivered from the bondage of corruption into the glorious liberty of the children of God" (NKJV). The following statistics, compiled by David Barret, show the desperate need for real answers to world problems:

"(1.)Megapoverty - 2.1 billion people (46% of world) live in poverty, of whom 800 million live in absolute poverty; 1.1 billion without adequate shelter, 2.1 billion without adequate water supply, 3 billion with unsafe water and bad sanitation, 800 million adults illiterate, 850 million with no access to schools, 1.5 billion with no access to medical care, 500 million on edge of starvation (20 million starvation-related deaths a year), 1.5 billion hungry or malnourished.

"(2.)Abortion - 75% of world's population live in countries where abortion is legal, though regarded by most Christians as murder; 25% of all pregnancies worldwide end in abortion, resulting in 65 million abortions a year of which 38% are illegal.

"(3.)Military coups - Armed forces' takeovers of governments escalate to over 50% of world's countries.

"(4.)Debt - Third World owes First World more than $1 trillion; corporate debt exceeds $1.5 trillion; possibility of global crash imminent.

"(5.)Human rights - Increasing vulnerability of human rights; widespread government use of torture, increasing from 98 countries in 1980 to 110 countries, especially in South America (Colombia, Peru, Paraguay, Chile), Africa and Asia (Syria, Pakistan, Iran, etc.).

"(6.)Refugees - World total of refugees of all kinds in asylum countries fluctuates around 20 million from 1965 to 1987.

"(7.)Megacrime - International crime now costs $400 billion a year; megafraud and computer crime $44 billion; illegal hard drug industry and traffic $110 billion, representing 38% of all organized crime; includes 25 million cocaine users in USA ($25 billion), 60 million marijuana users.

"(8.)Secret Police - Scores of national police forces around world (KGB,DINA,SAVAK,BOSS,SIS, as well as in less recent history OGPU,NKVD,Gestapo) use surveillance, terror, imprisonment and torture to destroy human rights and to persecute alleged enemies of state.

"(9.)Totalitarian Governments - The number of citizens killed by totalitarian or extreme authoritarian governments reaches 130 million since 1900 (1918-53, USSR kills 40 million citizens, China under Mao 45 million, 1975-79 Cambodia 2 million, et alia), far greater than 36 million combatants killed in wars since 1900; absolutist governments now mankind's deadliest scourge.

"(10.)Arms - Worldwide annual military expenditure (arms race) rises from $2 billion in 1969 to $650 billion in 1982, to $940 billion in 1985, with $4 trillion from 1983-88.

"(11.)Global terrorism - International terrorism proliferates around world: blackmail, bombings, kidnappings, assassinations, hijackings."[2]

## *The Answers Are Found in the Bible*

The truth of the Bible (John 8:32) provides mankind with a Theology of Liberty that brings real freedom to those individuals and nations who are oppressed. From the beginning of time, God created the earth and made man responsible to rule over it. Genesis 1:28 says: "And God blessed them; and God said to them, 'Be fruitful and multiply, and fill the earth and subdue it; and rule over... the earth.'" When man rejected God's Law, and lost the ability to not only govern himself, but also to govern society, public tyranny and oppression reigned through sinful men.

Through the ministry and death of Jesus Christ, however, the power for both self- and civil government was restored to mankind. Though internal liberty was a primary focus of Jesus Christ, it must not be overlooked that His inaugural and farewell sermons both emphasized external civil liberty. In Luke 4:18, Christ's first public message focused on "liberty" for "the poor... the captives... [and] those who are oppressed..." It is safe to assume that poverty, slavery, tyranny and injustice were on the Lord's mind when, in His final sermon, He commissioned His followers to "Go therefore and make disciples of all the nations..." (Matthew 28:19). The great Bible commentator studied by our Founding Fathers, Matthew Henry, explains that "the principal intention of this commission" is clear. It is to "... do your utmost to make the nations Christian nations."[3] This is God's plan for the nations.

The apostle Paul understood this plan very well and sought to communicate it to the Christians of the first century. In 1 Corinthians 6:2 Paul asks a vital question: "Do you not know that the Christians will one day judge and govern the world?" (Amplified Bible)" If this is true, Paul says, then they ought to at least be competent to hold public offices such as the local judgeships in Greece. To those Christians in Corinth, as well as in America today, who incorrectly assume that Paul means we should rule **only** in the next age after the second coming of Christ, the next question and answer of the apostle is aimed: "Do you not know that we shall judge angels? How much more the matters of this life?"(vs. 3). Paul then rebukes the Christians for their apathy and irresponsibility that allowed non-Christians to be in control: "If then you have

3

law courts dealing with matters of this life, do you appoint them as judges who are of no account in the church. I say this to your **shame**" (vs. 4-5).

This shameful situation has become the reality in America today. The battle for God's earth (Psalm 24:1) is being lost today mainly because Christians have thought that God does not really care about such things. They fail to see that Christ taught us to focus our prayers, not on heaven, but upon His kingdom coming "on earth as it is in heaven" (Matthew 6:9,10). The results of such ignorance and neglect of duty has been costly in the 20th century. America has experienced great revival since 1900, leading to over 60 million people claiming to be "Christian," yet simultaneously our nation has plummeted into debauchery and corruption at a rate unparalleled in our history. In 1900, Africa was about 1% Christian. By 1988 the Christian populace of that continent had grown to about 50%! However, in that same year 85% of Africa lived under Communist and totalitarian regimes. Historically, the gospel has liberated nations, but why not in Africa? One primary reason is that Christian missionaries have offered African nations a truncated Gospel message devoid of Biblical answers to anything not strictly of a pietistic or personal nature.

As a result, these and other nations of the world, have not been presented with a true Biblical theology of liberty and so are being increasingly deceived by Satan's counterfeit. The devil's "Liberation Theology" incorrectly identifies the root of public evil as the socio-economic environment, and claims that liberation comes through violent revolution, followed by the people's dependency on a government they can trust. Christ, in contrast, says the root of evil is the heart of man, and therefore, external liberty is possible only when it flows from the internal to the external. Revival therefore must precede Reformation.

Jesus Christ spoke of this "cause and effect" principle in Luke 6:43-45:

> "For there is no good tree which produces bad fruit; nor, on the other hand, a bad tree which produces good fruit. For each tree is known by its own fruit;... The good man out of the good treasure of his heart brings forth what is good; and the evil man out of the evil treasure of his heart brings forth what is evil."

Every effect has a cause. The fruit is determined by the root. Man's conduct is determined by man's heart. The external is determined by the internal. All external "forms" or structures come from some internal "power." We will call this "the principle of Power and Form." The Christian religion is the essential power needed to create and preserve a form of government that is free and just.

# *History is Shaped By the Heart of Man Under the Providence of God*

The external affairs of a nation are a reflection of the condition of the hearts of the people. Historian Charles Rollin reflects the view of most eighteenth century writers in stating that God is sovereign over history, but deals with nations dependent upon the heart and action of the people. He wrote: "Nothing gives history a greater superiority to many branches of literature, than to see in a manner imprinted, in almost every page of it, the precious footsteps and shining proofs of this great truth, viz. that God disposes all events as Supreme Lord and Sovereign; that He alone determines the fate of kings and the duration of empires; and that he transfers the government of kingdoms from one nation to another because of the unrighteous dealings and wickedness committed therein."[4]

You cannot understand history without understanding Divine Providence. George Bancroft, eminent historian of American history in the 19th century said, "Providence is the light of history and the soul of the world. God is in history and all history has a unity because God is in it." Providential history is true history. Many modern educators deny the Providential view of history and would have us believe that their promotion of one of several "secular" views of history is simply the recounting of brute facts. They fail to tell their students that their own humanistic presuppositions and religious doctrines determine their choice of people, places, principles, and events. They fail to communicate that neutrality is not possible in the teaching of history, for the historian's world-view will dictate his perspective. Even as there are not many interpretations of Scripture (2 Pet. 1:20, 21), neither are there of history - there is really only one correct view; that which is the Author's interpretation and perspective. God is the Author of Scripture and History.

*George Bancroft*

Reverend S.W. Foljambe, in 1876, defined history as "the autobiography of Him 'who worketh all things after the counsel of His will' (Eph. 1:11) and who is graciously timing all events after the counsel of His Christ, and the Kingdom of God on earth. It is His-Story."[5]

The Bible overwhelmingly affirms this truth. Let us examine just a few Scriptures along this line:

**Acts 17:24-26** - "The God who made the world... gives to all life and breath and all things; and He made... every nation..., having determined their appointed times, and the boundaries of their habitation..."

**1 Timothy 6:15-16** - "He is the blessed and only Sovereign, the King of Kings and Lord of lords;... To Him be honor and eternal dominion! Amen."

**Proverbs 16:9-10** - "The mind of man plans his way, but the Lord directs his steps. A divine decision is in the lips of the king."

**Job 12:23** - "He makes the nations great, then destroys them; He enlarges the nations, then leads them away."

**Psalms 22:28** - "For the kingdom is the Lord's, and He rules over the nations."

**Daniel 2:21** - "It is He who changes the times and the epochs; He removes kings and establishes kings."

**Daniel 4:17, 26** - "The Most High is ruler over the realm of mankind;... Your kingdom will be assured to you after you recognize it is Heaven that rules."

## *The Founders of the United States of America believed in the Providential View of History.*

Webster's 1828 Dictionary defines "Providence" as "the care and superintendence which God exercises over His creatures. By 'Divine Providence' is understood 'God Himself.'" This definition, written in the times in which our Founders lived, is significant, for it helps us to see what they meant when they used this term in their writings. They also used many other names for God other than simply "God" or "Jesus." George Washington's writings reveal 54 different titles, Abraham Lincoln used 49 and Robert E. Lee used 45. This reflects the depth of understanding our Founding Fathers had of God and His involvement in human affairs.

Here are some statements that reveal how America's Founders recognized God's hand in history:

### *William Bradford, Governor of the Pilgrims*

"But these things did not dismay them... for their desires were set on the ways of God, and to enjoy His ordinances; but they rested on His Providence and knew whom they had believed."[6]

### *Declaration of Independence*

"And for the support of this Declaration, with a firm reliance on the Protection of Divine Providence, we mutually pledge to each other our Lives, our Fortunes and our Sacred Honor."

### *Benjamin Franklin addressing the Constitutional Convention*

"How has it happened, Sir, that we have not hitherto once thought of humbly appealing to the Father of lights to illuminate our understandings? In the beginning of the contest with Great Britain, when we were sensible to danger, we had daily prayers in this room for Divine protection. Our prayers, Sir, were heard and

*Benjamin Franklin*

they were graciously answered...I have lived, Sir, a long time and the longer I live, the more convincing proofs I see of this truth - that God governs in the affairs of men. - <u>And if a sparrow cannot fall to the ground without His notice, is it probable that an empire can rise without His aid?</u> We have been assured, Sir, in the sacred writings that 'except the Lord build the house, they labor in vain that build it.'...I firmly believe this..."[7]

### The United States House of Representatives in 1854

"The people of these United States, from their earliest history to the present time, have been led by the hand of a Kind Providence, and are indebted for the countless blessings of the past and present, and dependent for continued prosperity in the future upon Almighty God... The great vital and conservative element in our system is the belief of our people in the pure doctrines and divine truths of the gospel of Jesus Christ."[8]

### George Washington's Thanksgiving Proclamation, 1789.

"It is the duty of all nations to acknowledge the Providence of Almighty God, to obey His will, to be grateful for His benefits, and humbly to implore His protection and favor."

*George Washington*

It is absolutely vital that our nation learns of its Providential history once again. Rev. A.W. Foljambe warns that, "The more thoroughly a nation deals with its history, the more decidedly will it recognize and own an over-ruling Providence therein, and the more religious a nation it will become; while the more superficially it deals with its history, seeing only secondary causes and human agencies, the more irreligious will it be."[9]

A lack of providential education contributes more than any other factor to the rise of secularism in a nation -- a separation of history from God as the Author of history.

# Chapter 2

# Providential Geography

God's plan for the nations has been unfolding in a specific geographic direction. This geographical march of history is called the **Chain of Christianity** or the **Chain of Liberty**. Another way to define the **Chain of Liberty** is the sequence of events in the lives of men and nations that are links or stepping stones in history which result in bringing forth internal and external liberty.

The Bible attests to this geographical march of the Gospel:

And they passed through the Phrygian and Galatian region, having been forbidden by the Holy Spirit to speak the word in Asia; and when they had come to Mysia, they were trying to go into Bithynia, and the Spirit of Jesus did not permit them; and passing by Mysia, they came down to Troas. And a vision appeared to Paul in the night: a certain man of Macedonia was standing and appealing to him and saying, 'Come over to Macedonia and help us.' And when he had seen the vision, immediately we sought to go into Macedonia, concluding that God had called us to preach the gospel to them" (Acts 16:6-10)

Why did God forbid Paul to speak the word in Asia? It is because He had other plans for the spread of the gospel. Paul and his companions were trying to go into Bithynia (northeast of where they were in Mysia) to preach the word, but God called them west into Europe. This was not by chance, but by God's choice in accordance with His plan for reaching the world with the gospel. From the beginning God has had a systematic plan for filling the earth with his glory.

We know from later Biblical events (see for example Romans 15:19,28 -- Illyricum is the Baltic region of Europe) and world history that the spread of Christianity (and hence civilization) has occurred in a westward direction. It is true that early disciples carried the gospel into Northern Africa and in much of Asia, but it was in Europe where Christianity firmly took root and affected the entire society. As we will see, Christianity produced internal and external liberty in a westward direction. This is why we speak of the westward move of the Chain of Christianity.

It seems as if God's direction is westward. Even as the sun rises in the east and travels to the west, so His Son rose in the east and has traveled to the west. It is interesting that the children of Israel entered the promised land, not traveling the shortest route, northeast, but traveling from east to west. In the tabernacle in the wilderness, the priests moved from east to west as they approached the presence of God in the Holy of Holies. Matthew 24:27 states that "just as the lightning comes from the east, and flashes even to the west, so shall the coming of the Son of Man be." Mark 16:21 says, "Jesus Himself sent out through them from east to west the sacred and imperishable proclamation of eternal salvation."

God had prepared Europe in many ways in order for it to fulfill its part in God's plan for the world. In particular, we want to look at Europe's geographic individuality--its unique placement on the earth in relation to the other continents, its unique geographic structure, coastline, and climate, and its unique people groups. Studying these, in conjunction with history, certainly reveals the sovereignty of God over the nations.

## The Individuality of the Continents

Like Europe, God has prepared all the continents for a specific purpose. Insight into the purpose of a continent or nation can be revealed by studying its geographic structure.

**What is geography?** The word "geography" is derived from two greek words meaning "the earth" and "to write". We could figuratively say that geography is God's handwriting on the earth. (He is the only one that I know who is big enough to write on the earth!)

"Christian" geography (which is true geography) is the view that the earth's origin, end, purposes, and physiography (physical structure, climate, plant and animal distribution) are for Christ and His glory.

Shakespeare was correct in saying that "all the world's a stage." God is the One who has created the props, placing the mountains, oceans, rivers, seas, deserts, islands, and continents just where He wanted them in order that they might assist in carrying out His plan for mankind on the earth.

## God's Principle of Individuality

All of God's creation is a reflection of his infinity, diversity, and individuality. God does not create carbon-copy entities, but distinct and unique individualities, be they animals, plants, humans, planets, stars, etc. While a unity exists among all creation, since all is created by God, there also exists a great diversity, since God himself is three, yet one. God displays the principle of individuality, and his creation does as well.

### People display the principle of individuality.

There are certain characteristics that all humans have (unity), yet no two people are alike (diversity):

- Each person has a unique purpose and call from God.
- Each person also has unique characteristics, both internal and external.

One external characteristic that you possess that no one else has are your fingerprints. Of the five billion people on the earth today, no two have the same fingerprints. You also have a unique profile, voiceprints, and nerve pattern on the inside of your eye. Internal characteristics that are uniquely yours include your thoughts, attitudes, and emotions. These are just a few characteristics you possess that reveal that God made you "the one and only you".

God gives us certain internal and external characteristics that enable us to fulfill our God-given purpose and call. (As an example, God made Eric Liddell physically fast so that he could win races and bring God glory through it.)

### Nations also display God's principle of individuality.

Like individuals, nations have a unique purpose. As an example, Babylon was used by God to bring his judgement upon Israel by taking them into captivity. We will see throughout this book how God has raised up and put down nations of the world for his purposes.

Nations also have unique characteristics, such as their time of existence in history, their power, national spirit, geographic location, boundaries, and structure. As with people, God gives nations unique characteristics in order that they can fulfill their divine purposes in history.

### Continents reflect the principle of design

Arnold Guyot, a nineteenth century scientist and professor of Geography at Princeton University, was an expert in the Providential view of Geography. In his book *The Earth and Man*, Guyot wrote:

"We must elevate ourselves to the moral world to understand the physical world: the physical world has no meaning except by and for the moral world...

"...it is correct to say that inorganic nature is made for organized nature, and the whole globe for man, as both are made for God, the origin and end of all things.... science may attempt to comprehend the purpose of God, as to the destinies of nations, by examining with care the theatre, seemingly arranged by Him for the realization of the new social order, towards which humanity is tending..."[1]

## Contrasting the Southern and Northern Continents

In his book *Physical Geography,* 1873, Guyot summarizes the distinction of the northern and southern continents and concludes the "the southern continents, may be designated the continents of nature" and "the northern continents, may properly be designated the continents of history."[2]

In *The Earth and Man,* Guyot gives these distinctions:

"The continents of the North are more indented, more articulated; their contours are more varied. Gulfs and inland seas cut very deep into the mass of their lands, and detach from the principal trunk a multitude of peninsulas...A great number of continental islands are scattered along their shores, and are a new source of wealth to them...

"The southern continents, on the other hand, are massive, entire, without indentations, without inland seas or deep inlets, scanty in articulations of every kind and in islands...

"The continents of the North are more open to maritime life, to the life of commerce; they are more richly organized; they are better made to stimulate improvement.

"The northern continents are brought nearer together, more consolidated.... whence the others appear to radiate in all directions, losing themselves as they taper off in the ocean.... Owing to this greater nearness, to the facility of communication between one continent and another... the three northern continents have a mutual relationship not to be mistaken...

"The continents of the South are more remote from each other than the foregoing. Broad oceans separate them even to isolation..."[3]

### The Southern Continents-- The Continents of Nature

Guyot calls the southern continents, the "continents of nature". These reflect the glory of God in various ways. As Guyot writes in the conclusion of *Physical Geography*, "the fullness of nature's life is typified by Africa, with its superabundant wealth and power of animal life; South America, with its exuberance of vegetation; and Australia, with its antiquated forms of plants and animals."[4]

### The Northern Continents--The Continents of History

*Australian Animals*

He refers to the northern continents as the "continents of history", for it is in the northern continents that man has progressed and developed throughout history. The southern continents are just beginning to enter into the historical development of mankind. This has not happened by chance, but by God's choice. He has even positioned and structured the continents so as to assist in the westward move of the *Chain of Christianity*.

## The climate affects the development of mankind

The climate, as well, has assisted in the progress of mankind. While the northern continents lie primarily in a temperate climate zone, the Southern Continents lie primarily in the tropical zone. This tropical climate is conducive for plant and animal life to flourish. Yet with man it is otherwise.

Guyot writes:

"Here is the reason, gentlemen, that the Creator has placed the cradle of mankind in the midst of the continents of the North, so well made, by their forms, by their structure, by their climate, as we shall soon see, to stimulate and hasten individual development and that of human societies; and not at the centre of the tropical regions, whose balmy but innervating and treacherous atmosphere would perhaps have lulled him to sleep the sleep of death in his very cradle. . ."[5]

The temperate climate incites man to action and challenges him to labor which assists in his development and growth.

"The man of the temperate regions is the... most favored. Invited to labor by everything around him, he soon finds, in the exercise of all his faculties, at once progress and well-being."[6]

"In the temperate climates all is activity, movement. The alternations of heat and cold, the changes of the seasons, a fresher and more bracing air, incite man to a constant struggle, to forethought, to the vigorous employment of all his faculties."[7]

## *The purpose of the continents of history*

### *Asia, the continent of origins*

In his conclusion to *Physical Geography*, Arnold Guyot summarizes the characteristics and functions of the continents of history:

"Asia is the largest of the continents, the most central, the only one with which all the others are closely connected; and the one whose different physical regions show the greatest contrasts, and are separated by the greatest barriers. This great and strongly marked continent is the continent of origins. The human family, its races and civilizations, and the systems of religion which rule the most enlightened nations, all had their beginning here. By the great diversity of its physical features and climate, and the strong barriers isolating them one from another, Asia was admirably fitted to promote the formation of a diversity of races; while its close connection with the other continents facilitated their dispersion throughout the earth.

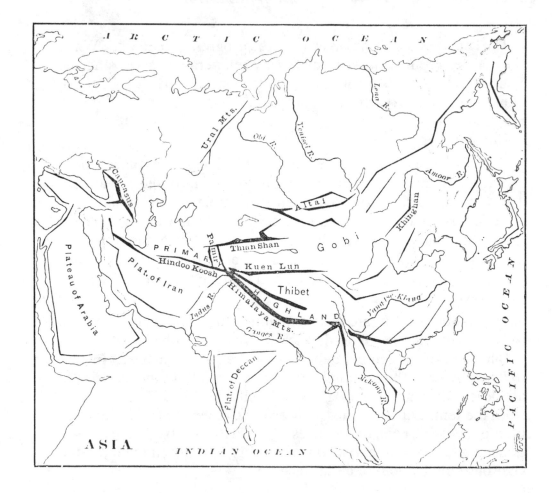

## Europe, the Continent of Development

"Europe shows a diversity of structure even greater than that of Asia; but with smaller areas, more moderate forms of relief, less extreme contrasts of climate, a more generally fertile soil, and everywhere an abundance of the most useful minerals; while the relative extent of its coast line - its maritime zone - is greater than that of any other continent. This continent is especially fitted, by its diversity, to foster the formation of distinct nationalities, each developing in an especial direction. Moreover, the proximity of these nations one to another, the greater facility of communication between them, and, above all, the common highway to the sea, nowhere very distant, facilitates mutual intercourse, the lack of which arrested the progress of the civilization of Asia. Though not the continent of origins, Europe is emphatically the continent of development. The Indo-European race - the people of progress - find their fullest expansion and activity, not in their original seat in Iran, but in Europe, whence they are spreading over all the quarters of the globe. The arts and learning of antiquity attained their highest development, not in western Asia and Egypt, the places of their origin, but in Greece and Rome. Christianity, also, only germinated in western Asia. Transplanted to Europe, it gradually attained its full development, and became the foundation on which is reared the vast and noble edifice of modern civilization."

As Guyot has noted, Asia (and particularly the Middle East) has been the center for the origins, from science, math, and languages, to Christianity, religions, and mankind.

While these things, and more, originated in Asia, they did not develop there, but in Europe. God had arranged the structure of the earth to assure that the *Chain of Christianity* would move, not south into Africa or east into Asia, but westward into Europe. Great physical barriers lie both in Africa (the Sahara Desert) and Asia that prohibited civilization from spreading into the heart of these continents.

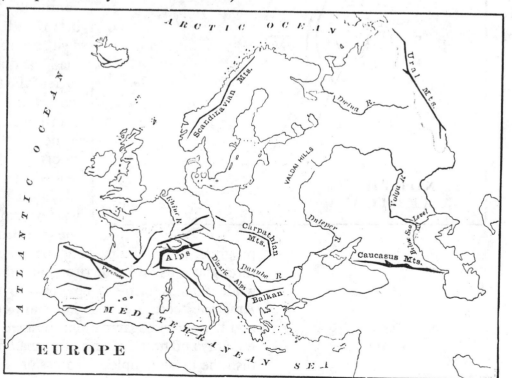

15

When Paul was called westward into Europe, he had no problem getting there, for the Mediterranean Sea provided easy access to the European Continent. It would have been quite different had he attempted to go into central Africa or Asia.

The physical structure of the continents has helped to assure that Europe would be the continent of development.

### North America, The Continent of Fulfillment and Propagation

"America, different in position, structure, and climatic conditions, from both the other northern continents, seems destined to play a part in the history of mankind unlike that of Europe and Asia, though not less noble than either. The structure of this continent is characterized by a unity and simplicity as striking as is the diversity of Europe. In its climate, those contrasts in temperature which are so violent in Asia, and still prevail in Europe, are obliterated. Nowhere do we find in America those local centres, each having a strongly marked individuality, which fostered the progress of the race in its infancy and its youth; but everywhere provision is made for mutual intercourse, a common life, and the blending of the entire population into one. Evidently this continent was not designed to give birth and development to a new civilization; but to receive one ready-made, and to furnish to the cultivated race of the Old World the scene most worthy of their activity. Its vast plains, overflowing with natural wealth, are turned towards Europe, and its largest rivers discharge into the Atlantic; while its lofty mountains, and less fertile lands, are removed far towards its western shores. Thus it seems to invite the Indo-European race, the people of progress, to new fields of action; to encourage their expansion throughout its entire territory, and their fusion into one nation; while it opens for them a pathway to all the nations of the earth. America, therefore, with her cultured and progressive people, and her social organization, founded upon the principle of the equality and brotherhood of all mankind, seems destined to furnish the most complete expression of the Christian civilization;

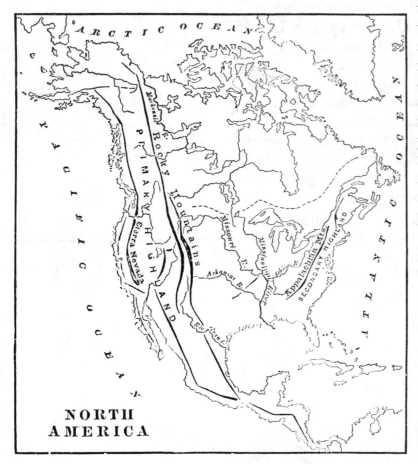

NORTH AMERICA

and to become the fountain of a new and higher life for all the races of men."[8]

That which originated in Asia and developed in Europe has had its greatest fulfillment in America. In addition, America has served as a propagator of those areas of fulfillment, from the Gospel and ideas of civil and religious freedom to scientific ideas and technological advancements: All the continents of the world have in recent history been affected by the things America has propagated.

America is the only nation in the world that is made up of people from every nation in the world. It is truly a melting pot. The physical geography of America promotes the blending together of all the peoples who came and settled this land.

Many historians have acknowledged the Providential preparation of America. Emma Willard stated: "In observing the United States, there is much to convince us, that an Almighty, Overruling Providence, designed from the first, to place here a great, united people."[9]

Alexis de Tocqueville wrote:

"Although the vast country which we have been describing was inhabited by many indigenous tribes, it may justly be said, at the time of its discovery by Europeans, to have formed one great desert. The Indians occupied, without possessing it. . . . Those coasts, so admirably adapted for commerce and industry; those wide and deep rivers; that inexhaustible valley of the Mississippi; the whole continent, in short, seemed prepared to be the abode of a great nation, yet unborn.

"In that land the great experiment was to be made by civilized man, of the attempt to construct society upon a new basis; and it was there, for the first time, that theories hitherto unknown, or deemed impracticable, were to exhibit a spectacle for which the world had not been prepared by the history of the past."[10]

## Conclusion -- the Earth Manifests God's Glory

Guyot concludes his *Physical Geography* book in the following way:

"Each continent has, therefore, a well defined individuality, which fits it for an especial function. The fullness of nature's life is typified by Africa, with its superabundant wealth and power of animal life; South America, with it's exuberance of vegetation; and Australia, with its antiquated forms of plants and animals.

"In the grand drama of man's life and development, Asia, Europe, and America play distinct parts, for which each seems to have been admirably prepared. Truly no blind force gave our Earth the forms so well adapted to perform these functions. The conclusion is irresistible -- that the entire globe is a grand organism, every feature of which is the outgrowth of a definite plan of the all-wise Creator for the education of the human family, and the manifestation of his own glory."[11]

Now, in the 20th and 21st Centuries, the travel and climactic barriers are being conquered by air travel and air conditioning, so that the historic development and purpose of the Southern continents are ready to come forth. Southeast Asia is now experiencing great revival. It appears that the internal preparation is taking place so that the *Chain of Liberty* and all its external blessings might continue its westward march from America around the globe.

---

# Chapter 3

---

# The Chain of Liberty: Origins

## Self-government and the Dominion Mandate

The history of government begins in the Garden of Eden with the first man. God placed man in the Garden and gave him a Dominion Mandate to subdue and rule all creatures including himself (Genesis 1:26-28). The test of man's self-government was his ability to resist eating of the forbidden tree without any type of external restraints. He had to internally govern himself to succeed (Genesis 2:16-17). Through Adam's failure to control himself, sin entered into the world and made it difficult for any man to govern himself. At this time there was no civil government yet established. The Dominion Mandate to Adam did not include the responsibility for ruling over other men. Therefore, when Cain did not control his anger and jealousy, he violently slew his brother. Who do we see taking responsibility for justice and protection? God Himself. (Genesis 4:1-16)

## Civil Government for Protection

After a period of time, however, the prevalence of sin and lack of self-government led to so much violence that God saw the end result would be all men destroying one another (Genesis 6:5-13). Therefore, God decides to intervene and bring a flood to destroy all but one righteous family. When God brings Noah through the flood to a new earth, He re-establishes the Dominion Mandate but now delegates to man the responsibility for governing other men in order

*When Cain killed Abel God took responsibility for justice.*

to protect human life (Genesis 9:5-7). He does this by instituting capital punishment--the backbone of civil government.

Civil government, then, is just as much a Divine institution as the Family and the Church. All were established by God with clear purposes and principles of operation revealed in Scripture. Here are some scriptures defining the purpose of civil government:

"Submit yourselves for the Lord's sake to every human institution, whether to a king as the one in authority, or to governors as sent by him for the punishment of evildoers and the praise of those who do right." (1 Peter 2:13-14)

"Let every person be in subjection to the governing authorities;...For rulers are not a cause of fear for good behavior, but for evil;...for it is a minister of God to you for good. But if you do what is evil, be afraid;...for it is a minister of God, an avenger who brings wrath upon the one who practices evil." (Romans 13:1,3,4)

The purpose of government therefore is to protect the life, liberty and property of all individuals, by punishing evildoers and encouraging the righteous. When governing rulers ever fail to do this, then they themselves are resisting the ordinances of God and are illegitimate authorities who should be resisted and replaced. The main functions, therefore, of the Family, church and civil government are procreation, propagation and protection respectively. Most Christians today sadly know much about the first two Divine institutions, but very little about the latter. Just one walk through a common Christian bookstore shows the lack of material on this subject although the Bible deals with it abundantly.

## The Origin of Nations

In Genesis 10:4,20,31,32 we find the first reference to "nations" arising from family groups. We also find the rise of pagan monarchy (kingdoms) as the form of civil government in these nations. Centralization of power is a pagan tendency and is also seen in the rise of the first cities such as at Ninevah (Genesis 10:11) and then Babel (Genesis 11:1). Egypt with its "Pharaohs" are mentioned in Genesis 12:10, 15 and nine kings are mentioned in Genesis 14:1,2.

## Centralization of Civil Government at Babel                    *c. 2300 B.C.*

Nowhere in Scripture is civil government said to have responsibility to be provider or savior for men by the centralization of its of powers; yet between 2300 - 2400 B.C. men began to pervert the purpose of civil government in this way. The men at Babel began to congregate together rather than spread out and "fill the earth." They wanted to make a name for themselves and save themselves through the state as their *counterfeit* Messiah. This was the first public expression of Humanism where sovereignty was placed in a man or a collection of men rather than God (Genesis 11:1-8). In order to prevent centralized, one-world government, God made diverse languages which are an effective deterrent to this day.

## The Hebrew Republic with Biblical Civil Laws                    *c. 1300 B.C.*

God called Abraham to establish a unique "nation" among the other pagan nations around 2000 B.C. (Genesis 12:2 and 17:6,10). Abraham becomes the "prince" (Genesis 23:6) or ruler of Israel and negotiates and battles with Pharoah (Genesis 12:18), kings of of Sodom and Salem (Genesis 14:17,18), and King of Gerar (Genesis 20:2 and 21:27).

When God gave Moses the Law around 1300 - 1500 B.C. to be interpreted by judges and prophets in Israel, the first representative republic on earth was established. From the beginning, God's purpose was not limited to Israel, but he desired that these laws and their blessings might be exported to all nations on earth who had perverted God's plan of civil government into pagan centralized monarchy. God established in Israel a decentralized, representative government where every group

*Babel was the beginning of the pagan tendency toward centralization.*

of 10, 50, 100 and 1,000 families could choose or elect someone to be their judge or ruler. All of their civil laws were based upon God's higher fixed law, and not majorities. This makes it a republic, not a democracy.

The Hebrew Republic also had an unelected civil body known as the "Sanhedrin" which was the 70 "elders" of the Republic. It is important to note that these elders were civil, not religious offices. There was a separation of "church and state." The clergy of the land were the "Priests" and the "Levites" and the "judges" were civil rulers. It is also important to note that the "prophets" were primarily social reformers and statesmen among the people and included both clergy and non-clergy in their ranks. All civil rulers in Israel, even kings, did not rule unless they obtained the consent of the governed by a covenant.

By 1120 B.C., however, as Israel backslid from God and their self and family government, there arose very poor and corrupt leadership under their judges (1 Samuel 8:19-20). Pagan monarchy was effective in keeping order but at the high price of oppression, taxation and the loss of much liberty (1 Samuel 8:10-20). Israel, however, conformed to this pagan form of civil government where dominion was turned into domination. From this point forward until the landing of the Pilgrims at Plymouth -- almost 3000 years -- the entire world would know nothing of full external liberty for the individual man.

## *Greece and Rome's Pagan Attempts at Civil Liberty*     *c. 500 B.C.*

The second major attempt at democratic government in history was in the Greek city-state of the sixth century before Christ. The Athenian lawgiver, Solon, drew up a legal system that would allow the people to make their own laws. Plato and Aristotle emphasized that a just society was one where every man is moved by concern for the common good. These concepts were also embraced by Roman statesmen such as Cicero and Seneca in the second century before Christ. They proposed an impartial system of laws based on Natural Law which, Cicero said, comes from God and originated before "any written law existed or any state had been established."

The Greek and Roman theories were never as democratic as the Hebrew, however, because of their belief in inequality of men. The ideas of democracy and freedom were only extended to certain classes and all others were denied basic rights. Such tyranny eventually produced conflicts in society that led to chaos and disorder. Cicero was murdered and they reverted to complete totalitarianism to restore order. Greek and Roman contributions to democratic ideas were therefore more theoretical than actual, but were helpful to later generations who learned from their mistakes.

The fundamental flaws of their attempts at democracy were rooted in their belief that man was naturally unequal and that only one or a privileged few were competent to govern the rest.

The pagan and Christian ideas of man and government are contrasted well by Historian Richard Frothingham. Of this pagan view that dominated the world at this time in history, he wrote:

> "At that time, social order rested on the assumed natural inequality of men. The individual was regarded as of value only as he formed a part of the political fabric, and was able to contribute to its uses, as though it were the end of his being to aggrandize the State. This was the pagan idea of man. The wisest philosophers of antiquity could not rise above it. Its influence imbued the pagan world;...especially the idea that man was made for the State, the office of which, or of a divine right vested in one, or in a privileged few, was to fashion the thought and control the action of the many."[1]

## The Gospel of Jesus Christ Introduces the Christian Idea of Man and Government

With the coming of Jesus Christ and His death on the cross for the sins of the world, man's ability to govern himself internally was restored. The Law of God was no longer an external thing, but now could be written on men's hearts and interpreted not by prophets and judges, but by the Spirit within them.

But in addition to this internal liberty, Christ also proposed principles for external civil liberty. As the church propagated these principles throughout the pagan world, the Christian idea of man and government became clear. As Frothingham states:

> "Christianity then appeared with its central doctrine, that man was created in the Divine image, and destined for immortality; pronouncing that, in the eye of God, all men are equal. This asserted for the individual an independent value. It occasioned the great inference, that man is superior to the State, which ought to be fashioned for his use;...that the state ought to exist for man; that justice, protection, and the common good, ought to be the aim of government."[2]

The Declaration of Independence states these Christian ideas this way:

> "We hold these Truths to be self-evident, that all Men are created equal, that they are endowed by their Creator with certain unalienable Rights, that among these are Life, Liberty, and the Pursuit of Happiness--That to secure these Rights, Govern-

ments are instituted by Men, deriving their just powers from the Consent of the Governed."

Few nations today operate their governments based on the Christian idea of man and government. But the pagan ideas are gradually being overcome.

## *Jesus Christ and Civil Government*

Why did Jesus come into the world? There are many answers to this question. He came to seek and to save those who are lost, He came to destroy the works of the devil, and He came to establish the Kingdom of God, to name a few.

We have seen how man lost his ability to be self-governed when he disobeyed God. This led to external governmental tyranny. Christ also came to restore to man the potential of being self-governing under God. As mankind begins to be self-governed, it will have an effect on the external government's operating on his life. Jesus came to not only bring internal salvation, but also external political freedom.

After Jesus had risen from the dead and before He ascended into heaven, He gathered His disciples together.

> Acts 1:6-8 states "And so when they had come together, they were asking Him saying, 'Lord, is it at this time You are restoring the kingdom to Israel?' He said to them, 'It is not for you to know times or epochs which the Father has fixed by His own authority; but you shall receive power when the Holy Spirit has come upon you; and you shall be My witnesses both in Jerusalem, and in all Judea and Samaria, and even to the remotest part of the earth.'" (Acts 1:6-8).

Of what type of kingdom were Jesus' disciples speaking? They were speaking of an external kingdom. For centuries the Hebrew people had read the prophecies of Scripture declaring a Messiah would come and set up His throne and deliver the people from bondage.

While Jesus walked on the earth, many of His followers thought He would set up His reign at any time. They even tried to make Him King. His disciples did not understand how His Kingdom was going to come.

While they had not seen it established during Jesus' ministry on earth, surely now that He had risen from the dead, He would restore the Kingdom. That's why they asked Him this question.

Jesus did not deny that an external expression of the Kingdom would come. In fact, He said that times and epochs would follow (which we can look back upon today) that would contribute to the establishment of the Kingdom and the extension of external and internal liberty "to the remotest part of the earth."

The "power" for this external establishment of liberty is the "Spirit of the Lord"; therefore, Jesus emphasized the receiving of this "power" through the Baptism of the Holy Spirit. He knew the inevitable result of internal liberty would be external liberty.

## God's Pathway to Liberty

God's pathway to liberty is from the internal to the external. God's desire is for an external expression of His Kingdom on earth. Yet it must first begin in the heart of man, and then it will naturally express itself externally in all aspects of society.

The Bible reveals that "where the Spirit of the Lord is, there is liberty" (2 Corinthians 3:17). When the Spirit of the Lord comes into the heart of a man, that man is liberated. Likewise, when the Spirit of the Lord comes into a nation, that nation is liberated. The degree to which the Spirit of the Lord is infused into a society (through its people, laws, and institutions), is the degree to which that society will experience liberty in every realm (civil, religious, economic, etc.)

Christ came to set us free (Gal. 5:1,3). Spiritual freedom or liberty ultimately produces political freedom. External political slavery reflects internal spiritual bondage.

## Gradual Leavening Principle

Christianity's method of change is the same for nations as it is for individuals. As Christians, we are gradually transformed as we apply the truth of His word to our lives.

Dr. Augustus Neander reveals in his 1871 book, *General History of the Christian Religion*, how Christianity has historically brought about change in various nations of the world. Neander writes:

"Again, Christianity, from its nature, must pronounce sentence of condemnation against all ungodliness, but at the same time appropriate to itself all purely human relations and arrangements, consecrating and ennobling, instead of annihilating them...That religion which aimed nowhere to produce violent and convulsive changes from without, but led to reforms by beginning in the first place within, --whose peculiar character it was to operate positively rather than negatively, --to displace and destroy no faster than it substituted something better..."[3]

Christian reforms within a nation do not begin with external or violent means (quite a contrast to Marxist/Communist "reforms" we see today), but they begin within.

In dealing with unbiblical situations in the nations today, we must remember that reform begins within, and as we remove the bad we must simultaneously substitute something. A government-controlled and funded welfare system is unbiblical, yet the solution is not to pass a law that immediately eliminates civil government support of the needy. Individuals and churches must begin to fulfill their God-given responsibility in this area (substitute the good) as we remove the role of our civil government.

Neander goes on to say:

"Yet Christianity nowhere began with outward revolutions and changes, which, in all cases where they have not been prepared from within, and are not based upon conviction, fail of their salutary ends. The new creation to which Christianity gave birth, was in all respects an inward one, from which the outward effects gradually and therefore more surely and healthfully, unfolded themselves to their full extent."[4]

## Civil Authority Comes Through Service and Work, Not Imposition

External liberty, then, must come gradually, not immediately. It was this mindset of immediate civil change that Christ sought to change in His parable found in Luke 19:11-17. The "nobleman" in the parable, who is a type of Christ, emphasizes to his servants that their responsibility is to "occupy" or "do business" with their earthly finances, time and talents until He returned. The reward for the faithful was that they would be given "authority over cities."

In other words, Jesus was giving a clue to Christians as to how to gain control of civil government. It is not to be imposing it upon people, but by consistent hard work and service to meet the needs of society around us. It comes about through democratic process, not by usurpation of power.

Through Christ, God releases the "Law of Liberty" into society through the cleansed hearts of men (James 1:25 & 2:12). The self-governing Christian is governed by the internal law written on his heart interpreted by the Holy Spirit.

This does not mean that the Old Testament law is done away with, but that man can now carry out the law, for God has empowered us to do so. The more a nation applies His law, the more that nation will prosper and walk in liberty. The degree which a people apply the law personally will be reflected through their governmental institutions, for the law flows from the heart of man out to the nation.

*Jesus giving one of His teachings on civil government.*

## Christ's Teachings on Politics and Government

Jesus did not specifically lay out external plans for setting up a godly civil government. He more importantly dealt with the "spirit" or "power" by giving certain principles, and knew that a godly "form" would follow.

Knowing that internal liberty would move outward, Jesus provided some principles and guidelines on civil government. These include:

### 1. The Lord is Sovereign in Human History and Government

In answer to Pilate, Jesus said, "You would have no authority over Me, unless it had been given you from above" (John. 19:11). Here Jesus asserts that civil authority is delegated and controlled by God. Paul states this in Romans 13:1 by saying, ". . . there is no authority except from God, and those which exist are established by God."

### 2. The Individual Has Inherent Value because He is made in the image of God (Matthew 22:17-21).

This contradicted the pagan idea that an individual was regarded as valuable only if he could contribute something to the state or he belonged to a certain social class or race.

### 3. Government exists to serve the common good of every individual

When we read the familiar passage of Matthew 20:25-28 in context, we receive a broader view of what Jesus meant. "But Jesus called them to Himself, and said, 'You know that the rulers of the Gentiles lord it over them, and their great men exercise authority over them. It is not so among you, but whoever wishes to become great [a governor (NKJV); a ruler (NIV)] among you shall be your servant. . ." (Mt. 20:25-26).

Jesus is making reference to civil authorities, and is declaring that they are to be public servants. Therefore, the purpose of civil government is to serve people. This was a radical, new idea, and it contrasted greatly with the pagan idea of rulers dominating the people, an idea which existed throughout the entire world at this time.

As we will see, this idea gradually leavened many nations of the world, especially the United States. Today we call our civil leaders "public servants." That the civil government is the servant of man is a Christian idea.

### 4. Civil Government and the Church have Separate Jurisdictions

While God cannot be separated from government, the Bible does speak of limits of jurisdiction of the state and church. Jesus taught that we are to render "to Caesar [the state] the things that are Caesar's, and to God the things that are God's." (Matt.22:17-21).

We have already seen that one thing that belongs to the state and not the church is the use of the sword to protect the citizenry (Rom. 13:1-4). Some things that belong to God and not the state include our worship of God, our children, and our own consciences and lives. In these matters, the state has no authority and should not interfere.

Three views of this "church/state" issue exist today. They can be summed up by the following:

### Pagan View

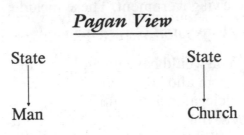

Here the state is sovereign over man and the church and dictates in civil and religious matters. Communism operates according to this idea.

### Modern "Christian" View

God        State

Church      State

Many Christians today acknowledge that God is sovereign over the Church, but do not believe He has anything to do with the state. God is separated by an impregnable wall from government.

### Biblical View

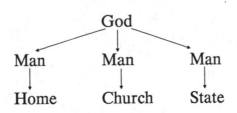

God is sovereign over man, out of which flows the government of the state and the church and the home. Each has a separate jurisdiction, and must be kept separate.

Jesus also taught that taxation is an appropriate function of civil government (Matthew 17:24-27), that people should try to settle disputes before going to court (Luke 12:58), and that when a government ruler acts in a tyrannical manner, he must be resisted (Acts 5:29).

## Christ's Guidelines for Resistance to Tyranny

There may come a time when we must resist unlawful authority. If so, we must be prepared to suffer the consequences, but we must also recognize that there are steps we should take in our resistance.

A tyrant is one who exercises unlawful authority. We should observe the following guidelines in resisting tyranny:

## 1. Protest or Legal Action

Our first means of recourse should be to protest and/or to take all legal action possible. Jesus protested when He remained silent before Pilate and refused to cooperate (Mt. 27:14) and when He publicly censured Herod for his death threats (Luke 13:31-32).

He also instructed His disciples to publicly protest if city officials denied them their inalienable right to religious speech. He told them to go out into the streets and say, "Even the dust of your city which clings to our feet, we wipe off in protest against you" (Luke 10:11). "Wiping off the dust" is equivalent to boycotting.

The free nations of the world generally have more means of legal recourse and of protesting ungodly action than do others. Examples of protesting include picketing abortion chambers, boycotting stores that sell pornography, and removing our children from public schools that deny God. We who live in free nations not only have the right to do this but are obligated to God to do so to keep our consciences clean.

The Apostles also protested and took legal action. When Paul and Barnabas were driven out of Antioch by the city officials, "they shook off the dust of their feet in protest against them" (Acts 13:51) as Jesus had instructed them.

Protesting unlawful action is a Christian idea. "Protestants" originally received this title due to their protesting action by authorities (civil and ecclesiastical) that God declared was wrong.

In Acts 16 we read how Paul and Silas were unlawfully thrown into jail. When the chief magistrates tried to cover this up, Paul, recognizing his civil liberties were a sacred cause, demanded restitution to be made. "Paul said to them, 'They have beaten us in public without trial, men who are Romans, and have thrown us into prison; and now are they sending us away secretly? No indeed! But let them come themselves and bring us out.'" (Acts 16:37). The chief magistrates did come and bring them out themselves.

The reason Paul appealed to Caesar in Acts 24-26 was because his civil rights had been violated. He was being a good steward of the civil liberties God gave to him. The whole course of Paul's life was changed due to his exerting his rights as a citizen. He saw this action as part of the Great Commission. Even when non-Christians apply Biblical methods for resisting tyranny they find some measure of success. An example is Gandhi in India.

*Paul being taken away from prison to Rome. His appeal to Caesar was a result of his civil rights being violated.*

## 2. Flight

If all avenues of protest or legal action are expended to right unlawful acts of civil authorities, than flight, if possible, is the next appropriate measure to take.

Jesus told His disciples that "whenever they persecute you in this city, flee to the next" (Mt. 10:23). He also warned them to flee the destruction that was to come upon Jerusalem (Mt. 24:15-18). The early church also took flight as persecution rose against them (Acts 8:1-4). This is not to say that we are to hide out in mountains, but that sometimes flight to other places will more surely allow us to fulfill God's will.

Many people who came to settle in America were fleeing civil and religious tyranny. After exhausting all means of protest and legal action, they saw that flight was the best means of accomplishing God's purpose. This principle is the basis of the Constitutional right of emigration.

### 3. *Force in self-defense*

As a last recourse in resisting tyranny, force is a legitimate biblical means. The Old Testament contains many examples of the Children of Israel using force to defend themselves. We will examine in a later lesson how a defensive war in a just cause is sinless, but for now we want to show that Jesus also considered force legitimate at certain times in resisting tyranny.

At the conclusion of the Last Supper, Jesus finished His instructions he began with the Seventy by instructing His disciples to prepare themselves militarily, "'Let him who has no sword sell his robe and buy one.' And they said, 'Lord, look, here are two swords.' And He said to them, 'It is enough.'" (Luke 22:36,38), implying the legitimacy of using force at certain times.

John Jay, the first Supreme Court Justice, commented on this incident in a letter written in 1818:

> "Although just war is not forbidden by the gospel in express terms, yet you think an implied prohibition of all war, without exception, is deducible from the answer of our Lord to Pilate, viz: 'If my kingdom were of this world, then would my servants fight, etc.'"

> "At the conclusion of the Last Supper, our Lord said to his disciples: 'He that hath no sword, let him now sell his garment and buy one.' They answered: 'Lord, here are two swords.' He replied: 'It is enough.'"

> "It is not to be presumed that our Lord would have ordered swords to be provided, but for some purpose for which a sword was requisite."

> "When the officers and their band arrived, with swords and with staves, to take Jesus, they who were about him saw what would follow. 'They said unto him: Lord, shall we smite with the sword?'" (Luke 22:49). It does not appear that any of the eleven disciples were with him, except one, made the least attempt to defend him. But, Peter, probably inferring from the other swords, that they were now to be used, proceeded to 'smite a servant of the high-priest, and cut off his right ear'(vs. 50). Jesus (perhaps, among other reasons, to abate inducements to prosecute Peter for that violent attack) healed the ear."

*Jesus taught that the use of force was legitimate at certain times in resisting tyranny. Before His betrayal, Jesus told His disciples that if they owned no swords to purchase them (Luke 22:36).*

"He ordered Peter to put his sword into its sheath, and gave two reasons for it. The first related to himself, and amounted to this, that he would make no opposition, saying: 'The cup which my Father hath given me, shall I not drink?' The second related to Peter, viz., they who take the sword, shall perish by the sword; doubtless meaning that they who take and use a sword, as Peter had just done, without lawful authority, and against lawful authority, incur the penalty and risk of perishing by the sword. This meaning seems to be attached to those words by the occasion and circumstances which prompted them. If understood in their unlimited latitude, they would contradict the experience and testimony of all ages, it being manifest that many military men die peaceably in their beds."[5]

As Jay noted, Christ's mission precluded the use of force in this particular instance, nonetheless, Jesus taught the legitimacy of using the legal sword to restrain the illegal sword of an aggressor (Mt. 26:52).

The authority and responsibility of using the sword to punish evil or protect the righteous (either from within a nation or from aggression by an outside enemy) resides with the civil government (Rom. 13:1-4). That is why anytime we reach the step where force is necessary in resisting tyranny, we must go through legitimate governing officials. A lower representative must be convinced to ignore a higher decree in obedience to God's higher law. Those who disobey an ungodly law or ruler must be prepared to pay the price for such an action.

We will see that the American colonists were not in rebellion (from God's perspective) in their struggle for independence from Britain, but were acting in accordance with the Biblical guidelines for resisting tyranny. They followed the above three steps in order. If we do not follow these steps in order, we will bring undue harm to ourselves, to others, and to God's cause.

# Origins and Development of Civil Government

Creation    3000    2300   2000      1500    1120 1000        0   29     1000      1789 2000

B.C. | A.D.

**GREECE & ROME**
Man's highest efforts still fail to provide liberty for all

**DARK AGES**
Pagan influence perverts church government

**BABEL**
Pagan men turn civil government into a counterfeit Messiah through centralization

**REFORMATION**
Reformers restore the textbook of liberty - the Bible

**CREATION**
God establishes:
1. Self-government
2. Family for procreation
3. The Dominion Mandate

**CROSS
(The Gospel)**
Jesus provides:
1. Internal liberty
(ie. - internal law interpreted by the Spirit)
2. Principles for external civil liberty

**SIN**
Destroys self-government and perverts family government

**ISRAEL
(The Law)**
Moses provides explicit civil laws for a Theocratic Republic
(ie. - external law interpreted by prophets and judges)

**CHURCH**
For propagation of Jesus' principles

**CAIN**
God personally handles all civil matters

**AMERICA**
God provides external liberty in the first Christian Republic (civil government run by self-governing individuals)

**FLOOD**
God establishes civil government for protection

**KINGS**
Israel conforms to the pagan idea of man and government (dominion is turned into domination)

---
# Chapter 4
---

# The Chain of Liberty: Development

## The Chain of Liberty Moves Westward to Europe

### The Primitive Churches in the Roman Empire                    33-312

As the early Church applied the political principles that Jesus taught, they not only affected multitudes of lives, but also turned the entire known world upside down. Paganism was being overthrown throughout Europe as Christianity rapidly spread. By 500 A.D. about 25% of the world had become Christian and over 40% had been evangelized.

In the previous chapter we have already documented the frequent instances in the New Testament where the apostles resisted tyranny by various forms of civil protest and legal action (Acts 13, 16, 24, 25, 26). The first chapter of this book mentioned how the apostle Paul rebuked the Christians in Greece for their apathy and irresponsibility in regards to politics that allowed non-Christians to be in control (1 Corinthians 6:2-5). He urged them to seek public office such as in the local court system of Corinth. When the Christians found it difficult to make inroads in the Roman legal system, they began to form their own alternative courts, which were binding only upon those who voluntarily accepted the outcome by covenant agreement. Over time, the pagans began to reject the arbitrary Roman system and seek for real justice through the Christian courts. By the time of Constantine around 300 A.D., half of the empire's population had been converted to Christianity and consequently were involved in the "Christian" court system. Thus when Constantine made Christianity the official established religion of the empire, the Christian judges were also given legal status and therefore required to wear the official dark robe or gown worn by all civil magistrates. The modern practice of mainline denominational clergymen wearing "pulpit gowns" traces its origins to this act, because most of these "Christian judges" were clergymen. The "pulpit gown" therefore is a testimony and memorial of the primitive churches being involved in politics.

Paul's exhortation to these Christians in Corinth was so strong that one of Paul's own staff -- a man named **Erastus** -- eventually switched from being a gospel minister to become a civil "minister" (Romans 13:4,6 - "Rulers are servants of God. . .a minister of God to you for good . ."). Erastus had been a full-time apostolic assistant to Paul, just like Timothy, until he was sent by Paul over to Greece (Acts 19:22). While ministering to the churches there, Erastus began to feel God's calling into political office. Paul tells us what happened to him when, in the close of his letter to the Romans (written from Corinth), Paul says: "Erastus, the city treasurer greets you" (Romans 16:23). Archaeology has uncovered in Corinth a first-century tablet that reads: "Erastus, the Commissioner of Public Works, laid this pavement at his own expense." This is believed to be the Erastus of the Bible.[1]

What an exciting illustration of obedience to Christ's command to his disciples to be public **servants** once they gain positions in government! Here Erastus does something unprecedented in pagan Roman government -- he personally pays for the project instead of raising taxes -- and is honored with a special tablet. Here we have an example in the New Testament of Christians, not just protesting evil government, but taking the initiative to provide good government by seeking civil office -- and its sanctioned by the greatest apostle of all!

Besides all this, the primitive churches provided a model of self-government with union among their congregations. Although church government on the local level was predominantly self-governing, nonetheless, there were certain limited powers in the hands of the apostles and elders of the churches at large who met in council at Jerusalem (Acts 15:2,4,6 and 16:4) and approved special ministries such as a poor fund which was administered out of Jerusalem (Galatians 2:1,2,9 and 2 Corinthians 8:19,23). The relationship between the mother church in Jerusalem and all the other new churches was the first example of federalism, or dual governments working both at once in defined spheres of jurisdiction (local and national).

As the centuries went on, the church gradually lost its virtue and Biblical knowledge and thus embraced a pagan philosophy of government and education. This caused them to think that only they could understand God's Word and, therefore, must tell the people what God required of them, instead of allowing every person to be self-governing and learn for themselves.

Instead of sowing the truth in the hearts of the people and allowing the inevitable fruit to grow, the clergy simply tried to externally dictate to the people what they thought God commanded (and what they thought was often quite contrary to the Bible). The first pagan king to be converted was the king of Armenia in 295 A.D. He declared his nation to be "Christian" although it was not genuine. It was still a pagan form of monarchical government.

Constantine also attempted to accomplish God's will with pagan methods. After Constantine was converted (about 312 A.D.) he desired to make his empire Christian. Yet not understanding God's method of gradualism, he superficially united the Church and State and set up a national church declaring all citizens in his empire must be Christians. His attempt at accomplishing that which was good, hindered the work of God for centuries to follow in an era which became known as the "Dark Ages," which followed the fall of the Roman Empire in 410 A.D.

## Patrick, Alfred and the Law of Moses in Britain

Christianity was introduced in Britain in the first century, possibly by Joseph of Arimathea. As the Celts were converted they established decentralized churches, unlike those that developed in the Roman and Byzantine Empires. By A.D. 150 the Pastors of the Celtic Churches preached in the common language from interlinear Bible translations called glosses.

The greatest of the pastors was Patrick who left England and went to evangelize Ireland. King Loeghaire was converted and made Patrick his counselor (termed "Annchara") and thus Biblical Law began to be introduced into the civil realm. In 432 Patrick wrote Liber Ex Lege Moisi (Book of the Law of Moses) which was applied by local chieftains or kings throughout Ireland (as yet not a united political arrangement, only a Biblical/religious unity). It emphasized the rule of law and local self government.

The Anglo-Saxons first came to Britain around 428 A.D. when two brothers, Hengist and Horsa, were invited to bring their relatives and help the king of Kent fight off his enemies. They stayed in Britain, and after some time eventually took the island over and named it Anglo-land, or Engel-land (today England).

Initially the Anglo-Saxons turned on the Celts, killing many of them. One time they killed 1200 Celtic Pastors in prayer. However, while the Saxons conquered the Celts militarily, the Celts conquered

*Patrick greatly influenced government through writing the* Book of the Law of Moses.

the Saxons spiritually. The Saxons were thus converted to Celtic Christianity. Catholicism did not come to Britain until 597. After its introduction the church in Britain, due to the Celtic influence, still emphasized the Bible above Papal authority.

Around 565 a follower of Patrick, named Columba, left his Ireland and evangelized the king of the Picts (who lived in what is today Scotland). Columba also translated Liber in the Scottish language.

The first king who was revered enough to unite all of England into one nation was known as **Alfred the Great**, who ruled from 871 to 899. Just before Alfred became king, most of England had been conquered by the Vikings from Denmark through a long series of fierce battles. Wessex, in the southwest portion of England, was the only region that remained for Alfred to rule. Almost immediately, and for years to follow, Alfred found himself in thick battle with the Danes. David Chilton writes of this struggle:

"In 876 the Danish chieftain Guthrum attacked Wessex in earnest with a powerful host, aiming to break Alfred's hold on the country once and for all. The Vikings succeeded: in the winter of early 878, Guthrum pushed Alfred into the marshes, where the king and a small group of loyal followers were forced to hide out on the Isle of Athelney. Historians have called this time of testing Alfred's "Valley Forge," where he had to bide his time while virtually all England was overrun with pagan enemies of the faith who sacked churches and monasteries, wiping out the tattered remains of a Christian past. The legends say, however, that the bold and daring Alfred entered the Viking camp disguised as a minstrel and actually performed for Guthrum and his chiefs -- getting a chance to listen to their plans and plotting his own strategy. When spring came, Alfred rallied the English army for a final push against the invader's vastly superior forces. This time Alfred was victorious. As the *Anglo-Saxon Chronicle* puts it, 'he fought against the entire host, and put it to flight.' The Vikings agreed never to attack Wessex again, and they submitted to the terms of peace.

"Alfred did not banish Guthrum and his men. He didn't have them executed, either. His solution to the problem of the Vikings seems incredible to us, but it worked. The peace treaty he imposed on them included this provision: that Guthrum and 'thirty of the most honorable men in the host' become Christians! Guthrum accepted the conditions, and he was baptized into the Christian faith, Alfred standing as his godfather. At the conclusion of the ceremony, Alfred embraced his newborn brother in Christ and threw a twelve-day feast for him and his men. And then, as if this weren't enough already, Alfred made the strangest political move of all. He said to Guthrum, in effect: 'My brother, this land is much too big for me to rule all by myself; and the important thing isn't who's in charge. The real issue is a Christian England. So don't go back to Denmark. Stay here and rule this land with me, under the lordship of Jesus Christ.'

"That's exactly what Guthrum did. In fact, when later groups of Danes tried to launch invasions against England, Guthrum and Alfred stood together as Christian kings, united in defense of a Christian land. As the first Viking leader to become a Christian, Guthrum foreshadowed the conversion of all the Norse peoples and their incorporation into the civilizations of Christendom."[2]

With the coming of peace, Alfred instituted Christian reforms in many areas including establishing a government that served the people. Alfred was taught how to read by a Celtic Christian scholar known as Asser, and studied Patrick's Liber and thus established the Ten Commandments as the basis of law and adopted many other patterns of government from the Hebrew Republic. The nation organized themselves into units of tens, fifties, hundreds and thousands and had an elected assembly known as the "Witen." These representatives were called respectively: a tithingman (over ten families), a vilman (over 50), a hundredman, and an earl. The earl's territory which he oversaw was called a "shire," and his assistant called the "shire-reef," where we get our word "Sheriff" today. The Witen also had an unelected House made up of the nobleman, but the king was elected; he was not a hereditary king. Their laws were established by their consent. Alfred's uniform code of Laws was the origin of common law, trial by jury, and habeas corpus. Alfred's code was derived from Mosaic law and Jesus' golden rule.

*Alfred the Great*

Thomas Jefferson said that the Anglo-Saxon laws were "...the sources of the Common Law...[and] the wisest and most perfect ever yet devised by the wit of man, as it stood before the 8th century;..." The National Seal proposed by Jefferson in 1776 was to have on one side "the children of Israel in the wilderness, led by a cloud by day, and a pillar of fire by the night." But on the other side Jefferson proposed images of "Hengist and Horsa, the Saxon chiefs... whose political principles and form of government we have assumed."[3] This is true because of the Saxons' contact with the Celtic Christians (British natives), but the Saxon culture in Germany from which they originated provided no constitutionalism whatsoever. In the 800's the clergy began to serve as judges in England and build common law on the Bible.

Reaching its height in the late 800's under the Christian King Alfred, Anglo-Saxon law was eroding at the time of the Norman Conquest in 1066. The Normans, under William the Conqueror, established a royal dynasty -- a system which destroyed the rights of the people yet increased efficiency by centralization of common law under Henry II.

Meanwhile, in 1016, Iceland became a Christian nation by genuine democratic process. The "Holy Roman Empire," founded by Otto I, King of Germany, in 962 A.D., launched a series of 8 crusades to "liberate" the Holy Land from the Muslims (1095 - 1272). At the apex of the Medieval Papacy under Pope Innocent III, a significant step toward liberty occurred in England.

*1215*                    *Magna Charta*

In England, the Norman system of government removed the rights of the people. Consequently, the kings abused the people, barons as well as commoners.

Brown Bros.

*In 1215 King John signed the Magna Charta, which was written by Rev. Langton.*

Things worsened to the point under King John that the English barons drew up a contract that addressed the abuses and guaranteed the barons certain rights and privileges as contained in Biblical law. King John, needing the help of the barons to raise money, reluctantly signed the Magna Charta in 1215. It is interesting to note (but not surprising) that a clergyman, Stephen Langton, is likely the chief architect of the document. The Pope said it was illegal but the English Catholic Church, having Celtic origins, ignored the Pope and preserved the document and expounded it (rather than the government).

The Magna Charta embodied the principle that both sovereign and people are beneath the law and subject to it. Later, both Englishmen and American colonists cited the Magna Charta as a source of their freedom.

It is also notable that around 1200, a Catholic monk named Dominque in England instituted the first example of representative government on a national level in England in his Order of Monks. This was in great contrast to most of Catholicism. Around 1300 Parliament was created reflecting the representative principle.

In 1231 the Pope initiated the first phase of the Inquisition to identify and punish "heretics."

The time period from approximately 500 -1500 A.D. was called the Dark Ages because mankind generally was stagnant and saw little or no advancement in civil liberty, scientific discoveries, technology, and almost every other area. This lack of advancement was primarily a result of the light of the Word of God being "hidden" from the common people. The Word of God was completed by the apostles in the first century and canonized in the following few centuries; yet as the church "backslid" from God, His Word was further removed from the people. Nevertheless, "the textbook of Liberty" was providentially being preserved by scribes and monks who painstakingly spent their entire lives hand-copying the Bible.

*John Wickliffe translating the Bible*

The lack of access to the truth of the Bible kept the common people ignorant during the Dark Ages. Around 1348, the bubonic Plague killed one third of the population of Europe. Shortly after this a Catholic clergyman named John Wycliffe, who did have access to the truth, began to see that "Scripture must become the common property of all" that there might be "a government of the people, by the people, and for the people." To accomplish this goal, he translated the whole Bible from Latin into English. This was completed around 1382, one hundred fifty years before the Reformation occurred.

He not only translated the Bible, but set out to implant the truth of the Scriptures in the hearts of all men. This was accomplished by distributing Bibles, books of the Bible, and tracts throughout all England.

His followers, called "Lollards" (a derogatory term meaning "idle babblers"), would travel to towns and villages passing out Bibles and tracts and preaching and teaching on street corners, in chapels, gardens, assembly halls, and everywhere else they had an opportunity. As most people were uneducated, the Lollards taught many how to read, including many nobles.

In the words of Prof. G. V. Lechler, the Lollards "were, above all, characterized by a striving after holiness, a zeal for the spread of scriptural truth, for the uprooting of prevalent error, and for Church reform. Even the common people among them were men who believed; and they communicated, as by a sacred contagion, their convictions to those around them. Thus they became mighty."[4]

The translation of the Bible in the hands of the Lollards became such a power, that at the close of the century, "according to the testimony of opponents, at least half the population had ranged themselves on the side of the Lollards."[5]

As prevalent error in the church began to be addressed, the church leaders showed their appreciation by trying to eradicate this *heretical* movement. Over the decades, they were able to stomp out most of the effects of Wycliffe's work and drive his followers underground, but the seeds of truth had been planted, that would later spring forth and produce a Reformation that no man could stop.

In 1425, hoping to remove all the traces of Wycliffe's *treachery*, the church ordered his bones exhumed and burned along with some 200 books he had written. His ashes were then cast into the little river Swift, "the little river conveyed Wycliffe's remains into the Avon, the Avon into the Severn, the Severn into the narrow seas, they to the main ocean. And thus the ashes of Wycliffe are the emblem of his doctrine, which now is dispersed all the world over."[6]

With John Wycliffe, the "Morning Star of the Reformation", the first rays of the light of God's Word began to shine forth in the darkness. This coincided with the beginning of the "Renaissance" (1340 to 1540) or revival of Greek and Roman art and learning.

1455         *The Printing Press in Germany*

An event occurred in the 15th century that assured that the light of the truth would never be put out by any civil or ecclesiastical government. That event was the invention of the printing press by John Guttenberg around the year 1455.

The first book printed by Guttenberg was the Bible. Before this time, the only means of recording was by hand. It would take scribes over a year to hand copy one Bible. It's no wonder Bibles were scarce and expensive.

In the next century as the Reformation broke forth, the use of the printing press was instrumental in spreading the knowledge of liber-

*The first book printed on Guttenberg's press was the Bible.*

ty. Within 10 years of the invention of the press the total number of books increased from 50,000 to 10 million. Charles Coffin wrote:

"Through the energizing influence of the printing press, emperors, kings, and despots have seen their power gradually waning, and the people becoming their masters."[7]

## *Christopher Columbus in Spain* *1492*

The Catholic monarchs of Spain, however, came under the influence of a man  whose name meant "The Christbearer" who believed that it would be possible to reach the east by sailing west. In 1492, Christopher Columbus opened up the New World to civilization.

We all know of this event, but do we know what motivated Columbus to embark on such an arduous and dangerous journey? The following excerpts from his diary will tell us:

"It was the Lord who put it into my mind -- I could feel His hand upon me -- the fact that it would be possible to sail from here to the Indies...

"All who heard of my project rejected it with laughter, ridiculing me... There is no question that the inspiration was from the Holy Spirit, because He comforted me with rays of marvelous illumination from the Holy Scriptures... For the execution of the journey to the Indies, I did not make use of intelligence, mathematics, or maps. It is simply the fulfillment of what Isaiah had prophesied...

"No one should fear to undertake a task in the name of our Savior, if it is just and if the intention is purely for His Service... The fact that the Gospel must still be preached to so many lands in such a short time -- this is what convinces me."[8]

While Columbus discovered the New World, God did not allow the country from which he sailed to colonize the territory which originally comprised the United States. Columbus and other explorers carried with them the seeds of religious tyranny, and God had plans for America to be planted with seeds of liberty.

Historian Daniel Dorchester writes:

*Columbus said the Lord inspired him to make his voyage.*

"While thirst for gold, lust of power, and love of daring adventure served the Providential purpose of opening the New World to papal Europe, and Roman Catholic colonies were successfully planted in some portions, the territory originally comprised within the United States was mysteriously guarded and reserved for another -- a prepared people."[9]

During the century following the discovery of the New World, colonization occurred in much of South and Central America. In 1493 the Pope gave Africa, Asia, and Brazil to Portugal and the rest of Latin America to Spain. This is reflected in the colonization that followed. Every attempt to colonize the territory comprising the original United States met with failure. God was preserving this land for a people whom He had yet to prepare.

In 1497, John Cabot, landing near the St. Lawrence River, laid claim to America for England. At this time, England, as all of Europe, lived under civil and religious tyranny, yet as we have already seen, God would be at work in the sixteenth century to assure that this was changed.

B.F. Morris writes of God's Providential hand at work during this era:

"No era in history is more signally and sublimely marked than that of the discovery and Christian colonization of the North American continent.

" The intervening century was in many respects the most important period of the world; certainly the most important in modern times. More marked and decided changes, affecting science, religion, and liberty, occurred in that period than had occurred in centuries before; and all these changes were just such as to determine the Christian character of this country. Meantime, God held this vast land in reserve, as the great field on which the experiment was to be made in favor of a civil and religious liberty. He suffered not the foot of Spaniard, or Portuguese, or Frenchman, or Englishman to come upon it until the changes had been wrought in Europe which would make it certain that it would always be a land of religious freedom."[10]

1478      *The Spanish Inquisition*

In 1478, the Papacy began the Spanish Inquisition which wiped out virtually all Protestants in that nation by 1558.

Martin Luther was God's instrument to awaken the conscience of man. His act of nailing his 95 theses on the church door at Wittenberg in 1517 is often referred to as a beginning point of the Protestant Reformation. Yet seeds of the Reformation had been planted many years before. About 100 years before, Jan Hus was burned at the stake for stressing Scripture authority instead of corrupt papal authority.  He was directly influenced by Wycliffe's works.  Hus influenced Luther by his example.

Luther's defense at the Diet of Worms in 1521 reveals that which characterized his life:

"'I am,' he pleaded, 'but a mere man, and not God; I shall therefore defend myself as Christ did, who said, 'If I have spoken evil, bear witness of the evil'...For this reason, by the mercy of God I conjure you, most serene Emperor, and you, most illustrious electors and princes, and all men of every degree, to prove from the

*Luther at the Diet of Worms*

writings of the prophets and apostles that I have erred. As soon as I am convinced of this, I will retract every error, and will be the first to lay hold of my books, and throw them into the fire...I cannot submit my faith either to the Pope or to the councils, because it is clear as the day that they have frequently erred and contradicted each other. Unless, therefore, I am convinced by the testimony of Scripture, or by clear reasoning, unless I am persuaded by means of the passages I have quoted, and unless my conscience is thus bound by the Word of God, I cannot and will not retract; for it is unsafe and injurious to act against one's own conscience. Here I stand, I can do no other: may God help me! Amen.'"[11]

His life, and those of the reformers, can be summed up in the Latin phrase, *sola scriptura,* "Scripture alone." He translated the first German Bible in 1534. That was to be the basis of the reformers' thoughts and actions, rather than the decree of pope or king. It was Luther who brought forth out of darkness the great truth that we are justified by faith.

In 1540 Denmark, Norway, and Sweden became Lutheran nations.

1509-1564        *John Calvin and Switzerland*

In 1534, when the French Protestant, John Calvin was 25, after having met with his cousin Robert Olivetan and Lefevre (the Bible translators), he left the Roman church in Noyon, France and was put in prison briefly. After his release, he lived in Paris for awhile in disguise and worshipped at secret meeting places in homes and in the woods by using passwords. But, later that year, he fled to Germany and then to Geneva, situated next to Lake Leman. This city had officially voted to be Protestant as a result of seeds planted by Ulrich Zwingli who was killed in battle in 1531 while serving as chaplain in the Swiss army. In 1536, he wrote his famous *Institutes of Christian Religion.* In 1538, the Council of Geneva ordered Calvin to do something that he felt conscience bound to disobey. Then he was banished from Geneva and went to Strasbourg and pastored a French refugee congregation for three years where he also married a French refugee named Idelette. In 1541, Calvin was invited back to Geneva by the Council, and he wrote his *Ecclesiastical Ordinances,* which included policies for jails, education, and the physical health and safety of citizens, such as sanitation requirements.

The writings of John Calvin have probably had more impact upon the modern world than any other book, except the Bible. "No writing of the Reformation era was more feared by Roman Catholics, more zealously fought against and more hostilely pursued, than Calvin's Institutes."[12]

In his history of the Reformation, D'Aubigne writes:

"The renovation of the individual, of the church, and of the human race, is his theme...

"The reformation of the sixteenth century restored to the human race what the middle ages had stolen from them; it delivered them from the traditions, laws, and despotism of the papacy; it put an end to the minority and tutelage in which Rome claimed to keep mankind forever; and by calling upon man to establish his faith not on the words of a priest, but on the infallible Word of God, and by announcing to every one free access to the Father through the new and saving way -- Christ Jesus, it proclaimed and brought about the hour of Christian manhood.

*John Calvin*

"An explanation is, however, necessary. There are philosophers in our days who regard Christ as simply the apostle of political liberty. These men should learn that, if they desire liberty outwardly, they must first possess it inwardly...

"There are, no doubt, many countries, especially among those which the sun of Christianity has not yet illumined, that are without civil liberty, and that groan under the arbitrary rule of powerful masters. But, in order to become free outwardly, man must first succeed in being free inwardly...

"The liberty which the Truth brings is not for individuals only: it affects the whole of society. Calvin's work of renovation, in particular, which was doubtless first of all an internal work, was afterwards destined to exercise a great influence over nations.[13]

Calvin worked hard to make Geneva a model of Biblical government. He established the first Protestant university in history known as the Geneva Acadamy whose rector was Theodore Beza. Geneva became a centre of reform for not only Huguenot but also Protestant refugees from all over Europe. Puritan leaders of England, as well as John Knox of Scotland, studied under Calvin at Geneva.

The nation of the United States of America has been influenced greatly by Calvin, as D'Aubigne observed:

"Lastly, Calvin was the founder of the greatest of republics. The *pilgrims* who left their country in the reign of James I and, landing on the barren shores of New England, founded populous and mighty colonies, are his sons, his direct and legitimate sons; and that American nation which we have seen growing so rapidly boasts as its father the humble reformer on the shores of the Leman."[14]

*John Knox was largely responsible for directing the Reformation in Scotland. Mary Queen of Scots said of him, "I fear the prayers of John Knox more than an army of ten thousand men!"*

| 1523-1598 | *The Huguenots: The Protestants in France* |

In 1523, just one year after Luther's New Testament translation into the German language and two years prior to Tyndale's English translation, Jacques Lefevre d'Etaples published the New Testament in French. The whole Bible was available in 1530 known as the *Antwerp Bible*. Another translation by Pierre Robert Olivetan was published in 1535. (It was revived in 1557 and became known as the Geneva Bible.)

Olivetan's cousin, John Calvin, fled persecution in France and settled in Geneva where he established a training center for many French Protestants. These Protestants became known as "Huguenots" which is a term from a German word meaning "confederates". Despite severe oppression, the Huguenots grew until in 1553 five were publicly burned at the stake. This event, instead of quenching the movement, fueled it so that four years later one third of all Frenchmen were Protestants! ( 300,000).

Two years later in Paris, a national synod convened and wrote the *Confession of Faith of the Reformed Churches* and the Pope responded by making the reading of the Bible illegal. Three years after this, in 1562, churches grew from 300 to 2000 throughout the land, and because of severe violations of their religious freedom they formed a political alliance to protect it. This plunged the nation into civil war between Protestant and Catholic powers which did not end until the *Edict of Toleration of 1598*, which guaranteed religious and political freedom in certain partitioned areas of the country.

In 1572, 30,000 Protestants were massacred while worshipping on St. Bartholomew's Day. The Huguenots became convinced of the necessity of using force in self-defense and articulated their Biblical reasoning of this in their *Vindicae Contra Tyrannos (A Defense of*

*Tens of thousands of Huguenots were persecuted and martyred by civil and religious tyrants.*

*Liberty Against Tyrants*) in 1579. This document, drafted by Philippe DuPlessis Mornay, drawing from reasoning found in Calvin's writings, became a precedent for the American Colonists at the time of their Revolution in 1776. An old Huguenot song said: "Spirit who made them live, awaken their children, so that they will know how to follow them."

# LEX, REX,

OR

# THE LAW AND THE PRINCE;

A DISPUTE FOR

## THE JUST PREROGATIVE OF KING AND PEOPLE:

CONTAINING

**THE REASONS AND CAUSES OF THE MOST NECESSARY DEFENSIVE WARS OF THE KINGDOM OF SCOTLAND,**

AND OF THEIR

**EXPEDITION FOR THE AID AND HELP OF THEIR DEAR BRETHREN OF ENGLAND;**

IN WHICH THEIR INNOCENCY IS ASSERTED, AND A FULL ANSWER IS GIVEN TO A SEDITIOUS PAMPHLET,

ENTITULED,

## " SACRO-SANCTA REGUM MAJESTAS,"

OR

THE SACRED AND ROYAL PREROGATIVE OF CHRISTIAN KINGS ;

UNDER THE NAME OF J. A., BUT PENNED BY

### JOHN MAXWELL, THE EXCOMMUNICATE POPISH PRELATE ;

WITH A SCRIPTURAL CONFUTATION OF THE RUINOUS GROUNDS OF W. BARCLAY, H. GROTIUS, H. ARNISÆUS, ANT. DE DOMI. POPISH BISHOP OF SPALATO, AND OF OTHER LATE ANTI-MAGISTRATICAL ROYALISTS, AS THE AUTHOR OF OSSORIANUM, DR FERNE, E. SYMMONS, THE DOCTORS OF ABERDEEN, ETC.

### IN FORTY-FOUR QUESTIONS.

BY THE

## REV. SAMUEL RUTHERFORD.

SOMETIME PROFESSOR OF DIVINITY IN THE UNIVERSITY OF ST. ANDREWS.

"But if you shall still do wickedly, ye shall be consumed, both ye and your king."—1 SAM. xii. 25.

*The Scottish Reformation, begun by John Knox, gave rise to writings on Christian resistance to tyranny, such as Lex Rex, written by Rev. Samuel Rutherford in 1644.*

---
# Chapter 5
---

# The Chain of Liberty: Preparation for America

## Puritans and Separatists in England

God not only prepares people to shape history, but He also shapes history to prepare people so that they may fulfill their destiny and accomplish God's purposes in the earth. This latter aspect of God's principle of preparation is evident in English history of the sixteenth century. We will see God using various leaders and events to help prepare those people who would become the "Parents of the Republic of the United States of America."

## William Tyndale                                              1494-1536

God's chief instrument in bringing about the Reformation in England was William Tyndale. Much of Tyndale's life was spent fulfilling his vision: "If God preserves my life, I will cause a boy that driveth a plow to know more of the Scriptures than the pope." Tyndales's dream was accomplished, but only at a great cost.

He spent over twelve years in exile from his native country, all the time facing the possibility of being captured and put to death. During this time, he translated the Bible from the original languages with the idea of making it available for the common man. His New Testament was published in 1525. So scholarly was Tyndale's work that is has been estimated that our present English Bibles retain eighty percent of his original work in the Old Testament, and ninety percent in the New.

*William Tyndale*

In 1536 Tyndale was betrayed, arrested, and killed as a heretic. On the day of his death, Tyndale calmly stated: "I call God to record that I have never altered, against the voice of my conscience, one syllable of his Word. Nor would I this day, if all the pleasures, honors, and riches of the earth might be given to me."

Before he was strangled and burned at the stake he prayed for King Henry VIII who had persecuted and put to death many reformers and caused Tyndale to flee his country. As he was being fastened to the stake he cried out with these final words: "Lord, open the king of England's eyes!" Although his life was extinguished, the flames of liberty would burn brighter than ever, for the Word of God would be spread to all people throughout England.

During Tyndale's life many copies of his New Testament were circulated throughout England, but only under cover for the king had banned Tyndale's work. Shortly after Tyndale's death, Henry VIII "authorized the sale and the reading of the Bible throughout the kingdom", for he wanted "to emancipate England from Romish domination", and saw the "Holy Scriptures as the most powerful engine to destroy the papal system." Ironically, the king put his approval on the Matthew Bible (the revised to be called The Great Bible promoted by Henry VIII in 1539), which was in reality Tyndale's work under another name.

As the Word of God spread throughout the land, many people cried out with Tyndale, "We know that this Word is from God, as we know that fire burns; not because anyone has told us, but because a Divine fire consumes our hearts."[1]

These men and events all contribute to the movement of the Chain of Christianity and the beginning of liberty upon the earth. We will continue to trace the hand of God in history and see various links in the Chain of Christianity. As we do, "We should never forget that the prison, the scaffold, and the stake were stages in the march of civil and religious liberty which our forefathers had to travel in order that we might attain our present liberty."[2]

## Henry VIII

When Henry VIII became king of England in 1509, Roman Catholicism was the established religion, not only in England, but in all of Europe. The government of the church reached beyond its Biblical sphere of jurisdiction by exercising control in all areas of life.

Most people, when they hear of Henry VIII, think of his many wives. His first wife, Catherine of Aragon, had borne him no sons, plus he had acquired a particular fondness for Anne Boleyn, so he decided to divorce Catherine. Such action required permission from the pope, so Henry sent a petition asking for approval for the divorce. When he was denied approval, Henry, not being the submissive type, decided he would not only go on and divorce Catherine, but he would also divorce himself (and take England with him) from the Catholic Church.

Henry and England thus split from the Roman Catholic Church and around 1534 set up the Church of England in its place. At the time, the only difference in the two was that Henry was the pope over the Church of England instead of the Pope in Rome. However, this event would prove to be very important in the advancement of religious and civil liberty in England and throughout the world.

*Henry VIII*

God was using Henry, who was not a godly man, to fulfill His purposes. Henry's actions toward Tyndale and other reformers (His policies led to Tyndale's and many others' death) reveal that his split from Rome had nothing to do with godly reform, but only selfish desires; yet, God who governs in the affairs of men, was using this historical event to accomplish His will. We saw earlier how God even used Henry to distribute Bibles that Tyndale had translated. While Henry broke from Roman Catholicism, there was still no freedom for individuals to worship God. Due to Tyndale's translation of the Bible people throughout England were being awakened, yet the climate of Henry's England did not permit reform to flourish. Many saw that the Church of England needed reform as much as the Catholic Church, but little external reform occurred under Henry.

## Edward VI

When Henry VIII died in 1547, he left the throne in the hands of his son, Edward VI, and Edward's protectorates. They favored those who wanted further reform in the Church of England. Under Edward the Puritan movement was born. Those people desiring to purify the Church of its errors and ungodliness were called "purifiers" or "puritans".

These reformers were overjoyed when Edward assumed power, for they could now begin to freely carry out their desired reform. Yet, they learned that one righteous ruler is not enough to ensure reform within a nation.

## *"Bloody" Mary*

1553

Edward died in 1553, having reigned only six years. His half-sister and Henry's daughter, Mary, succeeded him to the throne. She has earned the title, *Bloody Mary*, for she put to death hundreds of reformers including the "first Puritan", John Hooper. It was Hooper who first denied the right of the State to interfere with religion in 1553.

Mary not only detested the church reforms that occurred under Edward, but also never liked the fact that her father had separated from the Catholic Church. She set about to make amends with the Pope and purge England of the Puritan movement. She caused 286 Reformed Anglican leaders, including Thomas Cranmer, Nicholas Ridley, and Hugh Latimer, to be burned at the stake.

Consequently, thousands of Puritans fled England to places in Europe that harbored reformers, and in particular, Geneva. Due to the influence of Calvin, Geneva was one of the most free and advanced cities in the world. Internal liberty, resulting from Biblical truth, was affecting all aspects of society in Geneva -- from religious and civil freedom to education for the general populace and the best sanitation system in all of Europe.

It was in Geneva that the English Puritans were taught much Biblical truth that they were lacking, in particular ideas on civil liberty. God made sure that the people He was preparing were equipped in every way. He even used Bloody Mary to help accomplish His purposes.

## *Elizabeth I*

1558

Mary died in 1558, after reigning only five years, and was succeeded by her half-sister, Elizabeth. This began the Elizabethan Era.

Elizabeth did not want England to return to Catholicism, but she also was not interested in promoting the needed reforms within the Church of England. She did promise religious toleration which caused many Puritans to return to England who had fled during Mary's reign.

As the Puritans returned, they brought with them fuller ideas of civil and religious liberty, plus the Geneva Bible. While in exile in Geneva, a number of reformers translated and published a relatively compact and affordable Bible. The Geneva Bible would become the Bible of the masses. Since it was also the first English Bible to be divided into chapter and verse, it proved to be a good study Bible.

After a few years, Elizabeth saw her tolerance of reformers was causing many to cry out for more reform than she desired. So in 1562 she issued her *Articles of Religion* which prohibited further reform. At this, some of the Puritans gave up hope of ever seeing the needed church reform and separated themselves from the Church of England. Thus, the "Separatist" movement was born around 1580. The Pilgrims who first sailed to America in 1620 were English separatists.

The Separatist movement continued to grow throughout Elizabeth's long reign, although there were attempts from within England and from other nations to stop it.

## *The Miraculous Defeat of the Spanish Armada*                    1588

Satan hates revival and will try to stop it anyway he can. The Catholic monarchs of France caused 72,000 Protestants (Huguenots) to be massacred on one day in 1572. Finding that persecution only strengthened the movement in England, Satan attempted to stamp it out by war.

In 1588, Philip II of Spain sent the Spanish Armada to bring England again under the domination of Rome. A historian of the period, Richard Hakluyt writes of this event:

"It is most apparent, that God miraculously preserved the English nation. For the L. Admiral wrote unto her Majestie that in all humane reason, and according to the judgement of all men (every circumstance being duly considered) the English men were not of any such force, whereby they might, without a miracle dare once to approach within sight of the Spanish Fleet: insomuch that they freely ascribed all the honour of their victory unto God, who had confounded the enemy, and had brought his counsels to none effect.... While this wonderful and puissant navy was syling along the English coastes,... all people throut England prostrated themselves with humble prayers and supplications unto God: but especially the outlandish churches (who had greatest cause to feare, and against whom by name the Spaniards had threatened most grievous torments) enjoyned to their people continual fastings and supplications... knowing right well, that prayer was the onely refuge against all enemies, calamities, and necessities, and that it was the onely solace and reliefe for mankind, being visited with afflictions and misery..."[1]

Here is what happened: As the Spanish fleet sailed up the English Channel, they were met by the much smaller English navy. In the natural, the English had no hope, yet all of England had been fasting and praying. A storm arose which blew many of the Spanish ships up against the coast of Holland, causing them to sink. Oddly, the smaller English ships were not affected by the storm and were able to maneuver next to the Spanish ships and set many of them on fire. A few Spanish ships limped back to Spain without touching English soil.

God had providentially intervened to protect His people and ensure that England would fulfill its purpose as a nation. Even the nation of Holland acknowledged the hand of God. In commemoration of the event, they minted a coin. On one side were ships sinking; on the other, men on their knees in prayer with the inscription: "Man Proposeth, God Disposeth," and the date "1588".

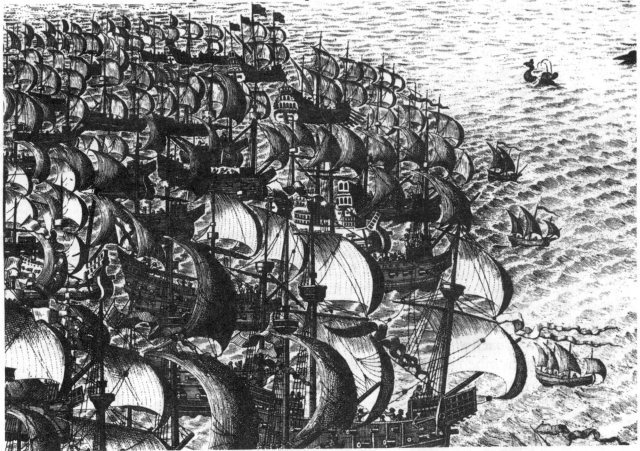

*The Spanish Armada*

1603                    *James I*

At Elizabeth's death in 1603, James I came to the throne. Intense persecution of Separatists under James' policies caused many of them to flee the country, this time to Holland. As we shall see, this was another Providential event that helped prepare those people who were to be "stepping stones" for the founding of a new nation -- one birthed by God.

---

## Chapter 6

# The Pilgrims: A Model of Christian Character

The Separatist Movement began in England in the latter part of the sixteenth century, as people began to embrace the idea of "reformation without tarrying for any." The many Separatists in and around the little town of Scrooby in the north of England were destined to have a great impact upon the world, for it was here that many of the Pilgrims had their roots. At Scrooby, these Christians wrote a church covenant - the first of its kind affirming church self-government in 1606.

Three of the most prominent leaders of the Pilgrims started on their great pilgrimage from Scrooby. As we briefly look at their lives, we will began to understand the heart of the Pilgrims.

### William Brewster

William Brewster was one of the only Pilgrims to have position in English society, and that was by no means an exalted one. After serving as a confidential secretary to a prominent member of Queen Elizabeth's court, he returned to Scrooby where he became

*William Brewster*

Postmaster and the overseer of a gentleman's estate in the area. "He set about trying to reform the Church of England from within by getting good Scriptural preachers for the local churches and paying for them out of his own pocket. (Many churches went without preaching for years on end, since Queen Elizabeth plainly preferred the reading of government-approved "homilies" to sermons that reflected individual interpretation of Scripture.) When the Church of England demanded more rigid conformity to its rituals and rejected the right of individuals to hear "unauthorized" preachers, Brewster finally decided to separate from the Church and to covenant with other Christians in his area to form a Scriptural congregation."[1]

Brewster later served as an elder in the congregation in England, Holland, and America. During the first year in America, the Pilgrims had no pastor, so Brewster effectively served in that capacity. According to Bradford, he was also a highly effective evangelist -- "He did more in this behalf in a year than many...do in all their lives."[2]

## John Robinson

*John Robinson*

More than anyone else, John Robinson prepared the Pilgrims to accomplish the great task of preparing the way for the settlement of a new nation. It was he who served as the Pilgrims pastor in England and Holland.

Robinson was trained as a clergyman in the Church of England, but was "dismissed from his first pastoral assignment for failure to conform to the Church of England's requirements regarding the wearing of priestly vestments."[3] Afterwards he took much time in considering whether he should remain in the Church of England. While he witnessed much that was unscriptural in the Church, he hesitated for there were many Godly men who still remained in the Church. Yet the truth of God burned in his heart. Robinson said:

> "...had not the truth been in my heart as a burning fire shut up in my bones, Jer. XX.9, I had never broken those bonds...wherein I was so straitly tied, but had suffered the light of God to have been put out in mine own unthankful heart by other men's darkness."

The truth did prevail, and the light within him burned brighter as he left the Church of England and joined the Separatist congregation that met in the home of William Brewster's in Scrooby.

Marshall Foster writes:

> "Though often neglected by historians, John Robinson should be known as one of the great Christian philosophers who propounded religious toleration in an intolerant age and representative government in an age of absolute monarchy. For twen-

ty years, he taught these principles in depth to his persecuted and beloved Pilgrim church. More than any other man, John Robinson prepared a people to take dominion over the wilderness to the glory of God. Through his godly wisdom, he taught the Pilgrims individual Christian unity."

"His love was great towards them, and his care was all ways bente for their best good, both for soule and body; for besids his singuler abilities in devine things (wherein he excelled), he was also very able to give directions in civill affaires, and to foresee dangers & inconveniences; by which means he was very helpful to their outward estats, and so was every way as a commone father unto them...."[4]

## William Bradford

One of the best known Pilgrim Fathers was William Bradford. He served as governor of Plymouth for 33 years and also wrote the *History of Plymouth Plantation,* the first great literary work of America.

As a young teenager, Bradford reasoned that the Church of England was unbiblical and so removed himself from it. He had such insight because a few years earlier, while confined to the bed with a long illness, he had read the Bible continuously. He attended the Church of England in Bobworth for some time simply because he was impressed by the Scriptural preaching of Rev. Richard Clyfton. When Clyfton withdrew and joined the Scrooby Congregation, Bradford followed, even though he faced enormous pressure. He decided:

"to withdraw from the communion of the parish-assemblies, and engage with some society of the faithful that should keep close unto the written word of God, as the rule of their worship...although the provoked rage of his friends tried all the ways imaginable to reclaim him from it, unto all...his answer was...'Nevertheless, to keep a good conscience, and walk in such a way as God has prescribed in his word, is a thing which I must prefer before you all, and above life itself.'"[5]

It was 1602 when Bradford started attending the Separatist Church in Scrooby. Six years later he would travel with part of the Church to Holland, and twelve years after that with a smaller number to America.

## History "Of Plymouth Plantation"

A book which every American and Christian should read, but whose title (not to mention the content) is rarely even mentioned in our schools today, is William Bradford's *Of Plymouth Plantation.* This history plainly reveals God's hand in the Pilgrim's lives and in the events they went through to settle in the north parts of America. We can see no greater human example of Christian character than in the lives of the Pilgrims.

To appreciate the price paid for liberty and to introduce you to one of America's greatest historical and literary writings, there follows many excerpts from Bradford's original manuscript, written in 1647 (from the 1901 edition printed by order of the General Court of Massachusetts by Wright & Potter Printing Co., State Printers):

## *"Of Plimoth Plantation" by William Bradford*

"When as by the travell & diligence of some godly & zealous preachers, & Gods blessing on their labours, as in other places of ye land, so in ye North parts, many became inlightened by ye word of God, and had their ignorance & sins discovered unto them, and begane by his grace to reforme their lives, and make conscience of their ways... So many therfore of these proffessors as saw ye evill of these things, in thes parts, and whose harts ye Lord had touched wth heavenly Zeale for his trueth, they shooke of this yoake of antichristian bondage, and as ye Lords free people, joyned them selves (by a covenant of the Lord) into a church estate, in ye felowhsip of ye gospell, to walke in all his wayes, make known or to be made known unto them, according to their best endeavours, whatsoever it should cost them, the Lord assisting them. And that it cost them something this ensewing historie will declare..."

### *"Of their departure into Holland"*

"Being thus constrained to leave their native soyle and countrie, their lands & livings, and all their freinds & famillier acquaintance, it was much, and thought marvelous by many. But to goe into a countrie they knew not (but hearsay), wher they must learne a new language, and get their livings they knew not how, it being a dear place,& subjecte to ye misseries of warr, it was by many thought an adventure almost desperate, a case intolerable, & a misserie worse then death. Espetially seeing they were not aquainted with trads nor traffique, (by which yt countrie doth subsiste,) but had only been used to a plaine countrie life, & ye inocente trade of husbandrey. But these things did not dismay them (though they did some times trouble them) for their desires were sett on ye ways of God, & to injoye his ordinances; but they rested on his providence, & knew whom they had beleeved."

"Ther was a large companie of them purposed to get passage at Boston in Lincoln-shire, and for that end had hired a shipe wholy to them selves, & made agreement with the maister to be ready at a certaine day, and take them and their goods in, at a conveniente place, wher they accordingly would all attende in readiness. So after long waiting, & large expences, though he kepte not day with them, yet he came at length & tooke them in, in ye night. But when he had them & their goods abord, he betrayed them, haveing before hand complotted with ye serchers & other officers so to doe; who tooke them, and put them into open boats, & ther rifled & ransaked them, searching them to their shirts for money, yea even ye women furder then became modestie; and then caried them back into ye towne, & made them a spectackle & wonder to ye multitude, which came flocking on all sids to behould them... After a months imprisonmente, ye greatest parte were dismiste, & sent to ye places from whence they came; but 7. of ye principall were still kept in prison..."

"The nexte spring after, ther was another attempte made by some of these & others, to get over at an other place. And it so fell out, that they light of a Dutchman at Hull, having a ship of his owne belonging to Zealand; they made agreemente with him, and acquainted him with their condition, hoping to find more faithfulness in him, then in ye former of their owne nation. He bad them not fear, for he would doe well enough. He was by appointment to take them in betweene Grimsbe & Hull, wher was a large comone a good way distante from any towne. Now aganst the prefixed time, the women & children, with ye goods, were sent to ye place in a small barke, which they had hired for yt end; and ye men were to meete them by land. But it so fell out, that they were ther a day before ye shipe came, & ye sea being rough, and ye women very sicke, prevailed with ye seamen to put into a creeke hardby, wher they lay on ground at lowwater. The nexte morning ye shipe came, but they were fast, & could not stir till about noone. In ye mean time, ye shipe maister, perceiving how ye matter was, sente his boate to be getting ye men abord whom he saw ready, walking aboute ye shore. But after ye first boat full was gott abord, & she was ready to goe for more, the mr espied a greate company, both horse & foote, with bills, & gunes, & other weapons; for ye countrie was raised to take them. Ye Dutchman seeing yt, swore his countries oath, 'sacremente, ' and having ye wind faire, waiged his Ancor, hoysed sayles, & away. But ye poore men which were gott abord, were in great distress for their wives and children, which they saw thus to be taken, and were left destitute of their helps; and them selves also, not having a cloath to shifte them with, more then they had on their baks, & some scarce a peney aboute them, all they had being abord ye barke. It drew tears from their eyes, and any thing they had they would have given to have been a shore againe; but all in vaine, ther was no remedy, they must thus sadly part. And afterward endured a fearfull storme at sea, being 14. days or more before yey arived at their porte, in 7. wherof they neither saw son, moone, nor stars, & were driven near ye coast of Norway; the mariners them selves often despairing of life; and once with shriks & cries gave over all, as if ye ship had been foundred in ye sea, & they sinking without recoverie. But when mans hope &: helpe wholy failed, ye Lords power & mercie appeared in ther recoverie; for ye ship rose againe, & gave ye mariners courage againe to manage her. And if modestie woud suffer me, I might declare with what fervente prayres they cried unto ye Lord in this great distres, (espetialy some of them,) even without any great distraction, when ye water rane into their mouthes & ears; & the mariners cried out, "We sinke, we sinke; they cried (if not with mirakelous, yet with a great hight or degree of devine faith), Yet Lord thou canst save, yet Lord thou canst save; with shuch other expressions as I will forbeare. Upon which ye ship did not only recover, but shortly after ye violence of ye storme begane to abate, and ye Lord filed their afflicted minds with shuch comforts as every one canot understand, and in ye end brought them to their desired Haven, wher ye people came flockeing admiring their deliverance, the storme having ben so longe & sore, in which much hurt had been don, as ye masters freinds related unto him in their congrattulations."

"But to returne to ye others wher we left. The rest of ye men yt were in greatest danger, made shift to escape away before ye troope could surprise them; those only staying yt best might, to be assistante unto ye women. But pitifull it was to see ye heavie case of these poore women in this distress; what weeping & crying on every side, some for their husbands, that were caried away in ye ship as is before related; others not knowing what shoud become of them, & their little ones; others againe melted in teares, seeing their poore litle ones hanging aboute them, crying for feare, and quaking with could. Being thus aprehended, they were hurried from one place to another, and from one justice to another, till in ye ende they knew not what to doe with them; for to imprison so many women & innocent children for no other cause (many of them) but that they must goe with their husbands, semed to be unreasonalbe and all would crie out of them; and to send them home againe was as difficult, for they aledged, as ye trueth was, they had no homes to goe to, for they had either sould, or otherwise disposed of their houses & livings..."

"But yt I be not tedious in these things, I will omitte ye rest, though I might relate many other notable passages and troubles which they endured & underwente in these their wanderings &

travells both at land & sea; but I hast to other things. Yet I may not omitte ye fruite that came hearby, for by these so publick troubls, in so many eminente places, their cause became famouss, & occasioned many to looke into ye same; and their godly cariage & Christian behaviour was such as left a deep impression in the minds of many. And though some few shrunk at these first conflicts & sharp beginings, (as it was no marvell,) yet many more came on with fresh courage, & greatly animated others. And in ye end, notwithstanding all these stormes of oppossition, they all gatt over at length, some at one time & some at an other, and some in one place & some in an other, and mette togeather againe according to their desires, with no small rejoycing.

### *"Of their setling in Holand, & their maner of living"*

*The Pilgrims consistently thanked God throughout their life.*

"Being now come into ye Low Countries, they saw many... faire & bewtifull cities, flowing with abundance of all sorts of welth & riches, yet it was not longe before they saw the grime & grisly face of povertie coming upon them like an armed man, with whom they must bukle & incounter, and from whom they; could not flye; but they were armed with faith & patience against him, and all his encounters; and though they were sometimes foyled, yet by Gods assistance they prevailed and got ye victorie...

"And when they had lived at Amsterdam aboute a year...they removed to Leyden, a fair & bewtifull citie, and of a sweete situation, but made more famous by ye universitie wherwith it is adorned, in which of late had been so many learned men.... And first though many of them weer poore... the Dutch (either bakers or others) would trust them in any reasonable matter when yey wanted money. Because they had found by experience how carfull they were to keep their word, and saw them so painfull & diligente in their callings; yea, they would strive to gett their custome, and to imploy them above others, in their worke, for their honestie & diligence....

### *"Ye reasons & causes of their remooval."*

After they had lived in this citie about some 11. or 12. years, (which is ye more observble being ye whole time of yt famose truce between that state & ye Spaniards,) and sundrie of them were taken away by death, & many others begane to be well striken in years, the grave mistris Experience haveing taught them many things, those prudent governours with sundrie of ye sagest members begane both deeply to apprehend their present dangers, & wisely to foresee ye future, & thinke of timly remedy. In ye agitation of their thoughts, and much discours of things hear aboute, at length they began to incline to this conclusion, of remooval to some other place. Not out of any newfanglednes, or other such like giddie humor, by which men are oftentimes transported to their great hurt & danger, but for sundrie weightie & solid reasons; some of ye cheefe of which I will hear breefly touch. And first, they saw & found by experience the hardnes of ye place & countrie to be such, as few in comparison would come to them... yea, some preferred & chose ye prisons in England, rather then this libertie in Holland, with these afflictions. But it was thought that if a better and easier place of living could be had, it would draw many, & take away these discouragements.

"They saw that though ye people generally bore all these difficulties very cherfully, & with a resolute courage, being in ye best & strength of their years, yet old age began to steale on many of them, (and their great & continuall labours, with other crosses and sorrows, hastened it before ye time,)... many of their children, by these occasions, and ye great licentiousnes of youth in yt countrie, and ye manifold temptations of the place, were drawne away by evill examples into extravagante & dangerous courses, getting ye raines off their neks, & departing from their parents. Some became souldiers, others tooke upon them farr viages by sea, and other some worse courses, tending to dissolutnes & the danger of their soules, to ye great greefe of their parents and dishonour of God. So that they saw their posteritie would be in danger to degenerate & be corrupted.

"Lastly, (and which was not least,) a great hope & inward zeall they had of laying some good foundatin, or at least to make some way therunto, for ye propagating & advancing ye gospell of ye kingdom of Christ in those remote parts of ye world; yea, though they should be but even as stepping-stones unto others for ye performing of so great a work.

"These, & some other like reasons, moved them to undertake this resolution of their removall; the which they afterward prosecuted with so great difficulties, as by the sequell will appeare.

"The place they had thoughts on was some of those vast & unpeopled countries of America, which are frutfull & fitt for habitation, being devoyed of all civill inhabitatnts, wher ther are only salvage & brutish men, which range up and downe, litle otherwise then ye wild beasts of the same. This proposition being made publike and coming to ye scaning of all, it raised many; variable opinions amongst men, and caused many fears & doubts amongst them selves.... For ther they should be liable to famine, and nakednes, & ye wante, in a maner, of all things. The chang of aire, diate, & drinking of water, would infecte their bodies with sore sickneses, and greevous diseases. And also those which should escape or overcome these difficulties, should yett be in continuall danger of ye salvage people, who are cruell, barbarous, & most trecherous, being most furious in their rage, and merciles wher they overcome; not being contente to kill, & take away life, but delight to tormente men in ye most bloodie maner that may be;....It was furder objected, that it would require greater sumes of money to furnish such a voiage, and to fitt them with necessaries, then their consumed estats would amounte too; and yett they must as well looke to be seconded with supplies, as presently to be transported. Also many presidents of ill success, & lamentable misseries befalne others in the like designes, were easie to be found, and not forgotten to be aledged; besids their owne experience, in their former troubles & haardships in their removall into Holand, and how hard a thing it was for them to live in that strange place, though it was a nieghbour countrie, & a civill and rich comne wealth.

"It was answered, that all great & honourable actions are accompanied with great difficulties, and must be both enterprised and overcome with answerable courages. It was granted ye dangers were great, but not desperate; the difficulties were many, but not invincible... and all of them, through ye help of God, by fortitude and patience, might either be borne, or overcome...

*"Preparation to this waightie vioage."*

"So being ready to departe, they had a day of solleme humiliation, their pastor taking his texte from Ezra 8. 21. 'And ther at ye river, by Ahava, I proclaimed a fast, that we might humble ourselves before our God, and seeke of him a right way for us, and

*William Brewster and Rev. John Robinson lead the Pilgrims in prayer before their voyage to America*

for our children, and for all our substance.' Upon which he spente a good parte of ye day very profitably, and suitable to their presente occasion....

"At their parting Mr. Robinson write a leter to ye whole company, which though it hath already bene printed, yet I thought good here likwise to inserte it;...

"Loving Christian friends, I doe hartily & in ye Lord salute you all,....

And first, as we are daly to renew our repentance with our God, expetially for our sines known, and generally for our unknowne trespasses,....sine being taken away by ernest repentence & ye pardon therof from ye Lord sealed up unto a mans conscience by his spirite, great shall be his securitie and peace in all dangers, sweete his comforts in all distresses, with hapie deliverance from all evill, whether in life or in death."

"Lastly, wheras you are become a body politick, using amongst your selves civill governmente, and are not furnished with any persons of spetiall eminencie above ye rest, to be chosen by you into office of governement, let your wisdome & godlines appeare, not only in chusing shuch persons as doe entirely love and will promote ye comone good, but also in yeellding unto them all due honour & obedience in their lawfull administrations; not be-houlding in them ye ordinarinesse of their persons, but Gods or-dinance for your good, not being like ye foolish multitud who more honour ye gay coate, then either ye vertuous minde of ye man, or glorious ordinance of ye Lord.

"I doe ernestly comend unto your care & conscience, joyning therwith my daily incessante prayers unto ye Lord, yt he who hath made ye heavens & ye earth, ye sea and all rivers of waters, and whose providence is over all his workes, espetially over all his dear children for good, would so guide & gard you in your wayes...John Robinson"

### "Of their vioage"

After 66 days at sea, in a space no larger than a volleyball court, these 102 passengers aboard the Mayflower finally reached America. The Pilgrims intended to settle just north of the Virginia Colony but were providentially blown off course and out from under the juris-diction of the Virginia Land Company. Being unable to sail south-ward due to the weather, they put ashore at Cape Cod. Had they arrived here some years earlier they would have been met by Patuxet Indians and would have found no place to settle. These Indians had murdered many white men who landed on their shores, but in 1617 a plague had mysteriously wiped them out (all except one, Squanto) and now neighboring tribes were afraid to come near the place for fear that some great supernatural spirit had destroyed them.

"Being thus passed ye vast ocean, and a sea of troubles before in their preparation (as may be remembred by yt which wente before), they had now no freinds to wellcome them, nor inns to entertaine or refresh their weatherbeaten bodys, no houses or much less townes to repaire too, to seeke for succoure. It is recorded in scripture as a mercie to ye apostle & his shipwraked company, yt the barbarians shewed them no smale kindnes in

*The Mayflower*

refreshing them, but these savage barbarians, when they mette with them (as after will appeare) were readier to fill their sids full of arrows then otherwise. And for ye season it was winter, and they that know ye winters of yt cuntrie know them to be sharp & violent, & subjecte to cruell & feirce stormes, deangerous to travill to known places, much more to serch an unknown coast. Besids, what could they see but a hidious & desolate wildernes, full of wild beasts & wild men? and what multituds ther might be of them they knew not. Nether could they, as it were, goe up to ye tope of Pisgah, to vew from this wildernes a more goodly cuntrie to feed their hops; for which way soever they turned their eys (save upward to ye heavens) they could have litle solace or content in respecte of any outward objects. For sumer being done, all things stand upon them with a wetherbeaten face; and ye whole countrie, full of woods & thickets, represented a wild & savage heiw. If they looked behind them, ther was ye mighty ocean which they had passed, and was now as a maine barr & goulfe to seperate them from all ye civill parts of ye world. If it be said they had a ship to sucour them, it is trew; but what heard they daly from ye mr. & company? but yt with speede they should looke out a place with their shallop, wher they would be at some near distance; for ye season was shuch as he would not stirr from thence till a safe harbor was discovered by them wher they would be, and he might goe without danger; and that victells consumed apace, but he must & would keepe sufficient for them selves & their returne. Yea, it was muttered by some, that if they gott not a place in time, they would turne them & their goods ashore & leave them. Let it also be considred what weake hopes of supply & succoure they left behinde them, yt might bear up their minds in this sade condition and trialls they were under; and they could not but be very smale. It is true, indeed, ye affections & love of their brethren at Leyden was cordiall & entire towards them, but they had litle power to help them, or them selves; and how ye case stode betweene them & ye marchants at their coming away, hath allready been declared. What could now sustaine them but ye spirite of God & his grace? May not & ought not the children of these fathers rightly say: Our faithers were Englishmen which came over this great ocean, and were ready to perish in this willdernes; but they cried unto ye Lord, and he heard their voyce, and looked on their adversitie, &c. Let them therfore praise ye Lord, because he is good, & his mercies endure for ever. Yea, let them which have been redeemed of ye Lord, shew how he hath delivered them from ye hand of ye oppressour, When they wandered in ye deserte willdernes out of ye way, and found no citie to dwell in, both hungrie, & thirstie, their sowle was overshelmed in them.

Let them confess before ye Lord his loving kindnes, and his wonderfull works before ye sons of men..."

## The Mayflower Compact and their 1st Winter

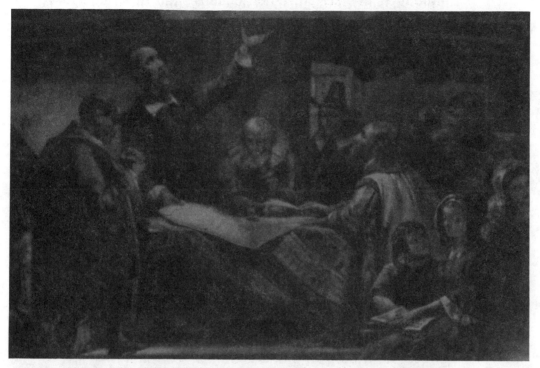

*The signing of the Mayflower Compact.*

"I shall a litle returne backe and begine with a combination made by them before they came ashore, being ye first foundation of their govermente in this place; occasioned partly by ye discontented & mutinous speeches that some of the strangers amongst them had let fall from them in ye ship - That when they came a shore they would use their owne libertie; for none had power to comand them, the patente they had being for Virginia, and not for New-england, which belonged to an other Goverment, with which Ye Virginia Company had nothing to doe. And partly that shuch an acte by them done (this their condition considered) might be as firme as any patent, and in some respects more sure. The forme was as followeth.

"In ye name of God, Amen. We whose names are underwriten, the loyall subjects of our dread soveraigne Lord, King James, by ye grace of God, of Great Britaine, France, & Ireland king, defender of ye faith, &c., haveing undertaken, for ye glorie of God, and advancemente of ye Christian faith, and honour of our king & countrie, a voyage to plant ye first colonie in ye Northerne parts of Virginia, doe by these presents solemnly & mutually in ye presence of God, and one of another, covenant & combine our selves togeather into a civill body politick, for our better ordering & preservation & furtherance of ye ends aforesaid; and by vertue hearof to enacte, constitute, and frame such just & equall lawes, ordinances, acts, constitutions, & offices, from time to time, as shall be thought most meete & convenient for ye generall good of ye Colonie, unto which we promise all due submission and obedience."

"After they had provided a place for their goods, or comone store, (which were long in unloading for want of boats,foulnes of winter weather, and sicknes of diverce) and begune some small cottages for their habitation, as time would admitte, they mette and consulted of lawes & orders..."

"But that which was most sadd & lamentable was, that in 2. or 3. moneths time halfe of their company dyed, espetialy in Jan: & February, being ye depth of winter, and wanting houses & other comforts; being infected with ye scurvie & other diseases, which this long vioage & their inacomodate condition had brought upon them; so as ther dyed some times 2. or 3. of a day, in ye foresaid time; that of 100. & odd persons, scarce 50. remained. And of these in ye time of most distres, ther was but 6. or 7. sound persons, who, to their great comendations be it spoken, spared no

*The Pilgrims thanked God for a safe Voyage.*

pains, night nor day, but with abundance of toyle and hazard of their owne health, fetched them woode, made them fires, drest them meat, made their beads, washed their lothsome cloaths, cloathed & uncloathed them; in a word, did all ye homly & necessarie offices for them wch dainty & quesie stomacks cannot endure to hear named; and all this willingly & cherfully, without any grudging in ye least, shewing herein their true love unto their freinds & bretheren. A rare example & worthy to be remembred..."

"But about ye 16. of March a certaine Indian came bouldly amongst them, and spoke to them in broken English, which they could well understand, but marvelled at it... He tould them also of another Indian whos name was Squanto, a native of this place, who had been in England & could speake better English then him selfe.

"Afterwards they (as many as were able) began to plant ther corne, in which servise Squanto stood them in great stead, showing them both ye maner how to set it, and after how to dress & tend it. Also he tould them excepte they gott fish & set with it (in these old grounds) it would come to nothing, and he showed them yt in ye midle of Aprill they should have store enough come up ye brooke, by which they begane to build, and taught them how to take it, and wher to get other provissions necessary for them; all which they found true by triall & experience.... And thus they found ye Lord to be with them in all their ways, and to blesse their outgoings & incomings, for which let his holy name have ye praise for ever, to all posteritie."

## The First Thanksgiving

In addition to teaching the Pilgrims how to plant corn and find fish, Squanto also taught them to stalk deer, plant pumpkins, find berries, and catch beaver, whose pelts proved to be their economic deliverance. He was also helpful in securing a peace treaty between the Pilgrims and surrounding Indian tribes, which lasted over fifty years. In the words of William Bradford, "Squanto... was a special instrument sent of God for their good beyond their expectation." His life story is amazing in itself.

In 1605, Squanto, a member of the Patuxet Indian tribe, was captured by an English explorer and taken to England. He remained there nine years, during which time he learned to speak English. In 1614, Captain John Smith took him back to New England, but shortly after this he was again taken captive and sold into slavery at a port in Spain. Providentially, some local friars bought and rescued him, and then introduced him to Christianity.

From Spain he eventually went to England where he remained until 1619, when he obtained passage back to his home in New England. As Squanto went ashore at what was to become Plymouth, he found his entire tribe had been killed by a plague. He was the only survivor of the Patuxet tribe. Joining himself to a nearby tribe, he remained there until the spring of 1621 when he joined himself with the Pilgrims, determining to see them survive at the place where his tribe had not.

Thanks to God, his instrument Squanto, and the character and determination of the Pilgrims, half of them had survived an unimaginably difficult first year. Moreover, they harvested a sufficient food supply for their second winter at Plymouth. Even though there was no surplus food, things looked much better than the preceding winter.

Governor Bradford appointed a day of Thanksgiving and invited the nearby Wampanoag Indians (Squanto's adopted tribe) to celebrate and give thanks unto God with them. Chief Massasoit and ninety of his men came and feasted with the Pilgrims. They ate deer, turkey, fish, lobster, eels, vegetables, corn bread, herbs, berries, pies, and the Indians even taught the Pilgrims how to make popcorn. The Pilgrims and Indians also competed in running, wrestling, and shooting games. Massasoit enjoyed himself so much that he and his men stayed for three days. It is easy to see where the American tradition of feasting at Thanksgiving began.

While many people today follow the Pilgrim's example of feasting at Thanksgiving, they too often ignore the entire reason that the Pilgrims set aside a special day -- that was to give thanks to Almighty God and acknowledge their utter dependence upon Him for their existence. While many today take ease in having plenty, never seeing a need to cry out to God, the Pilgrims relied upon God in their lack and thanked Him in their abundance. Their trust was in God and not in their abundant provisions.

## The Pilgrims --- An Example to All

As you have seen reading through the excerpts of Bradford's History, we can learn so much from the example of the Pilgrims. Following are only a few lessons we should learn:

1. The Pilgrims give us an excellent example of the Principle of Christian Character.

2. God will providentially prepare us to accomplish His destiny for our lives.

3. God will supernaturally protect and care for us as we walk in the way He's set before us.

4. Freedom of worship and liberty for ourselves and our descendants is worth any price we must pay.

5. The Pilgrims knew how to apply Biblical truth to civil affairs as seen in the Mayflower Compact, which was the first expression of civil government that recognized the Christian idea of man and government.

In the life of the Pilgrims, God had prepared those of humble beginnings to be a light of liberty to an entire nation. In the words of Bradford:

"Thus out of smalle beginings greater things have been prodused by His hand yt made all things of nothing, and gives being to all things that are; and as one small candle may light a thousand, so ye light here kindled hath shone to many, yea in some sorte to our whole nation; let ye glorious name of Jehova have all ye praise."

*Sunday at Plymouth*

In ye name of god Amen. We whose names are underwriten
the loyall subiects of our dread soueraigne Lord King Iame
by ye grace of God, of great Britaine, franc, & Ireland king
defendor of ye faith, &c

Haueing vndertaken, for ye glorie of god, and aduancemente
of ye christian faith and honour of our king & countrie, a voyage to
plant ye first colonie in ye Northerne parts of Virginia. Doe
by these presents solemnly & mutualy in ye presence of god, and
one of another, couenant, & combine our selues togeather into a
ciuill body politick; for our better ordering, & preseruation & fur=
therance of ye ends aforesaid; and by vertue hereof to enacte,
constitute, and frame such just & equall Lawes, ordinances,
Acts, constitutions, & offices, from time to time, as shall be thought
most meete & conuenient for ye generall good of ye Colonie: Vnto
which we promise all due submission and obedience. In witnes
wherof we haue here vnder subscribed our names at Cap=
Codd ye 11. of Nouember, in ye year of ye raigne of our soueraigne
Lord king Iames of England, franc, & Ireland ye eighteenth
and of scotland ye fiftie fourth, An: Dom: 1620.

**Facsimile of Governor Bradford's handwritten copy of the Mayflower Compact.**

---

## Chapter 7

# The Colonies: Seeds of a Nation

There is a direct causal relationship between the dispersion of the Bible in the hands of the people and the rise of civil liberty. A survey of civil government from the time of Christ to the present reveals a sudden profusion of documents such as the Mayflower Compact, English Bill of Rights, and the Constitution beginning in 1620. Before this there existed only pagan monarchies.

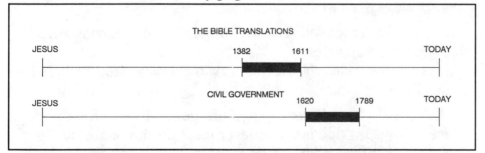

What produced these changes in ideas of government? How does one explain this? For two centuries prior to these changes, the Bible began to be translated and disseminated in the common language. It all began with John Wycliffe in 1382 who said of his new translation into English: "This Bible is for the government of the people, by the people, and for the people."[1]

As people began to read the Bible, two things occurred: The church began to return to Biblical Christianity, and society began to be reformed and enjoy civil liberty.

## Restoration of Biblical Church Government

Christians in the religious system of the 16th century began to study the Scriptural model of church government. They found that governing authority in the church was placed in the hands of apostles and elders:

"The brethren determined that Paul and Barnabas and certain others of them should go up to Jerusalem to the apostles and elders concerning this issue ... And the apostles and the elders came together to look into this matter." Acts 15:2,6 (see also vs. 1-6,23)

"Now while they were passing through the cities, they were delivering the decrees, which had been decided upon by the apostles and elders who were in Jerusalem, for them to observe." Acts 16:4 (See also: Acts 2:42; Acts 4:35; Acts 14:23)

The entire congregation could be involved and consulted in directional matters, but even here the final approval or appointing power remained with the apostles and elders:

"The **Twelve** summoned the congregation of the disciples and said, 'It is not desirable for us to neglect the word of God in order to serve tables. But select from among you, brethren, seven men of good reputation, full of the Spirit and of wisdom, whom **we** may put in charge of the task.' ...And the statement found approval with the whole congregation; And they brought (7 men) before **the apostles**; and after praying, they laid their hands on them." (Acts 6:2,3,6)

Note that even the requirements for nominating deacons were established by the apostles.

New Testament church government was characterized by three essentials in the original:

**1. Covenant Commitment** - A more general word for this was "love." It meant that **every** believer must do "his share" and participate in church activities. "Fellowship" meant partnership in the Gospel. The "body" of Christ is "held together by the joints and ligaments" (or "bonds") (Col. 2:19). The perfect "bond" or "ligament" of unity is "**love**" or covenant (Col. 3:14).

**2. Plurality of elders** - The government of the church is the responsibility of the elders. The Bible shows that these elders were appointed by God through apostles. Never is there an example of an elder ruling a church by himself; a plurality was always required to prevent poor decisions.

"And when they [the apostles] had appointed **elders** for them in every church, having prayed with fasting, they commended them to the Lord..." Acts 14:23

"For this reason I [Paul] left you in Crete, that you might set in order what remains, and appoint **elders** in every city as I directed you..." Tit. 1:5 (See also I Tim. 3:1-5 & Prov. 11:14)

**3. "Senior" elders, apostles and prophets** - Strong, decisive leadership is necessary at times in the plurality of elders. Jerusalem, which was a model for other local churches, had James as the "senior" elder:

- James was the one that people reported to (Acts 12:17).

- James moderated the council of elders (Acts 15:13,19).

- James was the one that Paul consulted for advice (Acts 21:18).

- James was the one with whom the Jerusalem believers identified themselves (Gal. 2:12).

And there were also apostles and prophets who exercised authority in the Body of Christ at large:

"God has appointed these in the church: first apostles, second prophets..." (I Cor. 12:28).

"The household of God is built on the foundation of the apostles and prophets" (Eph. 2:20).

## The Original Corrupted and Restored

These three New Testament elements of church government were corrupted over time as the church backslid. Fewer and fewer believers were willing to love or lay down their lives and serve in the church. As this covenant commitment waned, most church functions were being performed by leaders rather than all members. Laziness and unspirituality among common believers led to a clear clergy-laity distinction by the third century.

As time progressed, even the elders became less exemplary and therefore fewer. Authority became more centralized in the hands of the most prominent and spiritual elders known as "bishops." In the body of Christ at large, this same apostasy led to fewer qualified apostles, and therefore more centralization of apostolic authority. Within a few centuries it was all centralized in the hands of the "Popes."

After many centuries the dispersion of the Bible produced a revival in Europe and a rejection of the papal centralization of power. Catholic Reformers known as "Protestants" sprang up within the Catholic church throughout Europe. An ungodly king of England, Henry VIII, desired to divorce his wife but could not without being excommunicated by the Pope. Therefore in 1534, he decided to break off from Rome and start the Church of England.

The centralized form of church government, however, was the same, and became known as the Episcopal form.

In 1553 Protestants reestablished the role of elders in plurality (Presbytery) ruling the church instead of "popes." This became known as Presbyterian church government. In 1570, Protestants known as "Separatists" began emphasizing the role of the whole congregation in participating and ministering in the church. They placed church authority in the hands of the people through elections.

These three truths produced three distinct movements:

1. Episcopalians (1534) - emphasizing strong apostolic leadership.

2. Presbyterians (1558) - emphasizing plurality of elders.

3. Congregationalists (1570) - emphasizing covenant participation of all members.

## The Movements Planted In America

Each of these movements settled in the American colonies in three major geographical areas. This was significant because their views of church government determined their colonial forms of civil government. Let us examine just exactly how these Christian movements started America and gained dominance in three distinct regions.

## The Southern colonies -- Stronghold of Episcopalianism

*1607*

### Virginia

*John Smith*

Jamestown was the first permanent settlement in America. After the future settlers of Jamestown reached Virginia in April of 1607, one of the first acts of Captain John Smith and his soldiers was to erect a wooden cross on the shore at Cape Henry. It was at the foot of this cross that Reverend Robert Hunt led the 149 men of the Virginia company in public prayer, thanking God for their safe journey and recommitting themselves to God's plan and purpose for this New World. The Virginia Charter of 1606 reveals that part of their reason for coming to America was to propagate the "Christian Religion to such People, as yet live in Darkness and miserable Ignorance of the true knowledge and worship of God." In 1611, the colonists themselves wrote America's first civil document that was similar to the Constitution. That same year, the Rev. Alexander Whitaker built Virginia's second church in Henrico and preached a famous sermon entitled "Good News from Virginia" that encouraged Europeans to colonize America for the glory of God. He performed the celebrated marriage of John Rolfe and the Indian princess Pocahontas.

*Pocahontas providentially saved John Smith's life.*

When Pocahontas was a young teenager she providentially saved Captain John Smith from being killed by members of her Indian tribe. Jamestown would have probably not survived as a settlement had it not been for Pocahontas, for without Smith's leadership the colony would have likely died. In addition, she brought much needed food to Jamestown. Smith also took part in preserving the Pilgrims from extinction by carrying the Indian Squanto from England to America.

The first representative assembly in America began in a church in Jamestown with the Rev. Bucke leading the Burgesses in prayer that God would guide and sanctify their proceedings to his own glory and the good of the plantation. They issued laws requiring church attendance, believing that men's affairs cannot prosper where God's service is neglected. In that same year, 1619, they also observed the first American Day of Thanksgiving.

## North Carolina                                                    1653

Quakers and other religious dissenters from Virginia began to settle there in 1653 and nine years later obtained a Charter which acknowledged that the settlement was constituted for "...the propagation of the gospel ... in the parts of America not yet cultivated and planted ..."[2]

*The first representative assembly in the New World was held in the Jamestown Church in 1619.*

**1662**         *South Carolina*

The original Charter which established North Carolina as a colony also applied to South Carolina. But seven years later their own Fundamental Constitution of Carolina was drawn up by the great Christian philosopher John Locke. It required people to: (1) believe that there is a God, (2) in court, recognize Divine justice and human responsibility, and (3) be a church member in order to be a freeman of the colony.

**1731**         *Georgia*

*Oglethorpe*

Dr. Thomas Bray and General James Oglethorpe teamed up in 1731 to establish a colony ...for instructing the Negroes and the poor of this kingdom (England's imprisoned debtor and unemployed), and for other good purposes. [3]

The original 100 settlers were followed by Moravians and other persecuted Protestants in 1736 who, when they touched shore, kneeled in thanks to God. They said, "our end in leaving our native country is not to gain riches and honor, but singly this - to live wholly to the glory of God." The object of the devout Oglethorpe and others was "to make Georgia a religious colony" and so they laid out Savannah with numerous religious ceremonies and invited John and

Charles Wesley and Rev. George Whitefield over to serve as chaplains, oversee Indian affairs and build orphanages. When Whitefield died, the legislature attempted to have him buried there at public cost in honor of his influence.[4]

## Northern Colonies – Bastion of Congregationalism

### Massachusetts                                              1620

As we have seen, the Pilgrims established the first permanent settlement in New England at Plymouth in 1620. As was their desire, the Pilgrims were truly "stepping-stones" for those leaving Europe in search of religious and civil liberty. The Puritans soon followed their leading.

After decades of attempting to purify the Church of England with little result, many Puritans decided another plan was necessary. If they could not purify the Church from within, they would set up a model Church of England in America as an example of the true Church. They had not intended to break from the Church of England originally, as the Pilgrim Separatists had done, but after being some years in the new world they saw no other recourse if they desired to grow in God.

In the Spring of 1630 some 1000 Puritans (which was more than the total inhabitants of the ten-year Plymouth Colony) sailed to America. They were being led by John Winthrop, who served as the governor of Massachusetts Bay Colony for many years. John Fiske writes of him:

"When his life shall have been adequately written... he will be recognized as one of the very noblest figures in American history... From early youth he had the same power of winning confidence and commanding respect for which Washington was so remarkable; and when he was selected as the Moses of the great Puritan exodus, there was a wide-spread feeling that extraordinary results were likely to come of such an enterprise."[5]

While at sea in passage to America, Winthrop wrote "A Model of Christian Charity" which contains their reasons for starting a new colony and the goals they wished to accomplish. Winthrop spoke of their desire to be "as a city upon a hill", where all the people of the earth could look upon and say of their own nation, "the Lord make it like that of New England".[6]

President Reagan often spoke of this vision for America that our Pilgrim and Puritan Fathers had. We have been an example to the people of the world of what a Godly nation should be like. However, as we have forgotten that it was the Lord who made us a nation, we have also failed to be a "model of Christian Charity" in various ways. We must remember as Winthrop wrote, "that if we shall deal falsely with our God in this work we have undertaken and so cause Him to withdraw his present help from us, we shall be made a story and a byword through the world..."[7]

*Governor Winthrop desired to make New England "as a city upon a hill."*

## The Separatists at Plymouth and the Puritans at Boston Complement Each Other

When the Puritans first came to America they still held to a few pagan ideas of government, yet they also carried important scriptural truths. Over the years God would combine the strengths of both Puritan and Pilgrim as they began to populate New England.

The major Puritan weakness was their holding to the idea of a State Church. They saw nothing wrong with a National church and compelled religion (as in Europe). Their disapproval of affairs in England was that the Church and State were corrupt and unbiblical in many aspects. In Massachusetts they would set up right government, in church and state.

Here the Pilgrims and certain Puritan ministers would help leaven the thinking of the Puritans to allow more freedom of conscience and individual liberty. The advancement of Biblical truth that had begun to be recovered during the Reformation was continuing during the settlement of America.

The primary strength of the Puritans was their "spirit of dominion". They recognized the scriptural mandates requiring Godly rule, and zealously set out to establish that in all aspects of society. New

## Settlement of New England

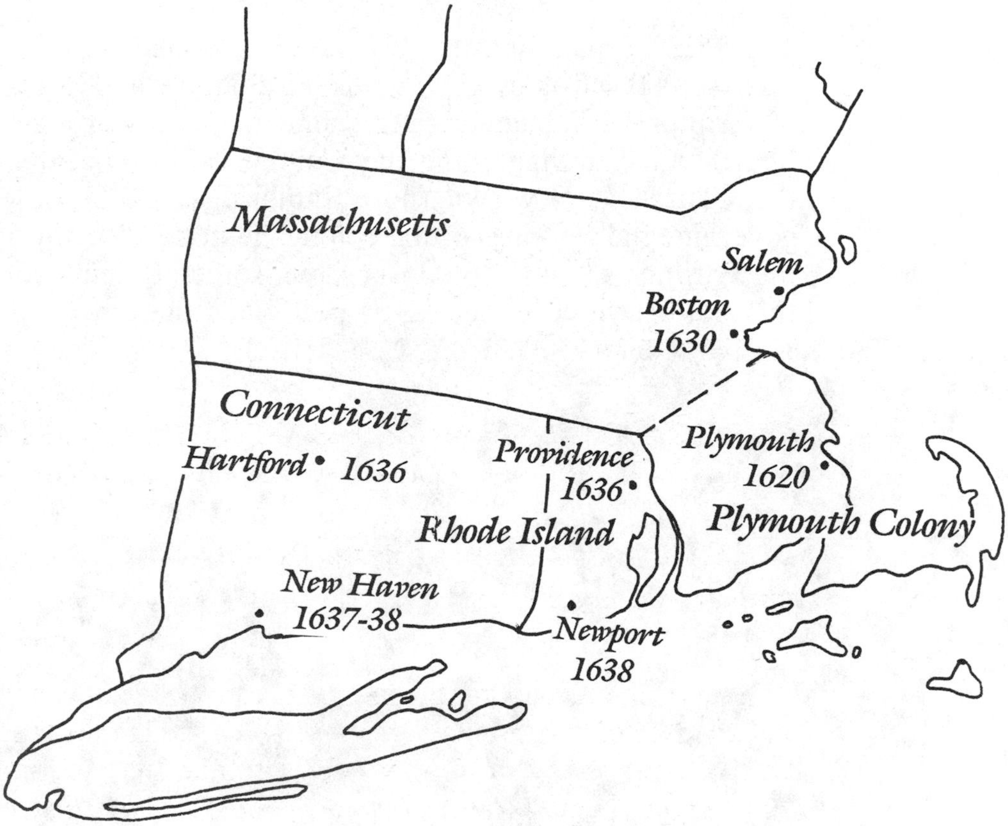

*Massachusetts' Colonies:*

*Connecticut Colonies:*

*Rhode Island:*

1. *Plymouth (1620) -- Pilgrims - Separatists*

2. *Bay Colonies (1628, 1629 - Charter) -- Puritans*

1. *Connecticut Colony (1636) -- Thomas Hooker - Puritan*

2. *New Haven Colony (1637) -- John Davenport - Puritan*

1. *Providence (1636) -- Roger Williams - Separatist*

2. *Newport (1638) -- John Clarke - Separatist*

England would become a blend of the best of these two movements -- Puritan mandates and Pilgrim principles of liberty. The Separatist influence brought about the gradual dominance of Congregational self-government throughout New England, and also greater liberty for everyone. In 1641, Massachusetts adopted the *Body of Liberties,* written by Rev. Nathaniel Ward, which was the first "bill of rights" in history.

*1636*                    *Conecticut*

In 1633 Puritan minister Rev. Thomas Hooker came to the Massachusetts Bay Colony. Rev. Hooker's eloquent and learned support of scriptural Christianity caused him to be driven from England. Shortly after arriving in the Bay Colony, Hooker became Pastor of the Church at Newtown (now Cambridge). After observing the governmental workings of the colony, he noticed the intolerance of the Puritans and attempted to correct some of their wrongs. When this resulted in little success, he petitioned the Bay Colony leaders

*Rev. Thomas Hooker's Sermon in Connecticut in 1638 shaped the framing of the first constitution in history.*

and was granted the right to migrate to the Connecticut Valley.

In June 1636, Rev. Hooker and most of his Newtown congregation of about 100 people settled in what would become Connecticut Colony. Many others followed in the months to come. By May 1637, eight hundred people had settled in the valley. In January 1639 the *Fundamental Orders of Connecticut* were adopted as the Constitution of Connecticut. Rev. Hooker chiefly formulated this document, "the first written constitution known to history."[8] This constitution, which contained many biblical rights and ideas expressed politically, would have a great influence on our nation. Historian John Fiske writes that the government of the United States is "in lineal descent more nearly related to that of Connecticut than to any of the other thirteen colonies."[9]

In 1637 Puritan minister, John Davenport, led the colonization of New Haven Colony. His reasons for coming were similar to those which led Hooker to settle the Connecticut Colony. These two colonies would later unite to form Connecticut.

## Rhode Island

1636

In many ways, Connecticut was a Puritan/Episcopal colony with Separatist/Pilgrim ideas, but Rhode Island was a Separatist colony through and through. A brilliant young Separatist minister, Roger Williams, came to the Bay Colony in 1631 as a refugee from the tyranny of Charles I. Williams served as Minister in Plymouth for a time, and then by mutual agreement left to pastor in Salem.

His firm convictions regarding liberty of conscience and his outspoken manner brought him into conflict with the intolerant Puritan leaders of the Bay Colony. After he was warned of causing trouble by spreading heretical ideas and failing to comply with the civil leaders, he was tried and banished from the Massachusetts Bay Colony. In 1636 he purchased some land from the Indians and founded Providence. In Williams' words, this was "in a sense of God's merciful providence unto me in my distress".

*State Seal of Rhode Island*

His belief that the civil power has no jurisdiction over the conscience, was reflected in the laws of Providence and later in the colony of Rhode Island. Many others who had been persecuted for their religious convictions began settling in Rhode Island.

In 1638 Rev. John Clarke led a group to found Newport "in the presence of Jehovah" by agreeing to "incorporate ourselves in a Body Politic, and as He shall help us, will submit our persons, lives, and estate unto our Lord Jesus Christ, the King of Kings, the Lord of Lords..."

One excellent truth that Roger Williams helped to advance was that a free and prosperous civil state is dependent upon individuals and a church that are grounded in Biblical truth and at liberty to worship God. This is revealed in the Royal Charter of Rhode Island of 1663:

> "The colonies are to pursue with peace and loyal minds their sober, serious, and religious intentions... in holy Christian faith;.... A most flourishing civil state may stand and best be maintained. .. with a full liberty in religious concernments... rightly grounded upon Gospel principles."[10]

In Connecticut and Rhode Island we see that God's people and God's Ministers were involved in formulating every aspect of the public affairs of these colonies. We also see the principles of liberty of the Separatists and the spirit of dominion of the Puritans coming together. As a result of this excellent blend, these two colonies were the only ones to remain self-governing all the way up to the American Revolution.

*1639*

### New Hampshire

The colonists of Exeter wrote in 1639:

"...considering with ourselves the holy will of God and our own necessity, that we should not live without wholesome laws and civil government among us, of which we are altogether destitute, do, in the name of Christ and in the sight of God, combine ourselves together to erect and set up among us such government as shall be, to our best discerning, agreeable to the will of God ..."

Later, in 1680, they proposed their "...glorious cause (to be) ... the glory of God ... and spreading the gospel among the heathen," so "a civil assembly was convened and a solemn public fast proclaimed and observed to propitiate the favor of Heaven" as they established themselves as a province independent of Massachusetts.

## The Middle Colonies -- Dominant Area of Presbyterianism

*1628*

### New York

This colony was originally started as two colonies in 1628 -- New Amsterdam and New Netherlands -- by Rev. Jonas Michaelius and others of the Dutch Reformed Church.

The first entry in New Amsterdam's city records (present day New York City) is Rev. John Megapolensis' prayer opening the court in 1653: "Graciously incline our hearts, that we exercise the power which thou hast given us, to the general good of the community, and to the maintenance of the church, that we may be praised by them that do well, and a terror to evil-doers."

In 1665, the legislature passed an act to uphold "...the public worship of God" and instruction of "...the people in the true religion."

*1633*

### Maryland

Maryland was started as a "reformed Catholic" colony, but became Protestant within a couple of decades. The governor, leading the expedition sent by Lord Baltimore, took possession of the country "for our Lord Jesus Christ" and made "Christianity the established faith of the land." One of the leaders wrote: "bearing on our shoulders a huge cross, which we had hewn from a tree, we moved in procession to a spot selected ... and erected it as a trophy to Christ our Savior; then humbly kneeling, we recited with deep emotion the Litany of the Holy Cross."

*The beginnings of Maryland.*

Father Andrew White wrote: "Behold the lands are white for the harvest, prepared for receiving the seed of the Gospel into a fruitful bosom; ...who then can doubt that by one such glorious work as this, many thousands of souls will be brought to Christ?"

In 1649, Maryland's Toleration Act stated that: "...No persons professing to believe in Jesus Christ should be molested in respect of their religion, or in the free exercise thereof ..."

## Delaware                                                                    *1638*

New Sweden was established along the Delaware River in 1638 due to the backing of the heroic king Gustavus Adolphus who envisioned such a Protestant "planting" in the New World. It was settled by Rev. John Campanius and others of the Lutheran Church of Sweden.

**1664**  *New Jersey*

An association of church members from New Haven, Connecticut settled New Jersey in order "...to carry on their spiritual and town affairs according to godly government." Leaders of the Dutch Reformed Church settled much of Eastern New Jersey in 1664.

Western New Jersey's constitution was developed by the Quakers. William Penn wrote: "There we lay a foundation for after ages to understand their liberty as men and Christians, that they may not be brought in bondage but by their own consent, for we put the power in the people."

In 1697, the governor made a proclamation "in obedience to the laws of God" to duly execute "...all laws made and provided for the suppression of vice and encouraging of religion and virtue, particularly the observance of the Lord's day ..."

The motto of New Jersey on their Provincial seal was Proverbs 14:34- "Righteousness exalteth a nation."

**1681**  *Pennsylvania*

*William Penn*

Quaker preacher William Penn was given the land between New York and Maryland in 1681. He said that "my God that has given it to me...will, I believe, bless and make it the seed of a nation."

In 1682 Penn wrote the colony's Frame of Government to establish "...laws as shall best preserve true Christian and civil liberty in opposition to all unchristian licentious and unjust practices, whereby God may have his due, Caesar his due, and the people their due..."

Thomas Jefferson called Penn "the greatest lawgiver the world has produced." Penn, whose wisdom was "derived from the book of the gospel statutes," recognized Christian character as the basis of good government. He states in the Frame of Government of Pennsylvania:

"Governments like clocks, go from the motion men give them; and as governments are made and moved by men, so by them they are ruined too. Wherefore governments rather depend upon men, than men upon governments...Let men be good, and the government cannot be bad; if it will be ill, they will cure it..."

At a later time William Penn told the Russian Czar, Peter the Great, that "if thou wouldst rule well, thou must rule for God, and to do that, thou must be ruled by him."[11] Penn also said that "those who will not be governed by God will be ruled by tyrants."

## Biblical Reformation of Civil Government

We can see a consistent Christian dominance in the settlement of every single colony. A joint statement made by all of the Northern Colonies in the *New England Confederation* of 1643 would just as well have been made by all 13 colonies. It stated: "We all came into these parts of America with one and the same end and aim, namely, to advance the kingdom of our Lord Jesus Christ, and to enjoy the liberties of the Gospel in purity with peace."[12]

Civil government is a reflection or a product of church government ideas. This relationship was clearly seen in the colonial civil governments.

The three religious movements settled in America in three geographical groupings: The Northern Colonies were settled predominately by Congregationalists, the Southern Colonies by Epis-

*When Penn received the Charter of Pennsylvania from Charles II he believed that God would "bless and make it the seed of a nation."*

copalians, and the Middle Colonies by Presbyterians.

Each of these colonies established civil government that coincided with their view of church government:

1. Northern Colonies were self-governing (Democratic).

2. Middle Colonies were proprietary governments (which tended to be Aristocratic).

3. Southern Colonies were royal provinces ruled by a Governor (Monarchial).

Each colony developed its form of government (and thoroughly understood the strengths and weaknesses of each) for 150 years until the Revolutionary period when they were blended together under our Constitution. Elements of *all three* forms of government are seen in America today:

1.  Episcopalian or Monarchial elements found in our President and Governors.

2.  Presbyterian or Aristocratic elements found in our Judges and originally in our U.S. Senators.

3.  Congregational or Democratic elements found in our U.S. and State Representatives.

Even as none of the forms of church government alone constitutes the Biblical model, so also the Christian form of civil government must be a composite of all three. Episcopalian, Presbyterian and Congregational forms *together* make Biblical Church government. Monarchy, Aristocracy and Democracy *together* make a Biblical civil Republic. This indeed was what God providentially arranged in the establishment of the United States of America.

*The first brick church built in Jamestown*
*Scene of the 1st Free Representative Assembly in America*

# Chapter 8

# Education in America: How the Principles are Planted

The Biblical principles upon which America was birthed were passed on to succeeding generations through education in the home, church, and school. Christian education assured a foundation of liberty. Our Founders understood that tyranny and bondage would result from ignorance of the truth. This truth was rooted in the Bible.

Benjamin Franklin said: "A nation of well informed men who have been taught to know and prize the rights which God has given them cannot be enslaved. It is in the region of ignorance that tyranny begins."

Rosalie Slater writes that "American Christian education was the foundation of our nation's great growth, progress, and success... The colonists brought with them a tradition of Biblical scholarship and the fruition of the Reformation -- the Scriptures in English. And with their Bibles they brought a determination to continue the individual study and practice of the Christian verities contained therein. Because of their sincere desire to teach their children to read the Scriptures they established schools. Their colleges were the culmination of the need for an enlightened ministry."[1]

## *Biblical Scholarship*

What was this "Biblical Scholarship" that formed the basis for all education in America for over two centuries? Simply stated, Biblical Scholarship is the ability to reason from Biblical principles and relate it to all of life. Not only did early American Christians reason from the Bible, but even non-Christians were trained in this manner and held to a Biblical worldview. This is quite the opposite of today for both non-Christians and even many Christians view life from a man-centered, humanistic worldview. Decades of humanistic teaching in schools and by the media have attempted to engrain this philosophy in all Americans.

### *What is a World-View?*

Gary Demar writes that "a world view is simply the way you look at yourself and the world around you. It includes your beliefs about God, yourself, your neighbors, your family, civil government, art, music, history, morality, education, business, economics, and all other areas of life."[2]

Another writer states: "Your world view, of course, is how you view the world. It is the set of presuppositions -- that which is believed beforehand -- which underlies all of our decisions and actions. These presuppositions (our world view) determine our thinking patterns, which in turn influence our actions . . . . Our world view may be conscious or unconscious, but it determines our destiny and the destiny of the society we live in."[3]

The Biblical worldview and scholarship of Colonial Americans provided the basis of a free and prosperous America. Miss Slater writes:

"The Pilgrims learned Biblical reasoning from Pastor John Robinson during their twelve years in Holland. Thus they were prepared to extend Christian principles into civil government and to deal with the problems that confronted them in the New World. Challenged on the Mayflower by rebellious "strangers," they wrote the Mayflower Compact, so that every man might voluntarily share in making and keeping the laws. Confronted with distrustful Indians, they made a mutual pact and maintained a long-lasting peace. Faced with starvation, William Bradford, Governor of Plymouth Plantation, 'had the courage and wisdom' to shift from 'labor in common' to the responsibility of individual enterprise and private property. For more than twenty years the Pilgrims labored to repay their original debt to venture capitalists in England who had financed the voyage of the Mayflower. There were many opportunities to escape from this responsibility but they held to the obligation as a matter of Christian conscience.

The Pilgrims were consistent because of their applications of Christian truths or principles.

"The ability to reason from the Word of God and to relate its principles to every area of life was characteristic of the American clergy prior to the American Revolution... Their election and artillery sermons identified 'the principles of civil government with the principles of Christianity.'

"At the time of the Declaration of Independence the quality of education had enabled the colonies to achieve a degree of literacy from '70% to virtually 100%.' This was not education restricted to the few. Modern scholarship reports 'the prevalence of schooling and its accessibility to most segments of the population.' Moses Coit Tyler, historian of American Literature, indicates the colonist's 'familiarity with history...extensive legal learning...lucid exposition of constitutional principles, showing, indeed, that somehow, out into that American wilderness had been carried the very accent of cosmopolitan thought and speech.' When the American State Papers arrived in Europe they surprised and astonished the 'enlightened men.' Americans had been dismissed as 'illiterate back-woodsmen' as, perhaps, 'law-defying revolutionists.' But when these papers were read they found to contain 'nearly every quality indicative of personal and national greatness.'

"Dr. Lawrence A. Cremin in his study of American Education from 1607 to 1789, credits the high quality of American education to the Bible, 'the single most important cultural influence in the lives of Anglo-Americans.'"[4]

## Christian Education

Colonial Americans exemplified qualities of "personal and national greatness" because of their Christian Education. To restore liberty and greatness to America, we must restore Christian Education to America. For education to be Christian, one's philosophy (why, what, who, when, and where), methodology (how), and curriculum (what) must be Christian, that is, be "Christ-like" or "pertain to Christ."

## Christian Philosophy

Abraham Lincoln once said, "the philosophy of the school room in one generation will be the philosophy of government in the next." Colossians 2:8 tells us that a worldly philosophy brings captivity:

"See to it that no one takes you captive through philosophy and empty deception, according to the tradition of men, according to the elementary principles of the world, rather than according to Christ."

A worldly, humanistic philosophy in the present educational system of many nations has produced bondage within individuals' lives. As an example of this, there are 30 - 40 million American adults today who are functionally illiterate. They cannot read a job applica-

*A Christian philosophy of education brings liberty.*

tion, a warning sign at work, or a label on a medicine bottle. That is bondage! This great illiteracy is the fruit of a humanistic method of teaching reading.

While a worldly philosophy brings captivity, the Bible tells us that a Christian philosophy brings liberty. In order to liberate our nation, individuals must be liberated first. True education is the primary means of imparting a Christian philosophy of life, and hence in bringing liberty to our nation.

### What is education?

In order to properly educate ourselves, we must first understand what true education is. If we were to define education from our experience in public schools, we would probably agree with most modern dictionary definitions of the word, which define it as teaching that primarily is concerned with imparting information. While education does involve imparting information, according to the Bible this is of secondary concern.

Noah Webster, in his original 1828 dictionary, reveals to us four minimal goals of education. He writes: "Education comprehends all that series of instruction and discipline which is intended to [1] enlighten the understanding, [2] correct the temper, [3] form the manners and habits of youth, and [4] fit them for usefulness in their future stations..."

We can see from his definition that education deals primarily with the inward man -- with forming character. The formation of character is inevitable. Bad character, not good, is the result of the failure of public schools to discipline.

## A Biblical Method of Education -- The Principle Approach

Methods of education are not neutral. Colonial America had a Biblical method of education. Noah Webster (1758-1843) helped to establish the Principle Approach as the standard method of education in the new Republic of America.

### What is the Principle Approach?

One thing it is not, is another program. It is not a pre-packaged, daily lesson plan that a teacher follows in instructing her students, where each step is given each day for each class. Briefly stated, the Principle Approach to education inculcates in individuals the ability to reason from the Bible to every aspect of life. As Christians, we know we are supposed to do this, but do we? Do we really know how to reason from the Bible to geography, astronomy, mathematics, or history, not to mention national defense, foreign policy, or civil government?

### *The Principle Approach restores the art of biblical reasoning.*

Many Christians of recent generations have read Romans 12:2 as follows: "Do not be conformed to this world, but be transformed by the *removal* of your mind..." We know that we are transformed by the *renewing* of our mind and not by its *removal*, yet many Christians over-responded to the decay of the institutionalized church in past generations into a "mental religion only" by rejecting the use of our minds in following God, desiring only to be "led by the Spirit."

We must again realize that as Christians we have the potential to be the greatest thinkers in all the world. Historically, Christians have been the leaders in almost every area of life (Johann S. Bach in music, Isaac Newton in science, Rembrandt in art, Adam Smith in economics, John Locke in civil government, to name only a few). Those men who founded America were only able to produce a free and prosperous society because they knew how to reason biblically to all areas of life.

We are in great need today of restoring the art of biblical reasoning to our educational system. We may have more facts taught in our schools today (even though in many fields, major facts are conspicuously missing), but we must teach more than just facts. We must teach how to arrive at those facts as well.

To more fully understand the Principle Approach, let's look at each of the words separately. A "principle", according to Webster's 1828 dictionary, is: "1. the cause, source, or origin of anything; that from which a thing proceeds; 2) Element; constituent part."

**A principle is like an element** in chemistry. An element is the lowest form in which matter can exist naturally -- it can be broken down no further. A principle is an absolute truth (and hence biblical) that is reduced to its most basic form. While the Bible contains thousands of truths, these can be broken down into a small number of principles from which the truths spring forth. If these principles are known, this provides parameters through which to view life, assuring that one truth is not forgotten while embracing a new one.

A *principle* and a *seed* are very similar in their meanings. A seed, being a plant in embryo, contains the entire plant -- the whole thing is there, albeit in a condensed form. After a seed is planted, given some time, water, sunlight, and care, a huge tree can be produced. Likewise, principles are first given in seed form to children, yet these principles contain the potential of giant trees of truth and application. God starts with a seed and produces a plant. Today most classes try to shove plants down children's throats.

The Principle Approach teaches seed principles over and over again in each subject and grade level with different illustrations, examples, assignments, educational methods, etc. This ensures that a child not only knows Biblical principles, but that he lives them -- that they are a part of his life.

"Approach" simply means "to come or go near, in place; to draw near." Therefore, the Principle Approach involves getting Biblical principles so near someone that they become a part of their life.

## A Wholistic Method

The Principle Approach is also a wholistic method of education, that is, it is instruction from the whole to the part. Take history, for example. Instead of teaching fragments of history throughout the various grade levels with seemingly no unifying factor among the different classes, a Biblical approach would look at the whole of history first, and then look at the parts in more detail, and those always in relation to the whole.

The whole of history can be looked at from a Biblical philosophy because there is an overall purpose in history which unifies all the specific events of history. From a humanistic viewpoint, there is no purpose in history and hence no unifying theme which ties events of history together.

A truly Biblical approach to education involves much more than just taking various academic subjects and trying to squeeze the Bible into them. A Principle Approach to education reveals that the source, origin, and purpose of all knowledge revolves around God and His plan for man.

## How do We Implant Principles

If we desire to have a Principle Approach education we must restore the 4 R's to teaching and learning:

**1) First R - RESEARCH:** We must research the subjects and topics of interest from the Bible and other resources to identify basic principles.

**2) Second R - REASON:** As we are researching a subject we must continually ask ourselves what is God's perspective and purpose for the subject and what does this information reveal to me of God and His purpose.

**3) Third R - RELATE:** As we are researching and reasoning we must also relate the truths uncovered to our own lives or to the situation at hand.

**4) Fourth R - RECORD:** The principles and truths uncovered and related must be recorded or written down to accurately and permanently preserve them.[5]

*Children are to be brought up in the instruction of the Lord.*

This process of researching, reasoning, relating, and recording ("4 R-ing") is the best way to implant truth within our hearts-- the best method by which to learn and be educated.

In most schools today students are seldom required to research, reason, relate or record in their pursuit of being educated. This is true in the every day study of subjects as well as the tests on the subjects. Most tests are fill-in-the-blank, matching, or True-False. (These type of tests were not used in our schools until the 1920's; before that, essays were the primary method of testing.) Students can take and pass these test for years and years without truly learning how to reason and think and be prepared for life after completion of school. Consequently, Americans today do not know how to reason and think.

### Practical Ways to Implement the 4 R's in our Educational Process

#### 1) Essays

Writing essays is an excellent way to implant within the student the ability to research, reason, relate, and record. Writing essays enables students to truly express themselves - to communicate what they really know and believe. As one writes his ideas in complete sentences, he is forced to reason and think for himself. This personal expression brings liberty to the individual. He will not be dependent upon the media, teachers, or anyone else for his ideas, for he will have learned how to search out the truth for himself.

#### 2) Notebooks

The compilation of notebooks by students on various subjects and topics is an excellent means of inculcating truth within them. Instead of being handed a textbook at the beginning of the year and memorizing pages of facts and information, in order to receive good grades, the student develops his own textbook by taking notes from the teacher and doing his own research and writing from various resources (which can include a textbook).

The notebook method not only assures that the student acquires knowledge, but it also builds character within the individual (which is the primary purpose of education). Self-government, industry, orderliness, discipline, and the ability to communicate and reason are only a few of the character qualities produced by the notebook method of education.

America's founding fathers were educated by the notebook method. Many of George Washington's early notebooks are still preserved in the Library of Congress. His life-time habits of orderliness, neatness, and consistency are readily seen within the pages of his manuscripts. His father required this of him from his first years of being educated.

In a letter to his father on June 2, 1777, at age 10, John Quincy Adams wrote:

> "P.S. -Sir, If you will be so good as to favor me with a blank-book I will transcribe the most remarkable occurrences I meet with in my reading, which will serve to fix them upon my mind."[6]

This is quite an amazing statement for a ten-year old, not only in that his literary level is beyond most college graduates today, but also in his educational insight. Our future sixth president was revealing the importance of a notebook approach to education.

There are may other practical educational methods that can be used to restore the 4-R's. Some include:

1) Verbal reports and tests

2) Complete sentences answers to classroom and test questions

3) Practical outlets for expression of all that is learned

4) Apprenticeship programs

5) Doing useful projects within the various classes

You can begin to see that a principle approach to education requires much work. While true education will be exciting and challenging, and not boring (one reason for the many discipline problems in schools today is that students are extremely bored), it will also, as Noah Webster felt, require severe effort.

If you have not exercised in many years and then participate in strenuous activity, your body will hurt. Likewise, if you haven't exercised your mind for years and begin to use it strenuously, it will also hurt. But the more you use your mind, the better in shape you will be to think.

Your mind is more than just a computer - garbage in, garbage out. It is like a womb, for you can get more out of your mind than you put in it. This is part of true reasoning.

## Three Essentials for Christian Education

To sum up what has been stated previously, these three elements are essential for an education to be truly Christian:

**1) Teacher** - A teacher who is a living witness or textbook (2 Cor. 3:3) is the most important aspect of education. When you teach, you impart more of who you are than what you know. Students will read you. Therefore, to be most effective as a teacher (we are all teachers, for we instruct all we come in contact with), you must master what you teach so that it is a living part of you.

**2) Content** - In the material we teach, the Bible must be our central text (as we have discussed, not in a superficial way). While the Bible doesn't contain all the facts on all the subjects, it does contain all the principles, and reveals God's purpose for each subject.

**3) Method** - In addition to a godly teacher and content, the educational method must also be Christian. This method should build Godly character, impart a love of learning, and prepare individuals to take dominion over the earth.

## Important Aspects of Education in Early America

### Home Education

Almost every child in early America was educated. This was largely due to the colonists' desire for their children to be able to read the Scriptures. Parents saw it as their responsibility, and not that of the government, to provide education. They understood the Biblical command of Deuteronomy 6:6-7 ("And these words, which I am commanding you today, shall be on your heart; and you shall teach them diligently to your sons...") and Ephesians 6:4 ("Fathers, do not provoke your children to anger; but bring them up in the discipline and instruction of the Lord").

For the first 150-200 years America's Education was primarily centered in the home. Home education was sometimes supplemented by tutors or schools, but even here the responsibility and bulk of a child's education rested in the home.

The model of education in Colonial America was very similar to the model used by ancient Israel. With both, education was centered in the home. This was solely the case until around the age of eight or nine. At this age some children had tutors to further instruct them, or an even smaller number attended a school. With the Israelites, the Levites and the Priests were the tutors; with colonial Americans, the ministers were generally the tutors. If there were too many children in the minister's community for him to go into each home to tutor, he would receive a group of children into his home. These were the first "grammar schools" and began in the late 1600's.

This would comprise a child's education until around age thirteen when they would enter an apprenticeship program or possibly enroll in a college.

## First School                                                                1636

In 1636 Rev. John Cotton of Boston willed half his property to establish a school to provide education for children who were disadvantaged or had no parents. The Boston Latin School was the first school established in America outside the home.

*Education is the responsibility of the parents.*

The Christians of Colonial America not only recognized that God required them to educate their own children, but also saw it as their responsibility to educate the general public. The Great Commission of Matthew 28:19-20, to "disciple the nations", was to be accomplished by "teaching them to observe all that I commanded you." As we have looked at the *Chain of Christianity* we have seen that education always accompanies the spread of the Gospel. The Lollards are an excellent example. Remember that they educated the common people in order that they could read the Scriptures for themselves. Education of the common man also followed the preaching of Luther, Tyndale, Calvin, and other Reformation preachers.

The desire to educate every individual accompanied the Pilgrims, Puritans, Quakers, and most others who came to settle America. One reason the Puritans came to America was to escape the ungodly influence that education in Europe had upon their children. Cotton Mather said, "The schools of learning and religion (in Europe) are so corrupted as most children, even the best and wittiest, and of the fairest hopes, are perverted, corrupted, and utterly overthrown by the multitude of evil examples and licentious behavior in these seminaries."

1647      *First Common Schools*

The "Old Deluder Law" of 1647 established the first free common schools in America. Historian John Fiske writes:

"In 1647 the legislature of Massachusetts enacted a law with the following preamble: 'It being one chief purpose of that old deluder, Satan, to keep men from the knowledge of the Scriptures,' it was therefore ordered that every township containing fifty families or householders should set up a school in which children might be taught to read and write, and that every township containing one hundred families or householders should set up a school in which boys might be fitted for entering Harvard College."[7]

Wages for the teachers were paid by the parents or the general inhabitants. These "public" schools ("public" in that they were required by law, although this was not enforced) were not under the control of a state government board, such as Horace Mann set up in Massachusetts 200 years later. The teacher's curriculum, methodology, and administration were completely under local control.

Free schools were also established in other towns and cities of New England over the next number of decades, but these always involved a small percentage of those being educated. The home, church, and private sector educated the vast majority of pupils. Samuel Blumenfeld writes that "by 1720 Boston had far more private schools than public ones, and by the close of the American Revolution many towns had no common schools at all."[8] Pennsylvania and New York had public schools like New England early but only in the cities, not in rural areas. There were no public schools in the Southern colonies until 1730 and only five by 1776.

Although public and private schools were established, the home was still where the majority of Colonial Americans were educated even up through the Revolution. Some of our greatest leaders and thinkers (not just of that era but including recent years) were primarily educated at home. This includes such men as George Washington, Thomas Jefferson, James Madison, Benjamin Franklin, Noah Webster, Abraham Lincoln, Thomas Edison, Alexander G. Bell, and many, many more.

Samuel L. Blumenfeld says: "Of the 117 men who signed the Declaration of Independence, the Articles of Confederation and the Constitution, one out of three had had only a few months of formal schooling, and only one in four had gone to college. They were educated by parents, church schools, tutors, academies, apprenticeship, and by themselves."[9]

### The New England Primer                                                    1690

The Pilgrims and Puritans' belief that all must seek the word of God in the Bible caused them to teach all boys and girls to read. For this purpose *hornbooks* were made, usually consisting of the alphabet

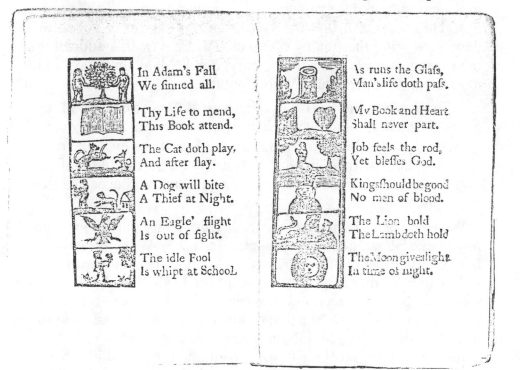

*A page from a New England primer.*

and a Bible text, mounted on a board and covered with a sheet of transparent animal horn. Later on, children used the New England Primer, printed in Boston in 1690.

The Primer, known as the "Little Bible of New England," is considered the most influential school book in the history of American education. The 3 x 5 inch, 88-page devotional was **the** school-book of America during the end of the 1600's and early 1700's. Over three million copies were printed with the alphabet and some verse. Simply viewing how the alphabet was taught using Biblical verse reveals the obvious Christian nature of this important book.

1783          *Noah Webster's Blue-backed Speller*

No single American has contributed so much to American education as has Noah Webster--the Founding Father of American Scholarship and Education. This expert in grammar and philology was known by more Americans than anyone except George Washington during the 19th century primarily due to his famous "blue-backed Speller" and his *American Dictionary of the English Language*. These, along with his self-teaching textbooks were produced out of his desire to make America intellectually independent of England and Europe.

After America won her Independence from Great Britain and established herself as a Constitutional Republic, Webster worked to see that our liberty and growth continued by providing educational tools that imparted the principles that originally gave birth to our nation. He recognized that the success of our system of government depended upon the quality of education. He saw this education as the responsibility of the parents and the individual, and that its basis must be upon Christianity. Webster stated:

> "In my view, the Christian religion is the most important and one of the first things in which all children, under a free government, ought to be instructed... No truth is more evident to my mind than that the Christian religion must be the basis of any government intended to secure the rights and privileges of a free people."[10]

While Webster is most known for his dictionary, this is only one of his phenomenal accomplishments. In 1783, Webster wrote his famous "Blue-backed Speller", which did more for American education than any other single book, except the Bible. His Speller, which sold over 100 million copies in a century, was written to instill into the minds of the youth "the first rudiments of the language and some just ideas of religion, morals, and domestic economy."

Its premise is that "God's word, contained in the Bible, has furnished all necessary rules to direct our conduct." It includes a moral catechism, large portions of the Sermon on the Mount, a paraphrase of the Genesis account of creation and other statements such as: "He who came to save us, will wash us from all sin; I will be glad in his name."

## *Webster's Dictionary*          *1828*

Noah Webster worked about twenty-six years on his *An American Dictionary of the English Language.* By the time of its completion and publication in 1828, Webster had mastered 28 languages. This colossal work reflects the diligence, scholarship, and Christian character of this great yet humble man.

His dictionary, which was the first American dictionary and the grandfather of all others, defines words biblically and generously uses scriptural references. The present day dictionary that bears Webster's name is a good example of how education has been secularized. A comparison reveals that not only have thousands of Scriptures been removed in modern editions, but biblical definitions have been replaced by definitions reflecting humanistic thought.

Noah Webster's life can be characterized as prolific. In addition to his dictionary and textbooks -- the "Blue-backed Speller", a "Grammar", and a "Reader" -- he wrote much more on many topics including religious, political, educational, musical, economic, commercial, medical, social, and scientific. He was also the first person to publicly promote the idea of a constitutional convention. His efforts brought about copyright legislation at state and national levels. He served in state government, published a magazine and newspaper, founded a college, and translated the first American revised version of the Bible. While doing all these things, his family was not neglected as he lovingly raised seven children.

In light of such an astoundingly productive life, Noah Webster's statement in the preface to his 1828 American Dictionary particularly reveals his Christian character. He said:

"And if the talent which (God) entrusted to my care, has not been put to the most profitable use in His service, I hope it has not been 'kept laid up in a napkin,' and that any misapplication of it may be graciously forgiven."[11]

*Noah Webster*

It was men with character like Noah Webster who educated the generations of Americans that secured this country as the most free and prosperous nation the world has seen. The continuance of a positive course for our nation will only occur as men like Noah Webster reestablish our educational system upon the Bible, removing any dependence upon man's own intellect.

This philosophy of education will produce leaders in all of life who will know how to properly guide our nation to secure life and liberty to all men.

1836                    *McGuffey and His Readers*

*Rev. William Holmes McGuffey*

Following Noah Webster came another educational reformer and university professor who was also a preacher. Rev. William Holmes McGuffey authored the *McGuffey Readers* -- which earned him the right to be called "The Schoolmaster of the Nation." His textbooks were designed to "fit the child's education to the child's world" and to build character as well as vocabulary. One hundred and twenty-two million copies were sold in 75 years. Since 1961, they still sell 30,000 a year and are still used in some public schools today. His readers continued to promote the theistic, Calvinist worldview and ideas of salvation, righteousness and piety that were found in the New England Primer the century before. The Readers "represent the most significant force in the framing of our national morals and tastes" other than the Bible. In the Preface to the Fourth Reader, he wrote:

"From no source has the author drawn more copiously, in his selections, than from the sacred Scriptures. For this, he certainly apprehends no censure. In a Christian country, that man is to be pitied, who at this day, can honestly object to imbuing the minds of youth with the language and spirit of the Word of God...."[12]

John Westerhoff writes:

"From the First to the Fourth Reader, belief in the God of the Old and New Testaments is assumed. When not mentioned directly, God is implied: 'You cannot steal the smallest pin... without being seen by the eye that never sleeps.' More typically, however, lessons make direct references to the Almighty.: "God makes the little lambs bring forth wool, that we may have clothes to keep us warm.... All that live get life from God.... The humble child went to God in penitence and prayer.... All who take care of you and help you were sent by God. He sent his Son to show you his will, and to die for your sake.'

"When we investigate the content of McGuffey's Readers, three dominant images of God emerge. God is creator, preserver, and governor."[13]

## *America's Christian Universities*

As with the private and public schools, the universities of America were established by the Christian community. One hundred and six of the first one hundred and eight colleges in America were founded on the Christian faith. By the time of the Civil War non-religious universities could be counted on one hand. College presidents were almost always clergymen until around 1900. A study entitled *An Appraisal of Church and Four-year Colleges* (1955) stated that "nearly all of those institutions which have exerted a decided influence, even in our literary and political history, were established by evangelical Christians".[14]

The first universities, which were really seminaries (not like most modern seminaries though), were started for the central purpose of perpetuating a learned clergy. Harvard, established in 1638, was our first university.

### *Harvard*                                                    *1638*

The Rev. John Harvard gave half of his property and his entire library to start this Congregational institution. "For Christ and the Church" is its official motto. Ten of its twelve presidents up to the Revolution were clergymen. The governing rules required both the president and professors to "open and explain the Scriptures to his pupils with integrity and faithfulness, according to the best light God shall give him... so that, through the blessing of God it may be conducive to their establishment in the principles of the Christian Protestant religion".[15]

The following report on Harvard College, from "New England's First Fruits" published in 1643, reveals the purpose for it's establishment:

> "After God had carried us safe to New England, and wee had builded our houses, provided necessaries for our liveli-hood, rear'd convenient places for Gods worship, and settled the Civil Government: One of the next things we longed for, and looked after was to advance Learning, and perpetuate it to Posterity, dreading to leave an illiterate Ministry to the Churches, when our present Ministers shall lie in the Dust."[16]

*Seal of Harvard College*

Following are a few of the "rules and precepts" that were "observed in the College":

> "Let every Student be plainly instructed, and earnestly pressed to consider well, the maine end of his life and studies is, to know God and Jesus Christ which is eternall life, (John 17:3), and there-

*Students at Harvard College were "to consider well, the maine end of (their) life and studies is, to know ... Jesus Christ."*

fore to lay Christ in the bottome, as the only foundation of all sound knowledge and Learning."

"And seeing the Lord only giveth wisedome, Let every one seriously set himselfe by prayer in secret to seeke it of him (Prov. 2:3)."[17]

Harvard was not unique in it's beginning. The following brief look at other universities reveals the same Christian foundation:

### College of William and Mary

1692

Through the efforts of Rev. James Blair, it received its Charter: "to the end that the Church of Virginia may be furnished with a seminary of ministers of the gospel, and...that the Christian faith may be propagated...to the glory of God..."[18] All presidents and professors were originally clergymen who taught the students and the Episcopal catechism.

*The Wren Building.*

### Yale University

1701

Rev, John Davenport began promoting the idea in 1652, and finally a plan and resources were provided by a synod of Congregational churches led by Rev. Pierport, Rev. Andrew, and Rev. Russell which led to an official Charter in 1701: "...for the liberal and religious education of suitable youth...to propagate in this wilderness, the blessed reformed Protestant religion..."[19]

Every president was a clergyman until 1898 and included such notables as Elisha Williams, Ezra Styles, and Timothy Dwight. *Yale's Rules* were modeled after Harvard's: "Seeing God is the giver of all wisdom, every scholar, besides private or secret prayer, where all we are bound to ask wisdom, shall be present morning and evening at public prayer in the hall at the accustomed hour..."[20]

### Princeton University

1746

Princeton was founded by Presbyterians, who called it the "Log College," but it was not officially chartered until 1746, when the Rev. Jonathan Dickinson became its first president, declaring: "Cursed be all that learning that is contrary to the cross of Christ." Every president was a clergyman until 1902 and included such notables as Jonathan Edwards, Samuel Davies, and John Witherspoon. The official motto is: "Under God's Power She Flourishes".

### Rutgers University

1766

Through the efforts of Rev. Theodore Frelinghuysen the Dutch Reformed Church established "Queen's College", "for the education of youth in the learned languages, liberal and useful arts and sciences, and especially in divinity, preparing them for the ministry and other good offices". Official motto: "Son of Righteousness, Shine upon the West also".[21]

## *The Need for Christianity in Our Public Schools*

A free nation must rest upon a Christian philosophy of education. This truth was recognized by the founders of our nation. Congress declared in the *Northwest Ordinance* of 1787 that "Religion, morality, and knowledge, being necessary to good government and the happiness of mankind, schools and the means of education shall forever be encouraged."

Congress recognized that the basis of happiness for mankind and good government was "religion, morality, and knowledge" and that these were to be taught in our schools. These schools were predominantly private and home-based, for this is the most effective way to educate our youth. Privatizing education would be a great step forward in correcting the problems of modern day education. With God and morality being ignored in most public schools today and true knowledge often "overlooked", it's no wonder Americans are losing their freedoms, government is becoming more corrupt, and the general state of happiness is declining.

Historian B.F. Morris says in his history:

"Education, next to the Christian religion, is an indispensable element of republican institutions, the basis upon which all free governments must rest. The state must rest upon the basis of religion, and it must preserve this basis, or itself must fall. But the support which religion gives to the state will obviously cease the moment religion loses its hold upon the popular mind. The very fact that state must have religion as a support for its own authority demands that some means for teaching religion be employed. Better for it to give up all other instruction than that religion should be disregarded in its schools."[22]

Every civil government is based upon some religion or philosophy of life. Education in a nation will propagate the religion of that nation. In America the foundational religion was Christianity, and it was sown in the hearts of Americans through the home, private, and public schools for centuries. Our liberty, growth, and prosperity was the result of a Biblical philosophy of life. Our continued freedom and success is dependent upon our educating the youth of America in the principles of the Christian religion.

Noah Webster understood this as he wrote:

"The foundation of all free government and of all social order must be laid in families and in the discipline of youth. . . The Education of youth, an employment of more consequence than making laws and preaching the gospel because it lays the foundation on which both law and gospel rest for success..."[23]

How we educate our youth has immeasurable consequences for the future of our nation. This can be for great good or great evil.

Samuel Adams said:

"Let divines and philosophers, statesmen and patriots, unite their endeavors to renovate the age, by impressing the minds of men with the importance of educating their little boys and girls, of inculcating in the minds of youth the fear and love of the Deity and universal philanthropy, and, in subordination to these great principles, the love of their country; of instructing them in the art of self-government, without which they never can act a wise part in the government of societies, great or small; in short, of leading them in the study and practice of the exalted virtues of the Christian system..."[24]

# In *Provincial Congress*,

## *Cambridge*, December 6, 1774.

RESOLVED, That the following Addreſs be preſented to the ſeveral Miniſters of the Goſpel in this Province.

REVEREND SIR,

WHEN we contemplate the Friendſhip and Aſſiſtance, our Anceſtors the firſt Settlers of Province (while over-whelmed with Diſtreſſ received from the pious Paſtors of the Churches of CHRIST, who, to enjoy the Rights of Conſcience, fled with them into this Land, then a ſavage Wilderneſs, we find ourſelves fill'd with the moſt grateful Senſations.---And we cannot but acknowledge theGoodneſs of Heaven, in conſtantly ſupplying us with Preachers of the Goſpel, whoſe Concern has been the temporal and ſpiritual Happineſs of this People.

In a Day like this, when all the Friends of civil and religious Liberty are exerting themſelves to deliver this Country from its preſent Calamities, we cannot but place great Hopes in an Order of Men, who have ever diſtinguiſhed themſelves in their Country's Cauſe ; and do therefore recommend to the Miniſters of the Goſpel, in the ſeveral Towns and other Places in this Colony, that they aſſiſt us, in avoiding that dreadful Slavery with which we are now threatened, by adviſing the People of their ſeveral Congregations, as they wiſh their Proſperity, to abide by and ſtrictly adhere to the *Reſolutions* of the *Continental Congreſs*, as the moſt peaceable and probable Method of preventing Confuſion and Bloodſhed, and of reſtoring that Harmony between Great-Britain and theſe Colonies, on which we wiſh might be eſtabliſhed not only the Rights and Liberties of America, but the Opulence and laſting Happineſs of the whole Britiſh Empire.

*Sign'd by Order of the Provincial Congreſs,*

## JOHN HANCOCK, Preſident.

*A true Extract from the Minutes.*

BENJAMIN LINCOLN, Secretary.

---

## Chapter 9

---

# The Role of the Church and Clergy in the Cultivation of Liberty

A statement by David Gregg describing the early American Republic states well the role of the church in a Christian nation: "The people made the laws, and the churches made the people."[1] The role of the church is not to directly hold power as an ecclesiastical body that makes civil law. The influence of the church on government is not by positional power, but by the influential power of its teachings.

This role was described by a French political philosopher, Alexis de Tocqueville, who came to the United States of America in the 1830's in search of her greatness. After a thorough examination he communicated in his book, *Democracy in America:*

"On my arrival in the United States the religious aspect of the country was the first thing that struck my attention; and the longer I stayed there, the more I perceived the great political consequences resulting from this new state of things."[2]

Elsewhere in his writings, de Tocqueville states:

"I sought for the greatness and genius of America in her commodious harbors and her ample rivers, and it was not there; in her fertile fields and boundless prairies, and it was not there; in her rich mines and her vast world commerce, and it was not there. Not until I went to the churches of America and heard her pulpits aflame with righteousness did I understand the secret of her genius and power. America is great because she is good and if America ever ceases to be good, America will cease to be great."[3]

In other words, de Tocqueville said that our civil government will not work without the people being virtuous, which is the product of the religious influence of the church.

Ministers were involved in every aspect of the public affairs of America. They colonized and formed many of our states, they wrote our laws and constitutions, they served as judges and lawyers, they established schools and universities, and they participated directly in civil government.

The Colonists considered that the greatest and most dreaded curse was for them to someday have impotent preachers who through ignorance of God's Word knew not how to make it relevant to any situation. In their thinking, this was the primary cause of the religious and civil tyranny of the Dark Ages.

In an election sermon of 1742, preaching before the governor of Massachusetts, Nathanial Appleton stated:

"As for you my Fathers and Brethren in the Ministry. . . surely it concerns us to be ready Scribes, well instructed in the Law of our God, and in the Gospel of his Son. . . Surely then, it is absolutely necessary for Ministers to be well acquainted with the holy Scriptures. Not only to have some certain Portions of Scripture by rote, to use upon all Occasions, but to understand the Meaning of Scripture, and to be able to give the Meaning of it to others -- And it was a Concern for a learned as well as godly Ministry, that stirred up such an early Care in our Fathers, to encourage Schools, and to erect a College, which has now for a Century of Years, conferred academical Honour upon the learned Youth, that have been trained up in it. God forbid, that an ignorant, and unlearned Ministry should ever rise up in this Land, especially a Ministry that should be ignorant of the Holy Scriptures; or that should think or speak disparagingly of them, or that should insinuate the Uselessness of them to unconverted Men; . . . And no less dangerous is it to insinuate, as if the Bible was not very necessary for the Saints, by Reason of their having the Spirit to inlighten and direct them. . . Accordingly we who are the Ministers of Christ, and have the glorious Gospel committed to our Trust, should be upon the Watch-Tower, to spy out every

Thing of such a dangerous Tendency, that we may give seasonable Warnings thereof."[4]

## Pastors in Public Affairs in the 1600's

We have already looked at significant clergymen who were links on the Chain of Liberty in America's beginnings. A brief review of those pastors who participated directly in politics follows:

1619 - Clergy serving in Virginia's First General Assembly.

1620 - John Robinson shaping the Mayflower Compact.

1636 - John Cotton starting the first public schools.

1636 - Roger Williams and John Clarke founding the state of Rhode Island.

1639 - Thomas Hooker and John Davenport founding the state of Connecticut and writing the first Constitution.

1638 - John Harvard founding the first University.

1641 - Nathaniel Ward writing the Massachusetts Body of Liberties.

1681 - William Penn founding Pennsylvania and writing its Frame of Government.

## Significant Preachers Who Cultivated Liberty in the 1700's:

### John Wise, Father of American Independence

In 1717 John Wise, who has been called a "Father of American Independence", wrote *The Law of Nature in Government*, which contained such important ideas that it was reprinted and studied by our Founders in 1772 and cited as legal authority by the Massachusetts Supreme Court. Sections of this work appear word for word in the Declaration of Independence.

### Elisha Williams, First Militant Clergyman                          *1744*

Elisha Williams was a significant force during the First Great Awakening. He served as a schoolteacher, a state representative, President of Yale University, a judge and an ambassador. He was a disciple of George Whitefield's and became chaplain of the New England forces in the French and Indian War. Whitefield blessed the troops as they marched off to battle and Williams even became a colonel who led the troops a year later in 1746. Elisha Williams wrote a 66-page pamphlet in 1744 which should be studied by every American Christian sometime in their life. Called *The Essential Rights and Liberties of Protestants*, it was one of the clearest and fullest explanations of the principles of equality, liberty and property. These ideas were influential in preparing people for the Revolution a few decades later.

1755

### Samuel Davies, Ambassador from the South

Rev. Samuel Davies was a bold ambassador for Christ. In his desire to see the Kingdom of God come "on earth as it is in heaven" he also became a lawyer, an ambassador to England, and President of Princeton. E.L. Magoon writes that "he had made himself a thorough master of English law, civil and ecclesiastical, and always chose to meet every persecuting indictment in the highest courts with his own plea...He went to England and obtained the explicit sanction of the highest authority with respect to the extension of the Toleration Law to Virginia. It was during this mission that...George II and many of his court were in the congregation of this" preacher. When his majesty spoke several times to those around him "Davies paused a moment, and then looking sternly at the king, exclaimed, 'When the lion roars, the beasts of the forest all tremble; and when King Jesus speaks, the princes of the earth should keep silence.'"[5] The boldness, eloquence and ideas of Davies had a great impact upon the life of his neighbor in Virginia, Patrick Henry.

*Samuel Davies*

1766

### Jonathan Mayhew, "Father of Civil Liberty"

Rev. Jonathan Mayhew has been called the Father of Civil Liberty in America for several reasons. He was the first clergyman to begin preaching resistance to England's tyranny in 1750. In his *Discourse Concerning Unlimited Submission* he said, "Although there be a sense...in which Christ's kingdom is not of this world, his inspired apostles have, nevertheless, laid down some general principles concerning the office of civil rulers. and the duty of subjects...It is the duty of all Christian people to inform themselves what it is which their religion teaches concerning that subjection which they owe to the higher powers."[6] After the passage of the Stamp Act, Mayhew became even more influential. George Bancroft wrote:

*Rev. Jonathan Mayhew*

"Whoever repeats the story of the Revolution will rehearse the fame of Mayhew. He spent whole nights in prayer for the dangers of this country. Light dawned on his mind on a Sabbath morning of July, 1766, and he wrote to Otis saying, 'You have heard of the communion [i.e. unity] of the churches; while I was thinking of

**118**

this...[the] importance of the communion of the colonies appeared to me in a striking light. Would it not be decorous in our Assembly to send circulars to all the rest (of the colonies) expressing a desire to cement a union among ourselves?...It may be the only means of perpetuating our liberties.' 'This suggestion,' said Bancroft, 'of a more perfect union for the common defence, originating with Mayhew, was the first public expression of the future Union which has been the glory of the American republic; and it came from a clergyman, on a Sabbath morning, under the inspiration of Heaven.'"[7]

### *Rev. John Witherspoon, Signer of the Declaration of Independence*      *1776*

Rev. John Witherspoon typified the Colonial Clergy who literally discipled the nation. Witherspoon served as a Minister, as President of Princeton College, as a signer of the Declaration of Independence, and on over 100 committees in Congress during our struggle for independence. He is said to have had more influence on the monetary policies found in the Constitution than any other man.

While President of Princeton he trained not only ministers but leaders in all areas of life. One man came to study theology, but Biblical principles of law and government were so impressed upon him that he went on to become the chief architect of the Constitution and the fourth President of the United States -- James Madison. Witherspoon's training enabled him to accomplish this.

Witherspoon also trained:

* 1 vice president

* 3 Supreme Court justices

* 10 Cabinet members

* 12 governors

* 60 Congressmen (21 Senators and 39 Congressmen)

* Plus many members of the Constitutional Convention and many state congressmen[8]

*John Witherspoon*

The following is an excerpt from a sermon entitled "The Dominion of Providence Over the Affairs of Men," that Witherspoon preached on May 17, 1776, in observance of a Day of Fasting and Prayer called for by Congress:

"Upon the whole, I beseech you to make a wise improvement of the present threatening aspect of public affairs and to remember that your duty to God, to your country, to your families, and to yourselves is the same. True religion is nothing else but an inward temper and outward conduct suited to your state and circumstance in Providence at any time. And as peace with God and conformity to Him, adds to the sweetness of created comforts while we possess them, so in times of difficulty and trial, it is in the man of piety and inward principle that we may expect to find the uncorrupted patriot, the useful citizen, and the invincible soldier, -- God grant that in America true religion and civil liberty may be inseparable, and the unjust attempts to destroy the one, may in the issue tend to the support and establishment of both."[9]

### Abraham Baldwin & Hugh Williamson, Delegates at the Constitutional Convention

*Abraham Baldwin*

Rev. Abraham Baldwin was a lawyer, a chaplain in the war, a member of the Georgia legislature, and a member of the Continental Congress before becoming Georgia's delegate to the Convention. Afterwards he was elected to the U.S, House of Representatives and the U.S. Senate and also founded the University of Georgia. Hugh Williamson was a licensed preacher of the Presbyterian Church who conducted church services.

### Other significant clergy/statesmen

Isaac Backus and John Leland were lobbyists for religious freedom in 1786. Manassas Cutler was the author of the Northwest Ordinance written in 1787. Approximately 50 clergy were part of the state ratifying conventions in 1788. William Provost was the first Chaplain to the United States Congress in 1789. Frederick A. C. Muhlenberg was the first Speaker of the United States House of Representatives in 1789.

*Frederick A. C. Muhlenberg*

## Clergy in Public Affairs in the 19th and 20th Centuries

The documentation of clergy actually holding public office is voluminous in the 18th century. (See Alice Baldwin's book, *The New England Clergy and the American Revolution*, for a partial list.) But this did not cease in the last 200 year period. Clergy such as Charles Finney led the fight against slavery, Lyman Beecher and D.L. Moody and Billy Sunday against alcohol use and for women's rights. Others helped to build hospitals and other charitable organizations such as the Salvation Army and the Red Cross. U.S. President James Garfield was a lay preacher before seeking public office. In recent times we have seen the political leadership of Martin Luther King against discrimination and Jerry Falwell against abortion and pornography. In 1988, Pat Robertson and Jesse Jackson, although opposites in political philosophy, were both clergymen who ran for President of the United States.

## Biblical Precedents

Were the American clergy following the Biblical example? Indeed. Clergy in the Old Testament who became politically active included Samuel, Jeremiah, Ezekiel, Zechariah and Ezra. They were clergymen who became statesmen and social reformers or in Biblical terms, Prophets. Many of God's people in the Bible not only influenced politics, but actually sought public office, such as Joseph, Daniel, Esther, Mordecai, Moses, Samuel and Erastus.

## How The Clergy Discipled the Nation in Principles of Liberty

*John Cotton*

While schools were established to train new generations in a Biblical worldview, the clergy continually clarified and applied that worldview to present day, relevant issues that faced the adults in the Colonies. For 150 years leading up to the Revolution, the Colonial pastors used every opportunity possible to educate the people in the principles of liberty. Various means included:

**1. The Weekday Lecture** - The most famous weekday class was held on Thursday in Boston, and was copied by pastors in many colonies. Historian Jonathan Trumbull wrote that the clergy "were the principal instructors of those who received an education for public life. For many years they were consulted by the legislature in all affairs of importance, civil or religious. They were appointed on committees with the Governor and magistrates to assist them in the most delicate concerns of the Commonwealth. . .So influential and authoritative were their teachings, that it is said of one of the Puritan ministers, John Cotton, 'That what he preached on the Lord's day was followed by the synod, and that what he preached in the Thursday Lecture was followed by the General Court.'"[10]

**2. The Election Sermon** - An annual event begun in 1633 in Massachusetts. They were their political textbooks. John Wingate Thornton writes of the Election Sermons and the clergy's influence in early America:

"The clergy were generally consulted by the civil authorities; and not infrequently the suggestions from the pulpit, on election days and other special occasions, were enacted into laws. The statutebook, the reflex of the age, shows this influence. The State was developed out of the Church.

"The sermon is styled the Election Sermon, and is printed. Every representative has a copy for himself, and generally one or more for the minister or ministers of his town. As the patriots have prevailed, the preachers of each sermon have been the zealous friends of liberty; and the passages most adapted to promote the spread and love of it have been selected and circulated far and wide by means of newspapers, and read with avidity and a degree of veneration on account of the preacher and his election to the service of the day. . . ."[11]

These election sermons were preached in America for about 250 years (into the 1870's).

**3. The Artillery Sermon** - These were periodic addresses given to the military on such topics as "a defensive war in a just cause is sinless" and the sin of cowardice.

**4. Special Fast, Thanksgiving, and Anniversary Sermons** - These sermons were preached in observance of victories, calamities, and special events.

The American political Science Review in 1984 showed that 10% of all Political writings in the Founding Era were sermons, and asserted therefore that colonial clergymen must be considered part of our "Founding Fathers" in America.[12]

In an adult's lifetime in Colonial America, the average adult listened to about 15,000 hours of Biblical exposition by the clergy. Their influence on public opinion was equivalent to what is held today by the modern media. If we ever hope for a restoration of the American Christian Republic, political educational efforts such as these must once again become a regular part of the clergy's weekly responsibilities in their churches.

## The Pulpits Produced the American Revolution

An example of an artillery sermon preached to General Washington and his troops on the eve of the Battle of Brandywine reveals the force that motivated the colonists. Rev. Jacob Troute's sermon was titled "They That Take the Sword Shall Perish by the Sword".

Soldiers, and countrymen, we have met this evening perhaps for the last time. We have shared the toils of the march, the peril of the flight, and the dismay of the retreat, alike. We have endured the cold and hunger, the contumely of the internal foe, and the scourge of the foreign oppressor. We have sat night after night by the campfire. We have together heard the roll of the reveille which calls us to duty, or the beat of the tattoo which gave the signal for the hardy sleep of the soldier, with the earth for his bed and the knapsack for his pillow.

And now, soldiers and brethren, we have met in this peaceful valley, on the eve of battle, in the sunlight that tomorrow morn will glimmer on the scenes of blood. We have met amid the whitening tents of our encampments; in the time of terror and gloom we have gathered together. God grant that it may not be for the last time.

It is a solemn moment! Brethren, does not the solemn voice of nature seem to echo the sympathies of the hour? The flag of our country droops heavily from yonder staff. The breeze has died away along the green plaid of Chadd's Ford. The plain that spreads before us glitters in the sunlight. The heights of Brandywine arise gloomy and grand beyond the waters of yonder stream. All nature holds a pause of solemn silence on the eve of the uproar and bloody strife of tomorrow.

*"Give them Watts boys"*

"They that take the sword shall perish by the sword."

And have they not taken the sword?

Let the desolate plain, the blood-sodden valley, the burned farmhouses, blackening in the sun, the sacked village and the ravaged town, answer. Let the withered bones of the butchered farmer, strewed along the fields of his homestead, answer. Let the starving mother, with her babe clinging to the withered breast that can afford no sustenance, let her answer,-with the death-rattle mingling with the murmuring tones that marked the last moment of her life. Let the mother and the babe answer.

It was but a day past, and our land slept in the quiet of peace. War was not here. Fraud and woe and want dwelt not among us. From the eternal solitude of the green woods arose the blue smoke of the settler's cabin, and golden fields of corn looked from amid the waste of the wilderness, and the glad music of human voices awoke the silence of the forest.

Now, God of mercy, behold the change. Under the shadow of a pre-text, under the sanctity of the name of God, invoking the Redeemer to their aid, do these foreign hirelings slay our people. They throng our towns, they darken our plains, and now they encompass our posts on the lonely plain of Chadd's Ford.

"They that take the sword shall perish by the sword."

Brethren, think me not unworthy of belief when I tell you the doom of the British is sealed. Think me not vain when I tell you that, beyond the cloud that now enshrouds us, I see gathering thick and fast the darker cloud and thicker storm of Divine retribution.

They may conquer tomorrow. Might and wrong may prevail, and we may be driven from the field, but the hour of God's vengeance will come!

Ay, if in the vast solitudes of eternal space there throbs the being of an awful God, quick to avenge and sure to punish guilt, then the man George Brunswick, called king, will feel in his brain and heart the vengeance of the eternal Jehovah. A blight will light upon his life - a withered and an accursed intellect; a blight will be upon his children and on his people. Great God, how dread the punishment! A crowded populace, peopling the dense towns where them men of money thrive, where the laborer starves; went striding among the people in all forms of terror; an ignorant and God-defying priesthood chuckling over the miseries of millions; a proud and merciless nobility adding wrong to wrong, and heaping insult upon robbery and fraud; royalty corrupt to the very heart, and aristocracy rotten to the core; crime and want linked hand in hand, and tempting the men to deeds of woe and death;

- these are a part of the doom and retribution that shall come upon the English throne and English people.

Soldiers, I look around upon your familiar faces with strange interest! Tomorrow morning we go forth to the battle - for need I tell you that your unworthy minister will march with you, invoking the blessing of God's aid in the fight? We will march forth to the battle. Need I exhort you to fight the good fight - to fight for your homesteads, for your wives and your children?

My friends, I urge you to fight, by the galling memories of British wrong. Walton, I might tell you of your father, butchered in the silence of the night in the plains of Trenton. I might picture his gray hairs dabbled in blood. I might ring his death-shrieks in your ears. Shaefmyer, I might tell you of a butchered mother and sister outraged, the lonely farmhouse, the night assault, the roof in flames, the shouts of the troops as they dispatched their victims, the cries for mercy, and the pleadings of innocence for pity. I might paint this all again, in the vivid colors of the terrible reality, if I thought courage needed such wild excitement.

But I know you are strong in the might of the Lord. You will march forth to battle tomorrow with light hearts and determined spirits, though the solemn duty -- the duty of avenging the dead -- may rest heavy on your souls.

And in the hour of battle, when all around is darkness, lit by the lurid cannon-glare and the piercing musket-flash, when the wounded strow the ground and the dead litter your path, then remember, soldiers, that God is with you. The eternal God fights for you; He rides on the battle-cloud. He sweeps onward with the march of a hurricane charge. God, the awful and infinite, fights for you, and you will triumph.

"They that take the sword shall perish by the sword."

You have taken the sword, but not in the spirit of wrong or revenge. You have taken the sword for your homes, for your wives and your little ones. You have taken the sword for truth, justice and right, and to you the promise is, be of good cheer, for your foes have taken the sword in defiance of all that men hold dear, in blasphemy of God; they shall perish by the sword.

And now, brethren and soldiers, I bid you all farewell. Many of us will fall in the battle of tomorrow, and in the memory of all will ever rest and linger the quiet sense of this autumnal eve.

Solemn twilight advances over the valley. The woods on the opposite height fling their long shadows over the green of the meadow. Around us are the tents of the Continental host, the suppressed bustle of the camp, the hurried tramp of the soldiers to and fro, and among the tents the stillness and awe that mark the eve of battle.

When we meet again, may the shadows of twilight be flung over the peaceful land. God in heaven grant it! Let us pray.[13]

Without a doubt, the moral force and unified biblical worldview exhibited in the American Christian Revolution was a product of the Pastoral Cultivation of liberty for 150 years. Historian Alice Baldwin said, "The Constitutional Convention and the written Constitution were the children of the pulpit."

*Jefferson's Seal*

# Chapter 10

# The American Christian Revolution

## *The Origins of the American Christian Revolution*

Without the Great Awakening (1740-1760) there would have been no American Revolution (1760-1790). The ideas, the motivation, the Biblical worldview, and the great virtuous statesmanship seen in the Founder's Era were all birthed in this great revival led by Jonathan Edwards and George Whitefield. George Washington, Samuel Adams, Thomas Jefferson and others who guided us through out independence and beginnings as a nation were young men during this time period. The Godly environment of the Awakening deeply affected and helped prepare them for their destiny.

During this Great Awakening the Spirit of God swept mightly throughout the colonies. The numbers of people in the churches more than doubled. Whole towns were literally converted to Christ. Benjamin Franklin wrote in his *Autobiography* that "it seem'd as if all the world were growing religious, so one could not walk thro' the town in an evening without hearing psalms sung in different families of every street."

Many new revivalist universities were established to cultivate and propagate seeds of liberty and raise up a learned clergy. The clergy trained at these universities helped to spread Biblical principles to

*George Whitefield*

all the colonies. They continued to cultivate the Christian ideas of Liberty up to the Revolution.

1772                    *The Harvest of Christian Ideas of Liberty*

Although Rev. Jonathan Mayhew was the first to propose the idea of using circular letters to unite the colonies, he died shortly thereafter. It was brought to pass by the man who became known as the "Father of the Revolution" -- Samuel Adams. George Bancroft wrote that Adams "...was a member of the church; and the austere purity of his life witnessed the sincerity of his profession. Evening and morning his house was a house of prayer; and no one more revered the Christian sabbath...The walls of his modest mansion never witnessed anything inconsistent with the discipline of the man whose desire for his birthplace was that 'Boston might became a Christian Sparta.'"[1]

*Samuel Adams, the Father of the American Revolution*

The title, the "Father of the American Revolution," was applied to Samuel Adams due to his unequaled efforts promoting the Revolution. He understood the conflict between the colonies and England was more than an economic or political struggle. He recognized, as only a Christian truly could, that the British government had violated the colonists' rights as men, Christians, and subjects.

Not only did Samuel Adams understand the principles upon which the American Revolution was based, but he also saw that in order for independence to be realized these ideas would have to be dispersed throughout the colonies. He worked for twenty years promoting the cause of liberty.

In 1772 Samuel Adams proposed "Committees of Correspondence" to be established throughout the colonies because he desired all people to be educated in order that they could reason out their rights and political convictions based upon Biblical principles. His desire was for the colonies to be united "not by external bonds, but by the vital force of distinctive ideas and principles."[2] This unity of ideas and principles helped to promote union among the colonists. The common ideas sown within the colonists by Samuel Adams and many other Christian thinking men of that and earlier generations resulted in the external union of the colonies into the United States of America.

The response of other colonies to Adams' "Committees of Correspondence" was not immediate because to educate in principles, as Adams desired, is much more difficult and requires more time than just teaching issues. Nevertheless, Samuel Adams did not lose heart for he had faith in the cause of independence. One incident revealing his faith was seen when Adams received a letter from a Plymouth patriot concerning establishing a committee in that area of Massachusetts. In the letter, the patriot expressed fear that most people would not join in the effort for "they are dead, " he wrote, "and the dead can't be raised without a miracle." Adams replied that there was no place for despair within their lives and that "all are not dead; and where there is a spark of patriotic fire, we will rekindle it."[3]

The first letter circulated among the Colonists in 1772 was called the *Rights of the Colonists* and was written by Sam Adams himself.  It was the "most systematic presentation of the American cause and the first public denial of the right of the British Parliament to tax the Colonists." He wrote: "The supreme power cannot justly take from any man any part of his property, without his consent in the person or by his representative." He said that "the natural rights of the Colonists are these: First, a right to life; Secondly, to liberty; Thirdly, to property; together with the right to support and defend them in the best manner they can. . .The rights of the Colonists as Christians," he said, "may be best understood by reading and carefully studying the institutes of the great Law Giver and Head of the Christian Church, which are to be found clearly written and promulgated in the New Testament." Samuel Adams, understood that the principles necessary for changing a society are discovered through "...the study and practice of the exalted virtues of the Christian system..."[4]

## *American Christian Ideas Lead to American Christian Unity*

For many decades England had embraced a philosophy of government that gave the Colonies representation in matters relating to themselves. This begin to change with the  Stamp Act in 1765. To raise revenue for the war debt, accrued through defending the Colonies from the French and Indians, England's Parliament imposed a tax upon the colonists without their having any say in the matter. The Colonists recognized that it was their responsibility to pay for the cost of their defense, but they opposed the principle of the Parliament being able to tax them without their consent, or the consent of their representatives. Due to their protest the Stamp Act was repealed, but England's change in governmental policy continued with the Townsend Act in 1767 and then the Tea Act in 1773. The Colonists would tolerate no longer this arbitrary power of the King or Parliament to take their property without their consent. They claimed it violated the English Constitution guaranteeing the fundamental right of property. It was not that they were poor and would not pay, but rather they were free and would not submit to tyranny.

*December, 1773*    ### The Boston Tea Party

After Parliament imposed a tax upon all British tea sold in the colonies, the colonists gathered together and determined that they would boycott the tea and not purchase it. As ships full of tea were on their way to America, patriots in Philadelphia, Boston, New York, and Charleston, the major destination ports for the ships, held town meetings. When the ships arrived in Boston, the patriots put a guard at the docks to prevent the tea from being unloaded. Almost 7,000 people gathered at the Old South Meeting House to hear from Mr. Rotch, the owner of the ships. He explained that if he attempted to sail from Boston without unloading the tea, his life and business would be in danger. The Colonists decided, therefore, that in order

*The Boston Tea Party... a protest of taxation without representation.*

to protect Mr. Rotch, they must accept the tea, but they wouldn't have to drink it! By accepting the shipment they were agreeing to pay for it, but they would make a radical sacrifice in order to protest this injustice before the eyes of the world. Thus ensued the "Boston Tea Party." To make it even more newsworthy as well as to protect individuals involved, the men disguised themselves as Indians.

Richard Frothingham records the incident:

"The party in disguise...whooping like Indians, went on board the vessels, and, warning their officers and those of the custom-house to keep out of the way, unlaid the hatches, hoisted the chests of tea on deck, cut them open, and hove the tea overboard. They proved quiet and systematic workers. No one interfered with them. No other property was injured; no person was harmed; no tea was allowed to be carried away; and the silence of the crowd on shore was such that the breaking of the chests was distinctly heard by them. 'The whole,' Hutchinson wrote, 'was done with very little tumult.'"[5]

*Old South Meeting House*

Soon after this, ships arrived at Philadelphia, New York and Charleston and were convinced to return to England. This confrontation brought about much unity throughout the colonies, and brought the first proposal for a Continental Congress.

## Boston Port Bill                                         June, 1774

England, however, embarrassed and infuriated, decided to retaliate. They passed the **Boston Port Bill** which was intended to shut down all commerce on June 1st and starve the townspeople into submission. "Committees of Correspondence" spread the news by letter through all the colonies. The colonies began to respond. Massachusetts, Connecticut and Virginia called for days of fasting and prayer. Thomas Jefferson penned the resolve in Virginia "to invoke the divine interposition to give to the American people one heart and one mind to oppose by all just means every injury to American rights."

Frothingham writes:

"...On the day [June 1] the Port Act went into effect, a cordon of British men-of-war was moored around the town of Boston. Not keel nor a raft was permitted to approach the wharves. The wheels of commerce were stopped. The poor were deprived of employment. The rich were cut off from their usual resources. The town entered upon its period of suffering. The day was widely observed as a day of fasting and prayer. The manifestations of sympathy were general. Business was suspended. Bells were muffled, and tolled from morning to night; flags were kept at half-mast; streets were dressed in mourning; public buildings and shops were draped in black; large congregations filled the churches.

"In Virginia the members of the House of Burgesses assembled at their place of meeting; went in procession, with the speaker at their head, to the church and listened to a discourse. 'Never,' a lady wrote, 'since my residence in Virginia have I seen so large a congregation as was this day assembled to hear divine service.' The preacher selected for his text the words: 'be strong and of good courage, fear not, nor be afraid of them; for the Lord thy God, He it is that doth go with thee. He will not fail thee nor forsake thee.' 'The people,' Jefferson says, 'met generally, with anxiety and alarm in their countenances; and the effect of the day, through the whole colony, was like a shock of electricity, arousing every man and placing him erect and solidly on his centre.' These words describe the effect of the Port Act throughout the thirteen colonies."[6]

*Virginia Capitol, where the members of the House of Burgesses declared a day of Prayer and Fasting in support of Boston.*

The colonies responded in material support as well, not by governmental decree but, more significantly, by individual action. A grassroots movement of zealous workers went door to door to gather patriotic offerings. These gifts were sent to Boston accompanied with letters containing phrases such as: "Stand firm, and let your intrepid courage show to the world that you are Christians." Out of the diversity of the colonies, a deep Christian unity was being revealed on a national level for the first time. In the *Boston Gazette* on July 11, 1774, the following words appeared in a published letter:

"My persecuted brethren of this metropolis, you may rest assured that the guardian God of New England, who holds the hearts of his people in his hands, has influenced your distant brethren to the benevolence."[7]

This was the greatest miracle of the Revolution: Unity out of Diversity. This is why *E. Pluribus Unum*, ("one from the many"), was such a significant motto. Rosalie Slater writes:

"The Colonies had grown up under the constitutions of government so different, there was so great a variety of religions, they were composed of so many different nations, their customs, manners and habits had so little resemblance, and their intercourse had been so rare, and their knowledge of each other so imperfect, that to unite them in the same principles in theory, and the same system of action, was certainly a very difficult enterprise. The complete accomplishment of it, in so short a time and by such simple means, was, perhaps, a singular example in the history of mankind - thirteen clocks were made to strike together; a perfection of mechanism which no artist had ever before effected. Within the space of two months, for the first time in Christian history, 3 million people achieved Biblical Christian Unity."[8]

Further evidence of national unity and union is found in the call for a Continental Congress to convene for the first time on September 5, 1774. B.F. Morris writes:

"No doubt the assembly of the first Continental Congress may be regarded as the era at which the Union of these States commenced. This event took place in Philadelphia, the city distinguished by the great civil events of our early history, on the 5th of September, 1774, on which day the first Continental Congress assembled.

"The proceedings of the Assembly were introduced by religious observances and devout supplications to the throne of grace, for the inspiration of wisdom and the spirit of good counsels. The first act of the first session of the Continental Congress was to pass the following resolution:

'Tuesday, September 6, 1774-Resolved, that the Rev. Mr. Duche be desired to open Congress to-morrow morning with prayer, at Carpenter's Hall, at nine o'clock.

'Wednesday, September 7, 1774, A.M.-Agreeable to the resolve of yesterday, the meeting was opened with prayer by the Rev. Mr. Duche.'"[9]

A beautiful reminiscence of this event was recorded by John Adams in a letter to his wife:

"When the Congress met, Mr. Cushing made a motion that it should be opened with prayer. It was opposed by Mr. Jay of New York and Mr. Rutledge of South Carolina because we were so divided in religious sentiments -- some Episcopalians, some Quakers, some Anabaptists, some Presbyterians, and some Congregationalists -- that we could not join in the same act of worship. Mr. Samuel Adams arose and said 'that he was no bigot, and could hear a prayer from any gentleman of piety and virtue who was at the same time a friend to his country. He was a stranger in Philadelphia, but had heard that Mr. Duche deserved that character, and therefore he moved that Mr. Duche, an Episcopal clergyman, might be desired to read prayers to Congress tomorrow morning.' The motion was seconded, and passed in the affirmative. Mr. Randolph, our president, waited on Mr. Duche, and received for [an] answer that if his health would permit, he certainly would. Accordingly next morning he appeared with his clerk, and his pontificals, and read the Psalter for the seventh day of September, which was the 85th Psalm. You must remember this was the next morning after we had heard the rumor of the horrible cannonade of Boston. I never saw a greater effect

When the First Continental Congress met in September, 1774, they prayed fervently for America, for Congress, for Massachusetts, and for Boston.

produced upon an audience. It seemed as if Heaven had ordained that Psalm to be read on that morning. After this, Mr. Duche, unexpectedly to everybody, struck out into extemporary prayer which filled the bosom of every man present: 'Be Thou present O God of Wisdom and direct the counsel of this Honorable Assembly. Enable them to settle all things on the best and surest foundations; that the scene of blood may be speedily closed; that order, harmony and peace may be effectually restored, and truth and justice, religion and piety, prevail and flourish among the people. Preserve the health of their bodies, and the vigor of them in this world., and crown them with everlasting glory in the world to come. All this we ask in the name and through the merits of Jesus Christ Thy Son and our Savior, Amen.'

"Washington was kneeling there, and Henry, Randolph, Rutledge, Lee, and Jay, and by their side there stood, bowed in reverence, the Puritan Patriots of New England, who at that moment had reason to believe that an armed soldiery was wasting their humble households;...They prayed fervently 'for America, for Congress, for the Province of Massachusetts Bay, and especially for the town of Boston,' and who can realize the emotions with which they turned imploringly to Heaven for Divine interposition. It was enough to melt a heart of stone. I saw the tears gush into the eyes of the old grave pacific Quakers of Philadelphia."[10]

## Leadership of the Clergy in the Revolution

The primary force or catalyst to this miracle of unity and mutual support among the colonies were the preachers of the era. Jedidiah Morse writes in his *Annals of the American Revolution*:

"The prayers and public discourses of the clergy,...who were friends to their country, (and there were few who were not) breathed the spirit of patriotism; and as their piety and integrity had generally secured to them the confidence of the people, they had great influence and success in encouraging them to engage in its defence. In this way, that class of citizens aided the cause of their country; and to their pious exertions, under the Great Arbiter of human affairs, has been justly ascribed no inconsiderable share of the success and victory that crowned the American arms."[11]

A significant proclamation from the period affirms this crucial role of the clergy in shaping public opinion. On December 6, 1774, the Provincial Congress of Massachusetts under the leadership of John Hancock, issued this statement:

"When we contemplate the friendship and assistance our ancestors -- the first settlers of this Province -- received from the pious Pastors of the Churches of Christ,... we cannot but acknowledge the goodness of Heaven in constantly supplying us with preachers of the Gospel whose concern has been the temporal and spiritual happiness of this people; In a day like this,... we cannot but place great hopes in an Order of Men, who have ever distinguished themselves in their country's cause, and do therefore recommend to the Ministers of the Gospel... that they assist us in avoiding that dreadful slavery with which we are now threatened by advising the people of their several congregations..."[12]

*A Minuteman leaving for action, as a minister bestows his blessing.*

The voluntary aid that came to Boston during the Port Bill and other instances throughout the war were primarily due to the leadership of the clergy. Alice Baldwin writes:

"Beginning in 1767 and continuing throughout the War, the ministers did all in their power to encourage the non-importation agreements and home manufactures. There are many instances in each of the New England colonies of all-day spinning bees held in the rooms and on the lawns of the minister's homes...One good clergyman [Rev. Judah Champion of Litchfield, Conn.] during the war felt so keenly the need of clothes for the soldiers [in the cold northern winter] at Quebec that he excused the women of the town from afternoon service and set them all to spinning on the Sabbath Day...Frequently before the end of the day the minister would address the women and girls on the issues of the time...In this manner the ministers showed knowledge of human nature by arousing competition between town and town, and between churches in the same town, and even between married and unmarried women, as well as by making the whole affair a great social occasion through having the men come to supper and join in an evening of fun with music and singing of songs written by the 'Sons of Liberty.'"[13]

But the clergy were also a motivating force behind the organization of militia for military defense. The churches would form *minute-men* from out of their male membership and the deacon of the church would often be responsible for drilling them. Richard Frothingham writes that, "On the days of drill the citizen soldiers sometimes went from the parade ground to the church where they listened to exhortation and prayer." He records part of an admonition given to these Minute-men by the Provincial Congress: "You are placed by Providence in the post of honor, because it is the post of danger;...The eyes not only of North America and the whole British Empire, but of all Europe, are upon you. Let us be, therefore, altogether solicitous that no disorderly behavior, nothing unbecoming our characters as Americans, as citizens and Christians, be justly chargeable to us."[14]

The Provincial Congress, led by John Hancock on April 15th called for a Day of Fasting and Prayer with these words:

"In circumstances dark as these, it becomes us, as Men and Christians, to reflect that, while every prudent measure should be taken to ward off the impending judgements;...at the same time, all confidence must be with-held from the means we use; and reposed only on that God who rules in the armies of Heaven, and without whose blessing the best human counsels are but foolishness -- and all created power, vanity. It is the happiness of his Church that, when the powers of earth and hell combine against it, and those who should be nursing fathers become its persecutors -- then the Throne of Grace is of easiest access -- and its appeal thither is graciously invited by the Father of Mercies, who has assured it, that when his children ask bread he will not give them stone."[15]

### Rev. Jonas Clark and the Battle of Lexington                    April, 1775

The most historic band of minutemen was led by Deacon Parker under the auspices of Rev. Jonas Clark. Clark was pastor of a church in Lexington, Massachusetts. Since the struggle over the Stamp Act in 1765, this clergyman had become this town's principal leader in its town meetings and issues of liberty and government. Almost every crucial state paper written to represent this town was authored by Jonas Clark. His home was a frequent meeting place for men like Samuel Adams and John Hancock when safe locations could not be assured inside Boston. Such was the case on the night of April 18th,

*Old North Church*

1775. Adams and Hancock were visiting for the night, unaware that the British had decided to send troops to Lexington to destroy the town's military supplies and capture these two men. One of Clark's house guests asked him on that night if the Lexington people would fight if necessary. Clark, who had laid a solid foundation concerning the duty of self-defense of inalienable rights for years through his sermons, responded confidently: "I have trained them for this very hour!"[16] Clark had prepared this people so well in the Scriptures as they related to the issues of the day, that the first shots of the entire war were providentially selected to be fired on his church lawn.

This first battle and the role of Paul Revere is recorded well in William Wells' book *The Life and Public Service of Samuel Adams:*

"Paul Revere had agreed to give the signal to the colonists across the Charles River by placing a lantern in the North Church Steeple."

"If the British went out by water, he would display two lanterns in the North Church Steeple, and if by land, one, as a signal that the news might be conveyed to Lexington, should the communication with the peninsula be cut off. Having instructed a friend to that effect, he was rowed across the Charles River. It was the young flood, the ship was winding, and the moon rising. Landing in Charlestown, Revere found that his signal had been understood. He then took a horse, and rode toward Lexington."

"After several adventures on the way, in which he narrowly escaped capture, he reached the house of Mr. Clark about midnight, and gave the alarm. He was just in time to elude the vigilance of the British in Boston; for Earl Percy, having accidentally ascertained that the secret was out, gave orders to allow no person to leave the town. Revere found the family at rest, and a guard of eight men stationed at the house, for the protection of Adams and Hancock. He rode up, and requested admittance, but the Sergeant replied that the family before retiring had desired that they not be disturbed by any noise about the house. 'Noise!' replied Revere, 'you'll have noise enough before long. The Regulars are coming out.' He was then admitted."

"About one o'clock on the morning of the 19th, the militia were mustered on the green near the meeting-house, and messengers sent for additional information. By two o'clock the countrymen numbered one hundred and thirty. The guns were loaded with powder and ball in the presence of Adams, Hancock, and Clark. One of the messengers returning with the report that no troops could be seen, and the weather being chilly, the men were dismissed with orders to appear again at the beat of the drum..."

"Colonel Smith had marched his column but a few miles, when the ringing of bells and firing of guns satisfied him that the country was alarmed. He immediately detached six companies of light infantry, under command of Major Pitcairn, with orders to press forward, and secure the two bridges at Concord, while he sent back for reinforcements. By capturing those whom he met upon the road, Pitcairn prevented the news of his approach from going before him, until he came within a mile and a half of Lexington meeting-house, when a horseman, who had succeeded in eluding the troops, galloped into the village. Then, about seventy townspeople assembled as the drums beat, and at the sound the British halted to load. The advance guard and grenadiers then hurried forward at double quick, and when within five or six rods of the Provincials, Pitcairn shouted, 'Disperse, ye villains! Ye rebels, disperse! Lay down your arms! Why don't you lay down your arms and disperse?' Most of the minute-men, undecided whether to fire or retreat, stood motionless, having been ordered by their commander not to fire first. Some were joining the ranks, others leaving them, when Pitcairn in a loud voice gave the word to fire, at the same time discharging his pistol. The order was obeyed at first by a few guns, which did no execution, and immediately after by a deadly discharge from the whole British force. A few of the militia, no longer hesitating, returned the fire, but without serious effect. Parker, seeing the utter disparity of forces, ordered his men to disperse. The Regulars continued their fire while any of the militia remained in sight, killing eight and wounding ten. The village green, where this event took place, has been aptly termed by the historian, 'a field of murder, not of battle.'"

"The firing was soon over, and the royal troops remained masters of the field; but the sacrifice of that little band revolutionized the world. It was the first scene in the drama which was to carry with it the destinies of mankind."

"Adams and Hancock, as the soldiers made their appearance, were persuaded to retire to the adjacent village of Woburn, their safety being regarded as of utmost importance. Passing through the fields, while the sunlight glistened in the dew of the fresh

The Battle of Lexington: "From this day will be dated the liberty of the World!"

spring morning, Adams felt his soul swell with uncontrollable joy as he contemplated the mighty future, and with prophetic utterance of his country's dawning independence, he exclaimed, 'O! what a glorious morning is this!'..."[17]

It *was* a glorious morning. Why? Because as Rev. Jonas Clark preached: "From this day will be dated the liberty of the world!"[18]

The Providential Hand of God is evident in this event. About one month earlier the Governor of Connecticut had called upon the colony to observe a "**Day of public Fasting and Prayer**...that God would graciously pour out his Holy Spirit on us, to bring us to a thorough repentance and effectual reformation;...That He would restore, preserve and secure the liberties of this, and all the other American Colonies, and make this land a mountain of Holiness and habitation of Righteousness forever.-(and) That God would preserve and confirm the Union of the Colonies in the pursuit and practice of that Religion and virtue which will honour Him..."[19]

What day had Governor Jonathan Trumbull selected for them to be praying? "**Wednesday, the nineteenth Day of April!**"

## *The Mecklenburg Declaration*          *May, 1775*

As soon as word of the battle of Lexington reached a convention of delegates in North Carolina, they declared independence from England. George Bancroft writes:

> "The first public voice in America for dissolving all connections with Great Britain, came not from the Puritans of New England, the Dutch of New York, nor from the planters of Virginia, but from the Scotch-Irish Presbyterians 'who were meeting in convention as delegates of Mecklenburg County, North Carolina.'"[20]

Over a year before the Declaration of Independence, these Presbyterians -- many of them preachers -- wrote the following declaration:

> "Resolved, That we do hereby declare ourselves a free and independent people, are, and of a right ought to be, a sovereign and self-governing Association, under the control of no power, other than that of our God and the General Government of the Congress; to the maintenance of which independence, we solemnly pledge to each other, our mutual cooperation, our lives, our fortunes, and our most sacred honor."[21]

## *Continental Congress Calls For a Day of Fasting and Prayer*    *July, 1775*

On June 12, 1775, England declared that the Colonies would now be put under martial law. The Christian Continental Congress, in response, employed their most trusted weapon: Prayer. They appealed to "The Great Governor of the World" who "frequently influences the minds of men to serve the wise and gracious purposes of His providential government." It was "recommended to Christians of all denominations to assemble for public...Humiliation, Fasting and Prayer" on the 20th of July.[22]

When the special day came, the entire Congress went as a group to the church of Jacob Duche and heard his sermon from Psalm 80:14. They were joined that day for the first time by delegates from Georgia who were led by Rev. John Zubly. Now all thirteen Colonies were united in Congress.

Elsewhere, on that day, **Rev. David Jones** preached one of the day's most eloquent sermons entitled, *Defensive War in a Just Cause Sinless.* In this sermon he appealed to the history of Israel and noted that "when vice and immorality became prevalent; when they forsook and rebelled against their God, (then) they lost their martial spirit." Then the nation experienced revival under the leadership of Nehemiah who stirred the people to arm themselves with these words: "Be not ye afraid of them: Remember the Lord, which is great and terrible, and fight for the brethren, your sons and your daughters, your wives and your houses!" Rev. Jones proved from many Scriptural examples how a defensive war is sinless before God, and when it is proper to use force against a tyrant. Then he says:

"The reason why a defensive war seems so awful to good people, is, they esteem it to be some kind of murder: but this is a very great mistake; for it is no more murder than a legal process against a criminal. The end is the same, the mode is different. In some cases it is the only mode left to obtain justice. And surely that religion is not from Heaven, which is against justice on earth. Remember all men are not converted; if they were, there could be no necessity of war in any sense. For, says the Scripture, 'they shall not hurt nor destroy.' But , remember, this is when the earth shall be filled with the knowledge of the Lord. Alas! this is not the case now; for darkness, gloomy darkness, prevails throughout the kingdoms of this world. Oh! that the kingdom of Jesus was come, when we should have occasion to learn war no more."[23]

*Patrick Henry making "an appeal to arms and to the God of Hosts."*

Just a few months prior to this sermon, **Patrick Henry,** the orator of the Revolution, urged the Virginia Convention of the delegates to take up arms since they had exhausted every means of protest and flight. He said:

"Sir, we have done everything that could be done to avert the storm which is now coming on. We have petitioned - we have remonstrated - we have supplicated - we have prostrated ourselves before the throne, and have implored its interposition to arrest the tyrannical hands of the ministry and parliament. Our petitions have been slighted; our remonstrances have produced additional violence and insult; our supplications have been disregarded; and we have been spurned, with contempt, from the foot of the throne. In vain, after these things, may we indulge the fond hope of peace and reconciliation. There is no longer any room for hope. If we wish to be free...we must fight! - I repeat it, sir, we must fight!  An appeal to arms and to the God of Hosts is all that is left us!...Three millions of people, armed in the holy cause of liberty...are invincible by any force which our enemy can send against us. Besides, sir, we shall not fight our battles alone. There is a just God who presides over the destinies of nations; and He will raise up friends to fight our battles for us. The battle, sir, is not to the strong alone; it is to the vigilant, the active, the brave...There is no retreat but in submission and slavery!"

"...Gentlemen may cry, 'Peace! peace!' - but there is no peace...Is life so dear, and peace so sweet, as to be purchased at the price of chains and slavery? Forbid it, Almighty God! I know not what course others may take; but as for me, give me liberty or give me death!"[24]

## *"The Black Regiment"*

The war effort was blessed with the inspirational leadership of the colonial clergy who became known by their opposition as "the Black Regiment" in reference to their wearing of pulpit gowns on the battlefront.

One month after the Battle of Lexington, **Rev. Samuel Langdon**, President of Harvard, preached to the leaders of Massachusetts an Election Sermon entitled, *Government Corrupted By Vice and Recovered by Righteousness*. He said that:

"...Vice will increase with the riches and glory of an empire; and this generally tends to corrupt the Constitution and in time bring on its dissolution. This may be considered not only as the natural effect of vice, but a religious judgement from Heaven, especially upon a nation which has been favored with the blessings of religion and liberty and is guilty of undervaluing them..."

*St. John Episcopal Church, Richmond. Here Patrick Henry in 1775 proclaimed "Give me liberty or give me death!"*

He went on to call for repentance, as well as action in faith that God had heard them, to set up their banners and fight in the name of the Lord. Langdon then personally led them to the heights of Bunker Hill to begin their entrenchments for that historic battle. Shortly after that battle Rev. Langdon felt called of God to devote himself full-time to ministering to the troops as their chaplain. He recorded in his journal the following:

"June 20, 1775--This has been one of the most important and trying days of my life. I have taken leave of my people for the present, and shall at once proceed to the American camp at Boston and offer my services as chaplain in the army. Ever since the battle of Bunker Hill my mind has been turned to this subject. God's servants are needed in the army to pray with it and for it. This is God's work; and his ministers should set an example that will convince the people that they believe it to be such. But the scene in the house of God today has tried me sorely. How silent, how solemn, was the congregation and when they sang the sixty-first Psalm, commencing--'When overwhelm'd with grief, My heart within me dies...' Sobs were heard in every part of the building. At the close, I was astonished to see Deacon S., now nearly sixty years of age, arise and address the congregation. 'Brethren,' said he, 'our minister has acted right. This is God's cause; and as in days of old the priests bore the ark into the midst of the battle, so must they do it now. We should be unworthy of the fathers and mothers who landed on Plymouth Rock, if we do not cheerfully bear what Providence shall put upon us in the great conflict now before us. I had two sons at Bunker Hill, and one of them, you know, was slain. The other did his duty, and for the future God must do with him what seemeth him best. I offer him to liberty. I had thought that I would stay here with the church. But my minister is going, and I will shoulder my musket and go, too.' In this strain he continued for some time, till the whole congregation was bathed in tears. Oh God must be with this people in the unequal struggle, or else how could they enter upon it with such solemnity and prayer, with such strong reliance on his assistance, and such a profound sense of their need of it? Just before separating, the whole congregation joined in singing-- 'O God our help in ages past, Our hope for years to come.'"[26]

*December, 1775*     *Peter Muhlenberg*

In the U.S. Capitol building today, there stands a statue honoring another one of "the Black Regiment." Benson J. Lossing writes:

"In those days politics were preached in the pulpits and men were led to action on the side of freedom by faithful pastors. The eminent General Muhlenberg was one of this stamp. When the war for independence was kindling, he was a clergyman in Virginia, and at the close of 1775, he concluded a sermon with the words of Scripture: 'There is a time for all things-- a time to preach and a time to pray;' but those times, he said, had passed away; and then, in a voice that sounded like a trumpet-blast through the church, he exclaimed: 'There is a time to fight, and that time has now come.' Then laying aside his sacerdotal gown, he stood before his flock in the full

*Peter Muhlenberg*

uniform of a Virginia colonel. He ordered the drums to be beaten at the church door for recruits; and almost the entire male audience, capable of bearing arms, joined his standard. Nearly three hundred men enlisted under his banner on that day."[27]

Rev. Peter Muhlenberg became one of Washington's primary Brigadier Generals in the Continental Army. Other clergymen followed Muhlenberg's example and led in battle: Rev. Robert Smith of South Carolina and Rev. John Craighead of North Carolina are examples.

J. Wingate Thornton declared in his book *The Pulpit of the American Revolution*:

"Thus it is manifest, in the spirit of our history, in our annals, and by the general voice of the fathers of the republic, that, in a very great degree, - to the pulpit, the Puritan pulpit, we owe the moral force which won our independence."[28]

Massachusetts affirmed this truth as they looked for the most effective way to promote the Declaration of Independence in that state. Large numbers of the Declaration were printed with the following addendum:

"Ordered, that the Declaration of Independence be printed; and a copy sent to the Ministers of each parish, of every denomination, within this state; and that they severally be required to read the same to their respective congregations, as soon as divine Service is ended;...And after such publication thereof, to deliver the said Declaration to the Clerks of their several towns or districts; who are hereby required to record the same in their respective town or district books..."[29]

John Quincy Adams said that "The highest glory of the American Revolution was this: it connected, in one indissoluble bond, the principles of civil government with the principles of Christianity."[30]

146

---

## Chapter 11

---

# How God Defends Christian Liberty

Christian character and principles were the foundation of the actions of the colonists which led to the American Revolution. The people, soldiers, and leaders exemplified the same Christian character during the war with Great Britain. In this chapter we will see the Christian Character of the Continental Congress and the Continental Army as well as witness how God providentially protected the Continental Army on numerous occasions. God was more than just supporting Christian individuals in the war; He was supporting the entire cause of liberty.

### The Christian Continental Congress                                    1775

Congress sought legal redress to be reconciled with England for 14 months even after war had begun. It was not until December of 1775, when King George rejected their petitions and declared them all rebels and enemies, that they realized their lives, liberty and property were no longer protected by the English government. This meant they were now in a "state of nature," and therefore, needed to establish their own government to protect their lives and liberty. The Declaration of Independence states that, "He [the King] has abdicated Government here, by declaring us out of his Protection and waging War against us."

Why the King and Parliament would treat the petitions of their own colonies in such a stupid way is incomprehensible. It can only be compared in history to the hardening of Pharaoh's heart so that God's purposes might be fulfilled.

*July, 1776*

During the first days of July in 1776 the Continental Congress was considering one of the most historical events of all time -- the declaration by thirteen colonies to become the new nation of the United States of America.

On the issue of independence all the colonies were agreed, but a few of the most cautious delegates still were not sure about the timing. **Rev. John Witherspoon,** a delegate from New Jersey, answered their concerns as he said:

"There is a tide in the affairs of men. We perceive it now before us. To hesitate is to consent to our own slavery. That noble instrument should be subscribed to this very morning by every pen in this house. Though these gray hairs must soon descend to the sepulchre, I would infinitely rather that they descend thither by the hand of the executioner than desert at the crisis the sacred cause of my country!"[1]

*John Hancock*

The delegates went on to approve the Declaration of Independence. After the announcement of the vote, silence moved over the Congress as the men contemplated the magnitude of what they had just done. Some wept openly, while others bowed in prayer. After signing the Declaration with unusually large writing, the President of the Continental Congress, **John Hancock,** broke the silence as he declared, "His majesty can now read my name without glasses. And he can also double the price on my head."[2] Then he went on to say at this tense moment, "We must be unanimous; there must be no pulling different ways; we must all hang together."

**Benjamin Franklin** responded in his characteristic wit, "Yes, we must indeed all hang together, or most assuredly we shall all hang separately!"[3]

A brief chuckle followed and then **Samuel Adams,** whom men of that day ascribed "the greatest part in the greatest revolution of the world,"[4] rose and stated:

"We have this day restored the Sovereign to Whom alone men ought to be obedient. He reigns in heaven and ... from the rising to the setting sun, may His kingdom come."[5]

The men who helped give birth to America understood what was taking place. They saw in the establishment of America the first truly Christian nation in history.

As Franklin suggested, they did "hang together", but even so, many of these signers as well as tens of thousands of colonists lost their lives, property, families, and reputations in order to purchase liberty for themselves and their posterity.

What was it that motivated these people to risk everything in order that they might have freedom? What was it that brought about the events leading to the colonists declaring their independence?

**John Adams**, our second President and a leader in the cause of independence, revealed what he and many others thought as he wrote on the day that the colonies declared their independence:

> "It is the will of Heaven that the two countries should be sundered for ever; it may be the will of Heaven that America shall suffer calamities still more wasting and distresses yet more dreadful. If this is to be the case, the furnace of affliction produces refinement in states as well as individuals; but I submit all my hopes and fears to an overruling Providence, in which, unfashionable as the faith may be, I firmly believe."[6]

**John Hancock** echoed the reliance upon God and the belief that the destiny of nations is in the hand of God as he said:

> "Let us humbly commit our righteous cause to the great Lord of the Universe ... Let us joyfully leave our concerns in the hands of Him who raises up and puts down the empires and kingdoms of the earth as He pleases."[7] STOP

This firm reliance upon God was so universally adhered to among those in America that the Continental Congress insisted it be included in the Declaration of Independence. While reviewing Thomas Jefferson's original draft of the Declaration, the committee assigned to the task added the words, "they are endowed by their Creator with certain unalienable rights." Then, when the Declaration was debated before Congress, they added the phrase, "appealing to the Supreme Judge of the World, for the rectitude of our intentions," as well as the words "with a firm reliance on the protection of divine Providence."[8]

Most of the revisions of Jefferson's original work had to do with the Lord. Thus we see the Continental Congress declaring to all the world their Christian convictions.

Not only does the Declaration of Independence reflect our Founders' faith in God, but as we have seen previously, this document only came into being as a result of Biblical ideas that had been sown in the hearts of the colonists for one hundred and fifty years.

The American Revolution was a revolution of ideas long before it was a revolution of war. As the clergy and other leaders taught the colonists their God-given rights as men, Christians, and subjects, the inevitable result was a nation birthed in liberty.

*The Signing of the Declaration of Independence. After President Hancock signed his name, Samuel Adams stated: "We have this day restored the Sovereign to Whom alone men ought to be obedient. He reigns in heaven and from the rising to the setting sun, may His kingdom come."*

# The Seal of the United States

The Seal of the United States (also known as "the Great Seal") is a symbol of our nation's sovereignty. It is affixed to various official national documents that are signed by the President.

Shortly after the adoption of the Declaration of Independence in 1776, a committee (composed of Thomas Jefferson, John Adams, and Benjamin Franklin) was appointed to formulate an official seal for the new nation. The seal was to reflect the heart of the new nation and the principles upon which she was built.

Franklin's description of his proposal for the seal was as follows:

"Moses standing on the shore, and extending his hand over the sea, thereby causing the same to overwhelm Pharaoh who is sitting in an open chariot, a crown on his head and a sword in his hand. Rays from a pillar of fire in the clouds reaching to Moses, to express that he acts by command of the Deity. Motto: Rebellion to tyrants is obedience to God."

Jefferson proposed that one side of the seal be "the children of Israel in the wilderness, led by a cloud by day, and a pillar of fire by night."

Both of these men saw that the birth of America, was accomplished sovereignly and miraculously by the hand of God, as He similarly had done with ancient Israel. While almost every member of Congress agreed with this, they also felt God was doing something more with America. Consequently, Congress did not immediately adopt any official seal. It was not until 1782 that a seal was approved. Both sides of the Seal are found on the back of our one dollar bill today.

Following is a description of the reverse side given in a Department of State bulletin which was taken from the *Journals of Congress:*

"Reverse. A pyramid unfinished -- of 13 layers of stone. In the zenith, an eye of Divine Providence, surrounded with a glory proper. Over the eye these words, "Annuit Coeptis" (Latin words that mean "He [God] has blessed our undertakings.") On the base of the pyramid the numerical letters MDCCLXXVI. And underneath, the following motto, "Novus Ordo Seclorum." (Latin for "A New Order of the Ages")[9]

Charles Thomson, the Secretary of the Congress that approved the Seal, wrote that "the Pyramid signifies Strength and Duration. The Eye over it and the Motto allude to the many signal interpositions of Providence in favour of the American cause."[10]

James Wilson, a Justice on the very first Supreme Court said that, "A free government has often been compared to a pyramid;... it is laid on the broad basis of the people."

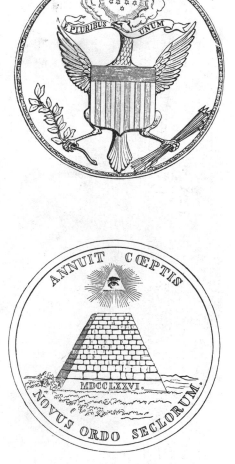

*The Great Seal*

## Chaplains Appointed

One of the first acts of the American Congress after declaring Independence was to appoint Chaplains to open the daily meetings of Congress in prayer. On July 9 Rev. Jacob Duche, Rev. Patrick Allison (a Baptist), and Rev. William White (an Episcopal) were among the first Chaplains appointed. Congress also ordered that chaplains be provided for the Continental Army and for the various hospitals and that they be paid at the rank of Colonel.

## Days of Fasting and Prayer

*A flag of the Revolutionary War*

Throughout the war with Britain, the American Congress frequently declared Days of Fasting and Prayer to beseech God for His aid and assistance in their struggle for freedom. They also declared Days of Thanksgiving to acknowledge the Hand of God after victories in battle and other significant events. We saw in the last chapter that this was their response to the Boston Port Bill of June 1, 1774 and to declaration of martial law on July 20, 1775. Later in this chapter, we will see a few more of the many times our Congress declared such days of acknowledgement of God. To date, our Congress has declared about 200 National Days of Prayer and Fasting.

*September, 1777*

## Importation of Bibles

In the book, *The Bible of the Revolution,* Robert Dearden and Douglas Watson wrote:

"...Revolutionary America without Bibles presented an impossible situation. In no country in the world was the Good Book then so relied upon. Faith in Divine Providence and the consolation and guidance of Holy Writ were necessary to all patriots in the struggle for Liberty...

"Before the rupture with the mother country, the Colonies had depended largely for their literature upon England, and entirely so for their Bibles in their native tongue. The Revolutionary War stopped importation, and at length the situation reached such an acute stage that the Chaplain of Congress, the Rev. Patrick Allison, D.D., placed before that body a petition praying for immediate relief. The memorial was assigned to a special committee which weighed the matter with great care, and on September 11, 1777, it reported:

". . . that the use of the Bible is so universal and its importance so great that your committee refer the above to the consideration of Congress, and if Congress shall not think it expedient to order the importation of types and paper, the Committee recommend that Congress will order the Committee of Congress to import 20,000 Bibles from Holland, Scotland, or elsewhere, into the different parts of the States of the Union.

"Whereupon it was resolved accordingly to direct said Committee to import 20,000 copies of the Bible. . ."[11]

This is another action of our early Congress that reveals their Christian values. The importance they gave to this legislation of importing Bibles is magnified when one considers the day upon which it occurred. The committee's report to import 20,000 Bibles took place on September 11, 1777, the same day that the Battle of Brandywine was claiming the lives of 1200 Americans and which resulted in a defeat for the Colonial Army. Congress was meeting within earshot of the cannon fire of this battle.

## The Christian Character of the Continental Army

The winter of 1777-1778 was one of the most important in our nation's history, for that winter was the turning point of the American Revolution. Yet during that winter the American Army faced a greater ordeal than any army throughout history.

Before the American Army moved into Valley Forge in December of 1777, it consisted of undisciplined men who had obtained few victories in their war with Britain, but the next spring they marched out as a well-disciplined band, committed more than ever to their General and the cause of liberty. They were now prepared to see victory through their efforts.

What was the ordeal this Army faced? How did such a change occur during the stay at Valley Forge? What was the cause behind this change?

As the American Army, under the command of George Washington, moved toward their wintering spot at Valley Forge, army troops had no clothes to cover their nakedness, nor blankets to lie on, nor tents to sleep under. Washington stated: "For the want of shoes their marches through frost and snow might be traced by the blood from their feet, and they were almost as often without provisions as with them."[12]

Their situation even worsened after their arrival at Valley Forge on December 19th. Lack of food and provisions for his men was central to Washington's appeals to Congress. In a letter to Congress dated December 23, 1777 Washington wrote, "Men are confined to hospitals, or in farmers' houses for want of shoes. We have this day no less than two thousand eight hundred and ninety-nine men in camp unfit for duty, because they are barefoot and otherwise naked..."[13]

About one third of all his troops were unfit for service, and this number increased as winter progressed. "The unfortunate soldiers were in want of everything. They had neither coats, hats, shirts, nor shoes," wrote Lafayette. "The men," said Baron Von Steuben, "were literally naked, some of them in the fullest extent of the word."[14]

Hunger was even a greater danger. "The army frequently remained whole days without provisions," said Lafayette. "One soldier's meal on a Thanksgiving Day declared by Congress was a "half a gill of rice and a tablespoonful of vinegar!" In mid-February there was more than a week when the men received no provisions at all.[15]

Dr. Waldo gives this description:

"There comes a soldier, his bare feet are seen through his worn out shoes, his legs nearly naked from the tattered remains of an only pair of stockings; his breeches are not sufficient to cover his nakedness, his shirt hanging in strings, his hair dishevelled, his face meagre. His whole appearance pictures a person forsaken and discouraged. He comes and cries with an air of wretchedness and despair, 'I am sick, my feet lame, my legs are sore, my body covered with this tormenting itch'..."[16]

Due to this lack of food and clothing, hundreds of the troops fell sick. Many men's "feet and legs froze till they became black, and it was often necessary to amputate them."[17] During most of January and February there were "constantly more than 4,000 soldiers who were incapacitated as a result of exposure, disease, and under-nourishment."[18]

And in the midst of all of this they persevered! Beyond this, the patient attitude with which they endured this misery was no less than supernatural. Washington wrote April 21, 1778 to a congressional delegate:

"...For, without arrogance or the smallest deviation from the truth, it may be said that no history now extant can furnish an instance of an army's suffering such uncommon hardships as ours has done, and bearing them with the same patience and fortitude. Their submitting without a murmur is a proof of patience and obedience which in my opinion can scarce be paralleled."[19]

What could possibly have held this army together through this ordeal? Baron Von Steuben said no European army could have held together in such circumstances. How then could an inexperienced American Army stick together? Was it due to good discipline? "With regard to military discipline," Von Steuben states, "no such thing existed."[20]

Could it have been the financial reward they would receive? Not hardly, for their meager pay was already four to five months past due, and complete payment would never come. What was it then?

Most historians agree that the reason for their perseverance at Valley Forge can be attributed to their love of liberty and to their General George Washington, and his amazing quality of leadership. George Bancroft states that "love of country and attachment to their General sustained them under their unparalleled hardships; with any other leader, the army would have dissolved and vanished."[21]

His character and encouragement inspired the army to follow his example. From the beginning he tirelessly traveled throughout the camp, his very presence bringing strength to the men. His heart was for his men as well as for his country. As Washington observed his naked and distressed soldiers, he said: "I feel superabundantly for them, and from my soul I pity those miseries which it is neither in my power to relieve or prevent."[22]

Washington knew that the cause for which they fought was well worth any price -- even the suffering at Valley Forge -- for they purchased liberty, not only for them, but for the generations to come. While at Valley Forge, blood was not shed in battle, yet the American Army shed much blood.

"The blood that stained this ground," writes Henry Brown, "did not rush forth in the joyous frenzy of the fight; it fell drop by drop from the heart of a suffering people. They who once encamped here in the snow fought not for conquest, not for power, not for glory, not for their country only, not for themselves alone. They served here for Posterity; they suffered here for the Human Race; they bore here the cross of all the peoples; they died here that freedom might be the heritage of all."[23]

It was Washington's character that helped sustain the army, but what sustained Washington? This question could easily be answered by Washington's troops or officers, for they knew his trust was completely in God. The army had frequently seen Washington order his men to attend church and to observe days of prayer and fasting and days of Thanksgiving.

Washington was also very instrumental in securing chaplains for the army. Rev. Henry Muhlenberg relates how General Washington "rode around among his army... and admonished each and every one to fear God, to put away the wickedness that has set in and become so general, and to practice the Christian virtues."[24]

It was said of Washington, in a sketch written by an American gentleman in London in 1779 that "he regularly attends divine service in his tent every morning and evening, and seems very fervent in his prayers."[25] General Knox was one among many who gave testimony of Washington frequently visiting secluded groves to lay the cause of his bleeding country at the throne of grace.

*General Washington "rode around among his army...and admonished each and every one...to practice the Christian virtues."*

A number of people have recorded the story of how a Tory Quaker, Isaac Potts, came upon Washington while he was on his knees in prayer in the woods. Benson J. Lossing relates that Potts later made the following remarks to his wife:

> "If there is anyone on this earth whom the Lord will listen to, it is George Washington; and I feel a presentiment that under such a commander there can be no doubt of our eventually establishing our independence, and that God in his providence has willed it so."[26]

On May 6, 1982, President Reagan remarked on this event in his National Day of Prayer Proclamation:

> "The most sublime picture in American history is of George Washington on his knees in the snow at Valley Forge. That image

personifies a people who know that it is not enough to depend on our own courage and goodness; we must also seek help from God, our Father and Preserver."

In this most difficult of times, General Washington constantly relied upon God and trusted in Him for success. God was faithful to answer his prayers, and through Washington He eventually established our independence and secured the beginning of the most free and prosperous nation the world has ever seen.

How did God answer Washington's prayer? One miracle occurred that winter which helped eliminate their near-starving situation. Bruce Lancaster relates the event as follows:

"One foggy morning the soldiers noticed the Schuylkill River seemed to be boiling. The disturbance was caused by thousands and thousands of shad which were making their way upstream in an unusually early migration. With pitchforks and shovels, the men plunged into the water, throwing the fish onto the banks. Lee's

*Using pitchforks and shovels to gather a miraculous supply of fish*

dragoons rode their horses into the stream to keep the shad from swimming on out of reach. Suddenly and wonderfully, there was plenty of food for the army."[27]

God's providence can again be seen as Baron Von Steuben, a veteran Prussian soldier, came to Valley Forge on February 23 and offered his services to the American Army. No one could have been more valuable at the time, for he trained the men to move together as a well-disciplined army.

His rigorous drilling and training of the troops gave them confidence in themselves as soldiers, even as Washington had given them confidence as men. Not only had godly character and strength been forged and tempered within the army, but military skill had also been imparted to them at last.

Another providential event occurred that winter when France became an ally to America. This meant much needed French money and troops would begin to pour into the new nation. The Continental Congress acknowledged this as the hand of God as they declared a National Day of Thanksgiving on May 7.

*Baron Von Steuben*

In Washington's orders issued at Valley Forge, May 5, 1778, he proclaimed:

"It having pleased the Almighty Ruler of the Universe propitiously to defend the cause of the United American States, and finally by raising up a powerful friend among the Princes of the earth, to establish our Liberty and Independence upon a lasting foundation; it becomes us to set apart a day for gratefully acknowledging the Divine Goodness, and celebrating the event, which we owe to His benign interposition."[28]

The troops' survival, the molding of a disciplined army, Washington's amazing leadership, and all the miraculous occurrences during the winter at Valley Forge can only be attributed to Almighty God. George Washington said following all this: "The hand of Providence has been so conspicuous in all this, that he must be worse than an infidel, and more than wicked, that has not gratitude enough to acknowledge his obligation."[29]

## The Hand of God Protects the Continental Army

During the Revolutionary War, God performed many miracles on behalf of the American Army, for God desired to see America win its struggle for freedom, become a nation, and fulfil its divine purposes. We will look at a number of these miracles.

*August, 1776*       *The Evacuation of Long Island*

One incident revealing God's supernatural care occurred shortly after the signing of the Declaration of Independence in August of 1776. During fighting on Long Island, British General Howe and his army of 32,000 men had inflicted heavy losses upon the American army but had not succeeded in capturing or destroying it. General Howe then prepared to attack the 8000 American troops on Brooklyn Heights.

The British Army had Washington surrounded in a great semicircle with their backs to the nearly mile wide East River. Here an amazing thing occurred, for General Howe remained in this position for two days and did not attack. Had he attacked, victory would have been certain for the superior British force.

Washington, greatly outnumbered, realized to fight would mean defeat... and the likely end of the war. Surrender was unthinkable. As difficult as it would be, he decided to retreat across the East River since all land routes were blocked by the British.

The American Army could have easily been surrounded by the British, but providentially, adverse weather conditions kept British

*Many providential occurrences took place during the retreat from Long Island.*

ships from sailing up the East River. As a result, the American army was able to escape.

To make sure the British did not discover their retreat, Washington set out to evacuate his army in great secrecy, even from his own troops. He sent orders for every rowboat, sailboat, and sea-going vessel to be collected in the area. At eight o'clock on the night of August 29, 1776, the evacuation of the troops began.

The day before about one thousand men had come over to reinforce Washington's army. Part of these reinforcements included Glover's regiment of Massachusetts fishermen. These men, some of the best mariners in the world, manned the boats that were evacuating not only the troops, but all their supplies, guns, carts, cattle, and horses.

A heavy rain was falling as the evacuation began and the adverse wind, which hindered the British ships, continued. In this weather the sailboats were of little use and only the few row boats were employed in the retreat. At this rate evacuation seemed impossible; but at eleven o'clock the northeast wind which had raged for three days amazingly stopped and the water became so calm that the boats could be loaded with extra weight. A gentle breeze also arose from the south and southwest which favored their travel across the river to New York.

However, as the adverse weather left, a new problem was created. Under the light of a full moon, the British were sure to see the American troops nearby. Yet, miraculously, the Americans retreated all night without being heard or seen. God's hand was surely upon the army and, as was stated in their newly ratified Declaration of Independence, their "firm reliance on the protection of Divine Providence" was proving invaluable.

During the pre-dawn hours of Friday, August 30, through mistaken orders, General Mifflin prematurely withdrew his men, who were the covering party for the retreat. They were to be the last to be evacuated. However, he ran into General Washington, who knew that they should not be removed, and he ordered them to return. Though they were gone 45 minutes from their post the British had not even noticed.

The retreat continued through the darkness of the pre-dawn, but as the sun began to rise many troops were yet to be evacuated. Their deaths seemed apparent, but again an astonishing thing occurred. Major Benjamin Tallmadge, who was still on the island, recorded what happened in his memoirs:

> "As the dawn of the next day approached, those of us who remained in the trenches became very anxious for our own safety, and when the dawn appeared there were several regiments still on duty. At this time a very dense fog began to rise (out of the

ground and off the river) and it seemed to settle in a peculiar manner over both encampments.

"I recall this peculiar providential occurrence perfectly well, and so very dense was the atmosphere that I could scarcely discern a man at six yards distance ... We tarried until the sun had risen, but the fog remained as dense as ever ..."[30]

The fog remained until the last boats left Long Island.

Another miraculous event occurring during this retreat was recorded by Washington Irving in his *Life of Washington*. Near the ferry where the troops were being evacuated, a family lived who favored the British cause. Upon seeing the army's embarkation the lady of the house sent a servant to warn the British of what was happening. The servant managed to slip past the American guards, but upon reaching the British lines he ran into an outpost of German speaking Hessian soldiers and was unable to communicate with them.

The servant was put under guard at the outpost as a suspicious person until early in the morning when a British officer examined him. Upon hearing his story, some soldiers were sent to validate it. They cautiously approached the American camp only to find it completely empty!

British troops were hurriedly dispatched to the river. As they arrived the fog had lifted enough for them to see four boats upon the East River. The only boat near enough to be captured contained three vagabonds who had stayed behind to plunder! Otherwise, 9000 men, with nearly all their supplies, had miraculously retreated to New York.

Here we see, as American General Greene said, "the best effected retreat I ever read or heard of."[31] This event was so astonishing that many (including General Washington) attributed the safe retreat of the American army to the hand of God. Surely God was defending American liberty.[32]

### Trenton and the Crossing of the Delaware                    *December, 1776*

A few months after the retreat from Long Island, Washington found himself in as desperate a situation as on Long Island. He was not engaged in battle or surrounded by the enemy, but his army was dwindling as the men's enlistment times were up. It was now December and at the first of the year most of the men's duty was over and few had re-enlisted. Defeat after defeat had brought the army's and the nation's morale to its lowest point. Washington knew he had to make a bold stroke and go on the offensive.

In a desperate move, Washington decided to cross the Delaware River in pre-dawn hours in order to surprise the enemy. He chose the early morning of December 26 to attack the Hessian garrison quartered at Trenton, for he knew their accustomed drinking on Christmas would help assure their deep slumber on that early morning.

As the troops prepared to cross the Delaware River, a violent snow and hailstorm suddenly came up. This hardship, however, worked in their favor by inducing the enemy's sentries to seek cover and reducing the visibility to near zero.

The Americans entered Trenton so unexpectedly and with such surprise to the Hessians that about 1000 prisoners were taken captive after only 45 minutes of battle. Only three Americans were wounded in the fighting. Two had died, but not in fighting; they froze to death on the march.

Henry Knox described the event as follows: "The hurry, fright and confusion of the enemy was not unlike that which will be when the last trump will sound."[33]

This much needed victory helped raise the spirit of the army and the nation, strengthening them to continue their struggle for liberty. As Knox wrote of the victory at Trenton, "Providence seemed to have smiled upon every part of this enterprise."[34] God was defending American liberty.

| *October, 1777* | *Defeat of Burgoyne at Saratoga* |

On October 17, 1777 British General Burgoyne was defeated by Colonial forces at Saratoga. This was a much needed victory and an answer to prayer. General Washington had experienced many defeats at the hands of the British, such as the Battle of Brandywine the month before where 1200 Americans lost their lives. In great need, Washington prayed fervently for a "signal stroke of Providence."

Others recognized the precarious position of the American cause. One Sunday in Sharon, Connecticut Rev. Smith proclaimed that though a long night of disaster had been occurring, God would soon bring a signal victory for the American army. Before the service ended, a messenger arrived with news that British General Burgoyne had surrendered at Saratoga!

The Providence of God was evident in this victory. Earlier, General Howe was supposed to have marched north to join Burgoyne's 11,000 men at Saratoga. However, in his haste to leave London for a holiday, Lord North forgot to sign the dispatch to General Howe. The dispatch was pigeonholed and not found until years later in the archives of the British army. This inadvertence, plus the fact that contrary winds kept British reinforcements delayed at sea for three months, totally altered the outcome at Saratoga in favor of America.

*The Continental Congress proclaimed a Day of Thanksgiving and Praise to God after the surrender of General Burgoyne.*

In response to the victory, the Continental Congress proclaimed a **Day of Thanksgiving and Praise to God**. In part, they stated:

"Forasmuch as it is the indispensable duty of all men to adore the superintending providence of Almighty God, ... and it having pleased Him in His abundant mercy ... to crown our arms with most signal success ... it is therefore recommended ... to set apart Thursday, the 18th day of December, for solemn thanksgiving and praise..."

They recommended for everyone to confess their sins and humbly ask God, "through the merits of Jesus Christ, mercifully to forgive and blot them out of remembrance" and thus He then would be able to pour out His blessings upon every aspect of the nation.[35]

### *Providential Discovery of Benedict Arnold's Treason*                *September, 1780*

Miss Hall and Miss Slater write of another miraculous event during the Revolutionary War:

"An example of God's Providential protection against such 'imminent, though unseen dangers' was in the amazing capture of the British spy Major Andre which revealed the treachery of Benedict Arnold. Of this event, Washington himself wrote to John Laurens:

'In no instance since the commencement of the War has the interposition of Providence appeared more conspicuous than in the rescue of the Post and Garrison of West Point from Arnold's villainous perfidy ... A combination of extraordinary circumstances.'

"Washington's letter of September 26, 1780 to Major General William Heath gives more details on what happened.

*Benedict Arnold*

'Major General Arnold has gone to the enemy. He had an interview with Major Andre, Adjutant General of the British Army, and had put into his possession a state of our Army; of the Garrison at this post; of the number of Men considered as necessary for the defence of it, a Return of Ordinance and the disposition of the Artillery Corps in case of Alarm. By a most Providential interposition, Major Andre was taken in returning to New York with all these papers in General Arnold's hand writing, who hearing the matter kept it secret, left his Quarters immediately under pretence of going over to West point on Monday forenoon, about an hour before my arrival, then pushed down the river in the barge, which was not discovered till I had returned from West point in the Afternoon...'

"Major Andre was finally brought to General Washington on the 26th, and then the full story of his capture came to light. On September 23, three young militiamen had posted themselves on the Old Post Road close to Tarrytown, waiting to waylay "cowboys" who were stealing cattle and driving them into the British lines. Suddenly, about 9:30 in the morning, they saw a solitary rider coming toward them. They stopped him and learned that he was on his way to New York. It was Major Andre who believed that they were loyalists who had established a look-out for the British. He didn't show them his pass and talked so freely that the young militiamen began to be suspicious. They made him strip off his clothes and discovered the incriminating papers stuffed in the feet of his stockings. Realizing the game was up, Andre then tried to bribe the boys, but they contemptuously dismissed his efforts and took him to the nearest outpost which was North Castle."[36]

The following is General Washington's message (delivered by General Greene) to his troops concerning Arnold's treason and its discovery:

"GENERAL ORDERS - Head Quarters, Orangetown, Tuesday, September 26, 1780

"Treason of the blackest dye was yesterday discovered! General Arnold who commanded at Westpoint, lost to every sentiment of honor, of public and private obligation, was about to deliver up that important Post into the hands of the enemy. Such an event must have given the American cause a deadly wound if not a fatal stab. Happily the treason has been timely discovered to prevent the fatal misfortune. The Providential train of circumstances which led to it affords the most convincing proof that the liberties of America are the object of Divine Protection."[37]

Following is the official response of Congress to this event:

Journals Of Congress     Wednesday, October 18, 1780

"...Congress took into consideration the resolution reported for setting apart a day of thanksgiving and prayer, and agreed to the following draught:

"Whereas it hath pleased Almighty God, the Father of all mercies, amidst the vicissitudes and calamities of war, to bestow blessings on the people of these states, which call for their devout and thankful acknowledgments, more especially in the late remarkable interposition of his watchful providence, in rescuing the person of our Commander in Chief and the army from imminent dangers, at the moment when treason was ripened for execution; in prospering the labours of the husbandmen, and causing the earth to yield its increase in plentiful harvests; and above all, in continuing to us the enjoyment of the gospel of peace;

"It is therefore recommended to the several states to set apart Thursday, the seventh day (of December next, to be observed as a day of public thanksgiving and prayer; that all the people may assemble on that day to celebrate the praises of our

*Major Andre's capture was, according to Washington, due to a Providential train of circumstances.*

Divine Benefactor; to confess our unworthiness of the least of his favours, and to offer our fervent supplications to the God of all grace; that it may please him to pardon our heinous transgressions and incline our hearts for the future to keep all his laws; to comfort and relieve our brethren who are any wise afflicted or distressed; to smile upon our husbandry and trade; to direct our publick councils, and lead our forces, by land and sea, to victory; to take our illustrious ally under his special protection, and favor our joint councils and exertions for the establishment of speedy and permanent peace; to cherish all schools and seminaries of education, and to cause the knowledge of Christianity to spread over all the earth.

"Done in Congress, the 18th day of October, 1780, and in the fifth year of the independence of the United States of America."[38]

**February, 1781**     ***Miraculous Retreat from Cowpens***

Marshall Foster, in *The American Covenant*, relates another event revealing the Providence of God:

"Led by George Morgan, the Americans defeated Colonel Tarleton's entire detachment at the Battle of the Cowpens, January 17, 1781. Lord Cornwallis, leading the large British army in the south, was infuriated by this defeat. Destroying his heavy baggage, he headed for the Catawba River to cut off the retreat of the small American army.

*Cornwallis*

"Cornwallis reached the Catawba River just two hours after General Morgan had crossed. Confident of victory, the British general decided to wait until morning to cross. But during the night a storm filled the river detaining his troops. Twice more in the next ten days Cornwallis nearly overtook the American Army. On February 3, he reached the Yadkin River in North Carolina, just as the Americans were landing on the eastern slopes. But, before he could cross, a sudden flood cut off the British troops again! On February 13, the Americans reached the Dan River that would lead them into friendly Virginia territory. They crossed and a few hours later, when Cornwallis arrived, rising waters once again stopped him from defeating the American Army. Even Clinton, the commander-in-chief of Lord Cornwallis, acknowledged that Divine Providence had intervened. He wrote: '...here the royal army was again stopped by a sudden rise of the waters, which had only just fallen (almost miraculously) to let the enemy over, who could not else have eluded Lord Cornwallis' grasp, so close was he upon their rear...'

"The significance of the Battle of Cowpens and the safe retreat of the patriots that followed is that our small army in the south was saved by God's providence so that it could harass General Cornwallis and drive him to the sea, which set the stage for the final defeat of the British at Yorktown in October 1781."[39]

**October, 1781**     ***The Battle of Yorktown***

In October of 1781, British General Cornwallis had his troops stationed at Yorktown, Virginia. While Cornwallis waited for reinforcements, Washington marched his troops from New York to Yorktown. Unknown to Washington or Cornwallis, a French fleet under Admiral De Grasse arrived just in time to defeat the British fleet sent to relieve General Cornwallis at Yorktown.

Without reinforcements, Cornwallis was barely holding out against the siege of the American and French forces. As a last resort he decided to attempt a retreat across the York River. At 10 o'clock on the night of October 17th, sixteen large boats were loaded with troops and embarked for Gloucester. After the first few boats had landed a great turn of events occurred. In the official dispatch to his superior, Cornwallis wrote: "...But at this critical moment, the weather, from being moderate and calm, changed to a violent storm of wind and rain, and drove all the boats, some of which had troops on board, down the river."[40] Due to this miraculous weather change, Cornwallis was unable to complete his intended retreat and found his force divided when Washington's batteries opened at daybreak. When the boats finally returned he ordered them to bring back the troops that had passed during the night. Later that day he surrendered his forces to General Washington. This essentially marked the end of the war.

General Washington and our Congress recognized the Providence of God in the battle of Yorktown. The Journals of the Continental Congress record this entry:

*A miraculous weather change stopped the escape of the British troops.*

"Resolved, that Congress will, at two o'clock this day, go in procession to the Dutch Lutheran Church, and return thanks to Almighty God, for crowning the allied arms of the United States and France, with success, by the surrender of the Earl of Cornwallis."[41]

And in his congratulatory order to the allied army on the day after the surrender, General Washington concluded:

"The General congratulates the army upon the glorious event of yesterday ... Divine service is to be performed tomorrow in the several brigades and divisions. The commander-in-chief recommends that the troops not on duty should universally attend with that seriousness of deportment and gratitude of heart which the recognition of such reiterated and astonishing interpositions of Providence demand of us."[42]

*The Surrender at Yorktown. In response, Congress went in procession to church "to return thanks to Almighty God, for crowning the allied arms. . .with success."*

# Chapter 12

# The Power Behind the American Republic

While the Battle of Yorktown was the last major battle of the war, a peace treaty between the United States and England was not signed until September 3, 1783. Fighting had stopped, yet the new nation of America still faced many difficulties. A number of the problems that existed were due to weaknesses in the *Articles of Confederation*, which was our national governing document from 1777-1789.

Some of the major weaknesses of the *Articles of Confederation* included:

1. Congress had no power to raise money

2. Congress had no power to enforce any of its decisions

3. There was a lack of supreme authority to lead -- no executive

As a consequence of these things, many times during the war, the army lacked supplies and received no pay. This was one reason why the troops suffered so at Valley Forge, and also contributed to members of the military threatening a coup in 1783.

As time went on it became evident that something must be done to correct the flaws of the *Articles of Confederation*. While many were proposing amending the Articles, some men, such as James Madison,

George Washington, and Noah Webster, felt we must draw up a whole new Constitution. When delegates from the various states met in the State House in Philadelphia in the spring of 1787, most of them were expecting to amend the *Articles of Confederation*. However, the Virginia delegates were prepared to propose a new form of government.

*1787*                    *The Constitutional Convention*

   Thirteen years earlier, on July 4th, men sat in the very same room and put their "lives, fortunes and sacred honor" on the line. The Pennsylvania State House would be renamed "Independence Hall" for that heroic act. Now, however, a different spirit prevailed among those delegates who had arrived in May. When they heard of the thorough reform proposed by Madison and Washington, hesitancy, fear and doubt surfaced. Many of them believed that half-measures would be far more acceptable in the eyes of the people-- any change this complete was sure to fail!

   **George Washington** rose and addressed the Convention in a brief but immortal speech. He agreed that it was "too probable that no plan we propose will be adopted." If so, then he believed that it was entirely possible that they would have to endure another dreadful war. But, he continued, "If, to please the people, we offer what we ourselves disapprove, how can we afterward defend our work?"[1]

   Washington then concluded by urging them to "raise a standard" of the best government they could devise and then trust in this fact: "THE EVENT IS IN THE HANDS OF GOD!"[2] This lofty statement by Washington was crucial during the first ten days of the Convention.

*The Constitutional Convention. Washington declares "the event is in the hands of God!"*

The Framers of the Constitution unabashedly declared that the forming of that document was a miracle of God. **Franklin** was the least orthodox of them all and yet he wrote:

"Our General Convention... when it formed the new Federal Constitution, [was]... influenced, guided, and governed by that omnipotent and beneficent Ruler in whom all... live, and move, and have their being."[3]

**James Madison,** the Father of the Constitution, was writing to Thomas Jefferson in France just a few weeks after the Convention. He said:

"It is impossible to conceive the degree of concord which ultimately prevailed, as less than a miracle."[4]

And later Madison wrote:

"It is impossible for the man of pious reflection not to perceive in it [the Constitutional Convention] a finger of that Almighty hand..."[5]

Perhaps the greatest affirmation of this came from the most influential of all the framers of the Constitution -- **George Washington.** In a letter to his good friend, Governor Jonathan Trumbull of Connecticut, he wrote that the "adoption of the proposed General Government" disposed him to be of the opinion "that miracles have not ceased." For, he said, one could "trace the finger of Providence through those dark and mysterious events, which first induced the States to appoint a general Convention and then led them one after another ...into an adoption of the system recommended by that general Convention..."[6]

On June 28, 1787, the Constitutional Convention was on the verge of complete rupture. For over a month the delegates wrestled with the issue of representation with no breakthroughs, and now patience was wearing thin, emotions were on edge.

A somber George Washington, presiding over this assembly, began to despair of seeing success in the Convention. But the oldest delegate in attendance, Dr. Benjamin Franklin, asked for permission to speak.

This was unusual. The 81-year-old Pennsylvanian up to this point wrote out his remarks and had someone else read them due to his infirmity. But this time he was stirred to rise and address the delegates himself:

"The small progress we have made after four or five weeks... with each other... is a melancholy proof of the imperfection of the human understanding.... In this situation of this Assembly, groping as it were in the dark to find political truth, and scarce able to distinguish it when presented to us, how has it happened, Sir, that

*On the brink of rupture, Franklin called the Constitutional Convention to prayer.*

we have not hitherto once thought of humbly applying to the Father of lights to illuminate our understandings?

"In the beginning of the contest with Britain, when we were sensible of danger, we had daily prayers in this room for Divine protection. Our prayers, Sir, were heard and they were graciously answered. All of us who were engaged in the struggle must have observed frequent instances of a superintending Providence in our favor.... Have we now forgotten this powerful Friend? Or do we imagine we no longer need His assistance?

"I have lived, Sir, a long time, and the longer I live, the more convincing proofs I see of this truth: that God governs in the affairs of man. And if a sparrow cannot fall to the ground without his notice, is it probable that an empire can rise without His aid? We have been assured, Sir, in the Sacred Writings that "except the Lord build the house, they labor in vain that build it (Psalm 127:1)." I firmly believe this, and I also believe that without His concurring aid we shall succeed in this political building no better than the builders of Babel. We shall be divided by our little partial local interests; our projects will be confounded and we ourselves shall become a reproach and bye word down to future ages.

"I therefore beg leave to move that, henceforth, prayers imploring the assistance of Heaven and its blessing on our deliberation be held in this assembly every morning...and that one or more of the clergy of this city be requested to officiate in that service."[7]

A delegate from New Jersey, Mr. Dayton, wrote:

"The doctor sat down; and never did I behold a countenance at once so dignified and delighted as was that of Washington at the close of the address; nor were the members of the convention generally less affected. The words of the venerable Franklin fell upon our ears with a weight and authority even greater than we may suppose an oracle to have had in the Roman Senate."[8]

Mr. Sherman seconded the motion for prayer, and it was carried with only one negative, but then Mr. Williamson of North Carolina pointed out that they had no funds to pay the salary of a full-time chaplain. This part of Franklin's motion, therefore, failed, but Mr. Randolph then proposed that they obtain clergy who would volunteer their time as much as possible to lead in prayer, and especially "that a sermon be preached, at the request of the convention, on the Fourth of July, the anniversary of Independence."[9]

They apparently were successful in obtaining clergymen to volunteer on some of the mornings, for Mr. Dayton refers to one opening the session on the first day after the three-day recess. Dayton also notes that "every unfriendly feeling had been expelled, and a spirit of conciliation had been cultivated which promised at least a calm and dispassionate reconsideration" of the representation issue.[10]

This speech marked the turning point of the Convention. Breakthroughs followed shortly and within a year the Constitution was ratified by eleven states to establish the first Christian form of government in history.

The nation as a whole distrusted any national centralization of power. The **Anti-Federalists** emphasized the fallen, carnal nature of man and fought against a national union under the Constitution. The **Federalists** on the other hand, acknowledging the sinful nature of man, emphasized the importance of Christian character, virtue, and morality in the rulers of a nation that delegated certain limited powers under the Constitution. More wisdom, trust and love is required when power is granted beyond the state level. In the Constitution's delicate balance between unity and diversity, the nation and the state can only be preserved by virtuous and knowledgeable representatives elected by virtuous and knowledgeable citizens.

The struggle between the Federalists and the Anti-Federalists was intense. Although the Federalist perspective prevailed in the ratification of the Constitution, many of the Anti-Federalist positions were established in the passage of the Bill of Rights. This brought a balance of both Christian perspectives. George Washington wrote:

> "I doubt whether the opposition to the Constitution will not ultimately be productive of more good than evil.... They have given the rights of man a full and fair discussion, and explained them in so clear and forcible a manner, as cannot fail to make a lasting impression."[11]

Within one month of Washington's statement five states ratified the Constitution, and six more followed within six more months! Over fifty clergy from various denominations were prominent in the state ratifying conventions, but they were especially numerous in Massachusetts, North Carolina and New Hampshire. In Massachusetts, twenty clergy served as delegates in their state convention and one of them urged ratification on the grounds that this "union" was the rock of their national "salvation." The support of these clergymen was crucial, since the Massachusetts convention ratified the Constitution by only nineteen votes! (187 to 168). In Connecticut, Rev. William Samuel Johnson preached to his state's convention that the one harmonious system of government that came out of Philadelphia was a sign of God's hand. In South Carolina, celebration broke out when the ratification vote was announced to the state delegates. When order was restored the elderly statesman Christopher Gadsden said that he would probably not live long enough to see the happy results, but declared: "I shall say with good old Simeon [when he saw the Christ child brought into the Temple], 'Lord, now lettest Thou Thy servant depart in peace, for mine eyes have seen the salvation of my country.'"[12]

Just prior to the official ratification of the Constitution by the ninth state which was New Hampshire, George Washington summed up the whole era by again referring to the hand of God:

> "Should everything proceed as we anticipate, it will be so much beyond anything we had a right to imagine or expect 18 months ago that it will demonstrate the finger of Providence in human affairs greater than any event in history."[13]

1789          *The First Inauguration*

Washington took the oath of office with his hand on a Bible opened to Deuteronomy 28, which promises blessings or curses on a nation according to its faithfulness to keep God's Word. At the end of the oath he added the words "So help me God" and leaned over and kissed the Bible. Every president since Washington has repeated this same appeal to God. Washington then gave his inaugural address to Congress and then obeyed their own official resolution on April 29th: "After the oath shall be administered to the President... the Speaker and the members of the House of Representatives, will accompany him to St. Paul's Chapel, to hear divine service performed by the chaplains [Rev. Provost]."[14]

A portion of **Washington's Inaugural Address** is as follows:

"It would be peculiarly improper to omit, in this first official act, my fervent supplications to that Almighty

*After being sworn in as the first President, Washington leaned over and kissed the Bible.*

Being who rules over the universe, [and] who presides in the councils of nations... No people can be bound to acknowledge and adore the Invisible Hand which conducts the affairs of men more than the people of the United States. Every step by which they have advanced to the character of an independent nation seems to have been distinguished by some token of providential agency.... We ought to be no less persuaded that the propitious smiles of Heaven can never be expected on a nation that disregards the eternal rules of order and right which Heaven itself has ordained..."[15]

Public acknowledgement and adoration of God was universally affirmed and practiced by every aspect of our government in its early years. Our Founders considered this an indispensable element to the success of our form of government. It was "the Spirit of the Constitution." All three branches of the government, both at the national and state level, emphasized its importance.

## Christianity and the Congress

The first Congress under the Constitution proposed a Bill of Rights on September 25, 1789. Foremost of these rights was the freedom of religion in the First Amendment. On that very same day, Congress also passed the **Northwest Ordinance** which said that, "religious liberty... [is] the basis whereon these republics, their laws and constitutions are erected" and that, being necessary to good government, "religion, morality and knowledge... shall forever be encouraged" through the schools. Also, on that same day, Congress passed a resolution for a National Day of Prayer. The *Journals of Congress* record that:

*St. Paul's Chapel, New York, where Congress and Washington worshiped after the first inauguration*

> "Mr. Sherman justified the practice of thanksgiving on any signal event, not only as a laudable one in itself, but as warranted by precedents in Holy Writ: for instance, the solemn thanksgiving and rejoicing which took place in the time of Solomon after the building of the temple was a case in point. This example he thought worthy of imitation on the present occasion."[16]

This resolution was unanimously adopted, and President Washington issued a proclamation for the people of the United States to thank "the great Lord and Ruler of Nations" for enabling us "to establish constitutions of government for our safety and happiness, and particularly the national one now lately instituted." He said it is "the duty of all nations to acknowledge the providence of Almighty God, to obey his will, to be grateful for his benefits, and humbly to implore his protection and favor."[17]

Our Congress and Presidents have fulfilled this duty over 200 times in our nation's history under the Constitution. We have seen that the Continental Congress had already established official Days of Fasting and Prayer on the national level beginning in 1775. These proclamations were not bland, "Deistic" documents; they were Christian. For example, on November 1, 1777, Congress called for a National Day of Thanksgiving and Prayer for the victory at Saratoga. In this, the people of the United States were urged to ask "...Jesus Christ mercifully to forgive and blot out (our sins)" and "to prosper the means of religion for the promotion and enlargement of that Kingdom which consisteth in righteousness, peace, and joy in the Holy Ghost." Three years later on October 18, 1780, Congress again called for a Day of Thanksgiving and Prayer for the discovery of Benedict Arnold's treason plot. Again the people were urged to ask God "...to cause the knowledge of Christianity to spread over all the earth." In 1782, Congress acted the role of a Bible society by officially approving the printing and distribution of the "Bible of the Revolution," an American translation prepared by Robert Aitken. In the same year that the Constitution was framed, 1787, Congress urged the people to thank God for providing us "... the light of Gospel truth..." and to ask Him to "...raise up from among our youth men eminent for virtue, learning and piety, to His service in the Church and State; to cause virtue and true religion to flourish; ... and to fill the world with His glory."

Congress renegotiated and ratified the "Treaty with Tripoli" in 1805 after repudiating and deleting the phrase: "The United States is not, in any sense, founded on the Christian religion."

In 1854, the House of Representatives passed a Resolution proclaiming that "the great vital element in our system is the belief of our people in the pure doctrines and divine truths of the gospel of Jesus Christ..."[18] Even recently, Congress and President Reagan proclaimed 1983 as the "Year of the Bible."

## Christianity and the Supreme Court

Both the Congress and the Supreme Court begin with prayer even to this day. A crier proclaims these words each day when the Supreme Court officially opens: "Oyez, Oyez, Oyez,. . .God save the United States and this honorable court!" Over the head of the Chief Justices is a carved marble relief containing a tablet on which are the Ten Commandments.

The Supreme Court of the state of Maryland recognized Christianity as the established religion in America and the basis of our form of government as early as 1799. In *Runkel vs. Winemiller* the

# "The Bible is the Rock on which our Republic Rests."
# President Andrew Jackson, June 8, 1845

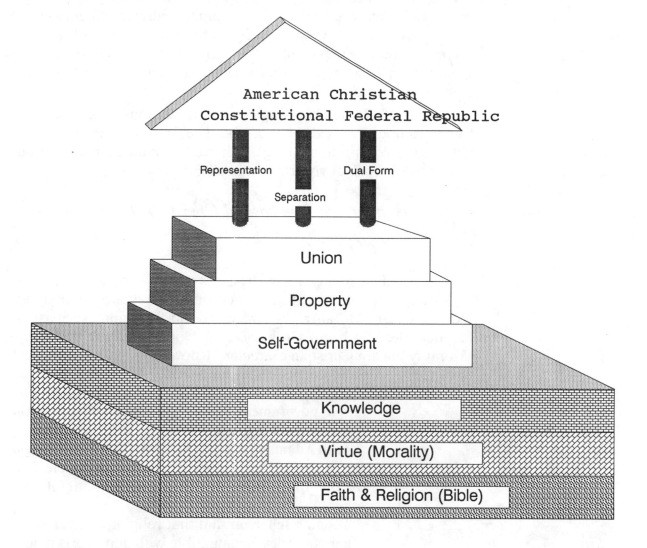

"Religion and morality are the essential pillars of society."
 George Washington 1797
"If Virtue and Knowledge are diffused among the People, they will never be enslaved."
 Samuel Adams 1779
"... in your faith supply moral excellence, and in your moral excellence, knowledge;
and in your knowledge, self-control ... "
 2 Peter 1:5-6

court stated that, "...By our form of government, the Christian religion is the established religion."[19]

In 1892, in *Church of the Holy Trinity v. The United States*, the U.S. Supreme Court declared that:

> "Our laws and institutions must necessarily be based upon the teachings of the Redeemer of mankind. It is impossible that it should be otherwise; and in this sense and to this extent our civilization and our institutions are emphatically Christian.... This is historically true. From the discovery of this continent to the present hour, there is a single voice making this affirmation... that this is a Christian nation. We are founded to legislate, propagate, and secure Christianity."[20]

Again in 1947, the Court said "we are a religious people and our laws presuppose" the existence of God. The Court upheld our national motto as constitutional in 1979, as well as paid chaplains in the Legislative branch of government in 1983.

## *Our Founding Fathers Emphasized Christian Faith and Morality*

"Virtue. . .Learning. . .Piety." These words are found throughout our official documents and statements of our Founders. Sometimes, they are called "Morality," "Knowledge," and "Religion," such as are found in the Northwest Ordinance. "Religion" meant Christianity. "Morality" meant Christian character. "Knowledge" meant a Biblical worldview. These were consistently emphasized by our Founders as the indispensable foundations or supports of our system of government. If they are lost, then our nation will eventually collapse.

**John Adams** said it best in 1798: "Our Constitution was made only for a moral and religious people. It is wholly inadequate for the government of any other."[21]

**Thomas Jefferson** said that religion is "deemed in other countries incompatible with good government and yet proved by our experience to be its best support." He believed that "the constitutional freedom of religion [is] the most inalienable and sacred of all human rights." He also maintained that "The Bible is the cornerstone of liberty; ...students perusal of the sacred volume will make us better citizens."[22]

The Father of the Constitution, **James Madison**, said in his *Memorial and Remonstrance* of 1785 that "religion... [is] the basis and foundation of govern-

*John Adams*

ment.... Before any man can be considered as a member of civil society, he must be considered as a subject of the Governor of the Universe."[23]

*James Madison*

**George Washington,** President of the Constitutional Convention, said in 1783 that "without an humble imitation" of the "characteristics of the Divine Author of our blessed religion... we can never hope to be a happy nation."[24] Later, in his Farewell Address in 1796, he said: "Of all the dispositions and habits which lead to a political prosperity, religion and morality are indispensable supports." He said they "are the essential pillars of society" in 1797.

The Father of the American Revolution was **Samuel Adams,** who said that to change any age in which we live we must simply "study and practice the exalted virtues of the Christian system." "While the people are virtuous," he said, "they cannot be subdued; but when once they lose their virtue they will be ready to surrender their liberties to the first external or internal invader.... If virtue and knowledge are diffused among the people, they will never be enslaved. This will be their great Security."[25]

**Abraham Lincoln** said: "The only assurance of our nation's safety is to lay our foundation in morality and religion."[26]

In a book entitled *American Political Writings During the Founding Era*, Dr. Donald Lutz and Charles Hyneman collected 76 of the most representative pamphlets and essays written by our Founders. In these 76 essays, "virtue" is emphasized as vital over 300 times!

## One Nation Under God

Many sincere people have the mistaken belief that our Constitution requires complete neutrality toward religion. Nothing could be further from the truth. Our Constitution establishes us as a nation "under God" in a variety of ways, but especially in Article 6.

Article 6 deals with supremacy. In paragraph one it declares that the national government had supreme responsibility for debts. In paragraph two it declares the Constitution to "be the supreme law of the land," but then in paragraph three it declares God to be supreme over both our laws and our leaders: "all... officers, both of the United States and of the several States, shall be bound by oath..." taken, of course, with their hand on a Bible.

The Framers of the Constitution wrote that the "definition of an oath is a solemn appeal to the Supreme Being, for the truth of what is said. In administering an oath, it is only necessary to inquire if the person who is to take it 'believes in a Supreme Being and in the future state of rewards and punishment'... otherwise there would be nothing to bind his conscience on."[27]

The Chairman of the Sesquicentennial Commission of the Constitution appointed by Congress fifty years ago was Sol Bloom. In his authorized book, *The Story of the Constitution*, Bloom asks the question: "Can an atheist become President of the United States?" Then he answers: "I maintain that the spirit of the Constitution forbids it. The Constitution prescribes an oath of affirmation which the President must take in order to qualify for his office. This oath or affirmation in its essence is a covenant with the people which the President pledges himself to keep with the help of Almighty God."[28] Since 1862, the words "so help me God" have also been legally required at the end of the oath.

The Constitution goes even further in its recognition of Christianity and Biblical law in Article 1, Section 7, Paragraph 2, where the President has "Sundays excepted" for deciding on legislation. A Senate Committee on the Judiciary commented on this provision in 1853:

> "In the law, Sunday is a *'dies non'*; it cannot be used for the services of legal process, the return of writs, or other judicial purposes. The executive department, the public establishments, are all closed on Sundays; on that day neither House of Congress sits;... Here is a recognition by law, and by universal usage, not only of a Sabbath, but of the Christian Sabbath, in exclusion of the Jewish or Mahammedan Sabbath;.... The recognition of the Christian Sabbath [by the Constitution] is complete and perfect."[29]

The final recognition of Christianity in the Constitution itself is found in the two-fold date employed by our Founders in Article 7: "... in the year of our Lord 1787, and of the independence of the United States of America the 12th." Our Founders dated this document in this way to deliberately recognize the two most significant sources of authority to our Constitution: the birth of Christ and the birth of Independence. Indeed, Scripture has said that "Where the Spirit of the Lord is, there is liberty." (2 Corinthians 3:17).

## Christianity and the States

After our Founders declared Independence in 1776, all but two states had written new constitutions by 1780. In many of these documents, not only was an oath required of public officials, but also a religious test which differed in each state according to the denomination that was officially established there. Of the thirteen states, eight had favored one denomination above others and four had required general affirmations of faith in Protestant Christianity in general. Only Rhode Island required no religious test whatsoever.

Let us look at some examples. Delaware's Constitution was non-denominational, yet emphatically Christian:

"Everyone appointed to public office must say, 'I do profess faith in God the Father, and in the Lord Jesus Christ his only Son, and in the Holy Ghost, one God and blessed forevermore; and I do acknowledge the Holy Scriptures of the Old and New Testaments to be given by divine inspiration.'"[30]

New Hampshire's Constitution was typical of the New England establishment of Congregationalism where the legislature was empowered to adopt measures "...for the support and maintenance of public Protestant teachers of piety, religion and morality."[31]

South Carolina's Constitution was typical of the establishment of Episcopal churches in the southern states: "The Christian Protestant religion shall be deemed, and is hereby constituted and declared to be, the established religion of the State... No person should be eligible to a seat in the Senate unless he be of the Protestant religion..."[32]

Most states had Sabbath laws and blasphemy laws. Maryland required of its public officials belief in Christianity until 1864, New Hampshire specifically required that only Protestants hold office until 1902, after which it was switched to any "Christian." These religious tests and established churches were not unconstitutional on the state level. However, a Christian movement toward disestablishment of favored denominations was growing in the states. This led the Framers of the Constitution to write Article 6, which first required an oath, but also prohibited any "religious test" on the national level.

In 1838, the Legislature of New York rejected by a nearly unanimous vote a petition calling for "a repeal of the laws for the observance of the Sabbath." Their report declared that:

"In all countries, some kind of religion or other has existed in all ages. No people on the face of the globe are without a prevailing national religion. Magistrates have sought in many countries to strengthen civil government by an alliance with some particular religion and an intolerant exclusion of all others. But those who have wielded this formidable power have rendered it a rival instead of an auxiliary to the public welfare, -- a fetter instead of a protection to the rights of conscience. With us it is wisely ordered that no one religion shall be established by law, but that all persons shall be left free in their choice and in their mode of worship. Still, *this is a Christian nation*. Ninety-nine hundredths, if not a larger proportion, of our whole population, believe in the general doctrines of the Christian religion. Our Government depends for its being on the virtue of the people, -- on that virtue that has its foundation in the morality of the Christian religion; and that religion is the common and prevailing faith of the people. There are, it is true, exceptions to this belief; but general laws are not made for excepted cases. There are to be found, here and there, the world over, individuals who entertain opinions hostile to the common sense of mankind on subjects of honesty, humanity, and decency; but it would be a kind of republicanism with which we are not acquainted in this country, which would require the great mass of mankind to yield to and be governed by this few."33

## The First Amendment

Justice Joseph Story, in his *Commentaries On the Constitution,* wrote that:

"The clause requiring no religious test for office is ...designed to cut off every pretence of an alliance between the Church and State in the administration of the National Government. The American people were too well read in the history of other countries, and had suffered too much in their colonial state, not to dread the abuses of authority resulting from religious bigotry, intolerance, and persecution.... The same policy which introduced into the Constitution the prohibition of any religious test, led to the more extended prohibition of the interference of Congress in religious concerns [i.e. the First Amendment]. We are not to attribute this prohibition of a national religious establishment to an indifference to religion in general, and especially to Christianity which none could hold in more reverence than the framers of the Constitution... Probably at the time of the adoption of the Constitution and of the Amendments to it, the general, if not universal, sentiment in America was that Christianity ought to receive encouragement from the State, so far as such encouragement was not incompatible with the private rights of conscience and the freedom of religious worship. An attempt to level all religions, and to make it a matter of state policy to hold all in utter indifference, would have created universal disapprobation, if not universal indignation.... In some of the states, Episcopalians constituted the predominant sect; in others, Presbyterians; in others, Congregationalists; in others, Quakers;... It was impossible that there should not arise perpetual strife and jealousy... if the national government were left free to create a religious establishment.... Thus the whole power over the subject of religion is left exclusive to the state governments..."[34]

The First Amendment to the Constitution is misunderstood today, even by the Supreme Court. It reads as follows: "Congress shall make no law respecting an establishment of religion..." The only government forbidden of favoring a particular denomination is the U.S. Congress, not the state legislatures.

Thomas Jefferson, who was never a strict separationist, wrote in the *Kentucky Resolutions of 1798* that "No power over the freedom of religion [is]... delegated to the United States by the Constitution;... All lawful powers respecting the same did of right remain, and were restored, to the states, or to the people."[35] In his 1805 Inaugural Address he said, "In matters of religion I... have left them, as the Constitution found them, under the direction and discipline of the church or state authorities acknowledged by the several religious societies." Again, in a letter in 1808, Jefferson said, "I consider the government of the United States as interdicted by the Constitution from intermeddling with religious institutions, their doctrines, discipline, or exercises... It must then rest with the states as far as it can be in any human authority."[36]

*Thomas Jefferson*

Jefferson never promoted the concept of a secular state. While serving in the Virginia House of Burgesses he was the one who personally introduced a resolution for a Day of Fasting and Prayer in 1774. Then while President, he also chaired the school board for the District of Columbia and authored its plan of education using the Bible and Watt's Hymnal as reading texts. He also proposed a treaty with the Kaskasian Indians which included using Federal money to build a church and support a clergyman. When he established the University of Virginia, he encouraged the teaching of religion and set apart space in the Rotunda for chapel services. He also praised the use of the local courthouse in his home town for religious services.

So our Founders' definition of "separation of church and state" was far different from the present way it is interpreted by the courts and secularists. The Courts today use the 14th Amendment as grounds to declare prayer, Bible-reading and other such traditions in the states as unconstitutional, but most of the same Congress that passed the 14th Amendment defeated the proposed Blaine Amendment and numerous other attempts to apply the First Amendment to the states. The Blaine Amendment in 1876 read: "No **state** shall make any law respecting the establishment of religion." What the people of the United States have **never done by due constitutional means, an activist liberal Supreme Court has done unconstitutionally. No matter how much the secularists may want to remove the influence of Christianity from public life, no matter how heterogenous or diverse we become, they have no real constitutional grounds for demanding the banishment of Christianity until an amendment is passed to that effect. The First Amendment does not guarantee freedom from** religion and a secular state, but **freedom of religion** and a truly non-denominational **Christian** state. It guaranteed that the "Spirit of the Constitution" would be forever free to flourish as the foundation of our Republic.

Harvey Cox, of Harvard University, has pointed out that secularism is a religion and a very intolerant one at that. It does not concede that any other religious perspective can be promoted in public, and it calls upon the government to enforce its beliefs. "Pluralism" today, although a Christian idea originally, now claims to protect the freedom of all religions, but this is a farce. There is one religion which does not have free exercise-- Christianity.

In 1952 Justice William O. Douglas wrote for the Supreme Court that "we find no constitutional requirement... for government to be hostile to religion and to throw its weight against efforts to widen the effective scope of religious influence."[37]

As recently as 1984 the Supreme Court made a surprising statement in *Lynch v. Donnelly:*

> "The Constitution [does not] require complete separation of church and state; it affirmatively mandates accommodation, not mere tolerance, of all religions, and forbids hostility toward any.... Anything less would require the 'callous indifference' we have said was never intended by the Establishment Clause.... Indeed, we have observed such hostility would bring us into 'war with our national tradition as embodied in the First Amendment's guarantee of the free exercise of religion.'"[38]

Patrick Henry stated:

"It can not be emphasized too strongly or too often that this great nation was founded, not by religionists, but by Christians, not on religions but on the gospel of Jesus Christ! For this very reason peoples of other faiths have been afforded asylum, prosperity, and freedom of worship here."

The Christian religion, Christian Virtue, and a Biblical Worldview are the "Spirit of the Constitution" -- the power behind our form of government.

# Chapter 13

# The Christian Form of Our Government

What makes America a Christian nation? Many Christians erroneously believe it depends on whether or not our Founders were Christians. Others believe it depends on if a vast majority of Americans are Christians. The problem with these criteria is when one or more of our Founders are found not to be Christians; does that negate the rest? Who determines the arbitrary percentage of a population that must be Christian to qualify? 100%? 51%? What about when even our Christian Founding Fathers came short of God's glory and sinned against the Indians or in other ways? Does the fallibility of Christians in a Christian nation negate the claim? Of course not. Even as an individual Christian fails morally now and then, he still can claim the name of Christ without reservation. Modern "Christian" books such as, *In Search of Christian America,* have made these fundamental mistakes in how one determines a Christian nation.

A Christian nation is determined by its **form** of government, not **who** formed it. If the form of a nation's government is shaped by Biblical ideas of man and government, in contrast to pagan or man centered ideas, then the nation is a Christian nation.

In 1867 *The North American Review* declared that "the American government and Constitution is the ... political expression of Christian ideas."[1] Our Founders were universally convinced of this truth.

Even unorthodox believers such as Benjamin Franklin often publicly cited Scripture. In the Constitutional Convention Franklin said:

> "We have been assured, Sir, in the Sacred Writings that 'except
> the Lord build the house, they labor in vain that build it'[Psalm
> 127:1]. I firmly believe this, and I also believe that without His
> concurring aid we shall succeed in this political building no bet-
> ter than the builders of Babel [Genesis 11]."[2]

The ideas embodied in our Constitution without a doubt, stem
primarily from the Bible. Our Founders reasoned from the Bible far
more than any other source. This was once taken for granted by
Americans until our modern revisionist historians began to promote
the view that rationalistic enlightenment thinkers were the major influence behind the Constitution. How can we know for sure?

Dr. Donald Lutz, a professor of political science from the University of Houston, conducted an exhaustive ten-year research of about
15,000 political documents of the Founders' Era (1760-1805), and
recorded every quote or reference to another written source. This
list of the 3,154 citations of the Founders was analyzed and published
in Volume #78 of the *American Political Science Review* in 1983. The
results would give quite an accurate measure of the influence of
various sources of thought on the Constitution. The results were
surprisingly contradictory to "modern scholarship." By far, the most
often quoted source of their political ideas was the Bible. This ac-
counts for over one-third of all their citations. The next most quoted
source is not even cited one-fourth as frequently. Another 60% of
all references can be attributed to authors which themselves derived
their ideas from the Bible. Therefore, it can be said that 94% of the
ideas in our Constitution are based either directly or indirectly on
the Bible.[3]

The Bible and Civil Liberty are inseparable. Even Newsweek, on
December 26, 1982, acknowledged after a major analysis of the
Bible's influence in America, that, "Now historians are discovering
that the Bible, perhaps even more than the Constitution is our
Founding document."[4] Honest historians are beginning to recognize
that Franklin's reference to "the Sacred Writings" and to "the
builders of Babel" in the Convention's search for "political truth" was
not an aberration.

## The Christian Constitution

The Preamble to the Constitution provides evidence that it is the
product of Christianity and its ideas of man and government. In the
Preamble is found a summary of the purpose of civil government.
These five basic functions are revealed in Scripture as legitimate.

The **first** is **"to establish justice."** This is the first purpose of civil government. The Bible says in 1 Peter 2:14 that civil rulers exist "for the punishment of evildoers and the praise of those who do right." Even back in Genesis 9:6, God told Noah that "Whoever sheds man's blood, by man his blood shall be shed." This is justice.

The **second** purpose of civil government is **"to insure domestic tranquility."** This is found in Scripture in 1 Timothy 2:1,2 where Paul urges Christians to pray for civil rulers "in order that we may lead a tranquil and quiet life in all godliness and dignity."

**Third**, government is **"to provide for the common defense."** The protection of innocent human life is at the base of not only capital punishment, and domestic police force, but also in this third provision of army for protection from external threats. In Romans 13:4, it is affirmed that civil government "does not bear the sword for nothing." The "sword" in Scripture is equivalent to any military weapon used today, even nuclear weapons. The only thing that would make any weapons "immoral" is if there is not a sufficient amount to bring "wrath upon one who practices evil." If external threats have a huge arsenal of nuclear weapons, there must be at least equal amounts to deter aggression upon innocent human beings. Even Jesus Christ taught His disciples the legitimacy of being armed militarily, saying in Luke 22:36, "Now... let him who has no sword sell his robe and buy one."

**Fourth**, government should **"promote the general welfare."** Romans 13:4 says civil rulers are servants "to you for *good*." The common good of all classes of citizens must be promoted by government passage of laws guaranteeing equal opportunity. Notice, our Framer's choice of words here: promote, not provide. Scripture makes it clear that God is the provider, not the state, and that needy individuals are to be cared for by private acts of charity. A Biblical free-enterprise system must promote compassionate use of wealth, but socialism or communism is contrary to Biblical definitions of civil government.

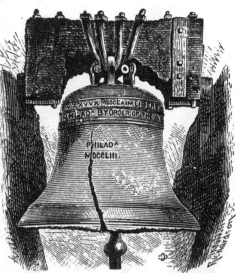

*Proclaim liberty throughout all the land, unto all the inhabitants thereof (Leviticus 25:10)*

Lastly, civil government exists to **"secure the blessings of liberty."** "Blessings" are a gift of one's Creator, not a privilege granted by government. The most basic of these Creator-endowed blessings were defined in the Fifth Amendment of the Constitution which mentions, "life, liberty and ...private property." Scripture defines God as the source of life in Genesis 1:27, "And God created man in His own image." He is the author of liberty as well -- 2 Corinthians 3:17 says, "Where the Spirit of the Lord is, there is liberty;" and Leviticus 25:10 says, "Proclaim liberty throughout the land to all its inhabitants." Scripture also defines God as the source of private property and "the pursuit of happiness" as expressed in the Declaration of Independence. Ecclesiastes 5:19 states, "For every man to whom God has given riches and wealth, He has also empowered him to eat from them ...and rejoice in his labor; this is the gift of God." Also in 1 Chronicles 29:12, "Both riches and honor come from Thee."

Contrary to the belief of a majority of Americans today, public education is **not** guaranteed in the Constitution. This is because our Founders knew that Scripture does not declare this as a function of civil government.

## Structures Based on Christian Presuppositions in the Constitution

Our Founders, while not all born-again Christians, firmly believed in the Biblical ideas of man and government. They believed that man's sinful nature meant that he should not be entrusted with too much power, even if he was regenerated through the blood of Jesus Christ.

The form of government you determine depends greatly on whether or not you believe mankind has an inherent sin nature. James Madison said, in the *Federalist* No. 51, "What is government itself but the greatest of all reflections on human nature?" One's view of human nature profoundly affects one's view of government.

Pagan governments, which are not based on the belief that men are sinners, establish too much centralized power in the hands of men. This has always resulted in awful oppression and tyranny at the expense of individual liberty. There are really only two types of national union-- pagan and Christian. Pagan union is held together by external force and intimidation. Christian union, in contrast, is held together by internal unity of purpose and principles. Christian union always protects diversity and individuality.

When our Founders declared independence from England, they were well aware that great oppression was possible, not only when power is concentrated in a monarchy, but also in the hands of an elite. Parliament was a national legislature with supreme authority. When our founders drafted the *Articles of Confederation* in 1777, a National Congress was established but with very little power. The Confederation placed supreme authority in the 13 state legislatures. The Continental Congress was merely a committee of the 13 sovereign states and its "president" was simply a chairman elected annually. Our Founders wanted to keep power decentralized.

## Federalism

The problem with a confederation or confederacy, however, is that it is too weak or inefficient to maintain a strong nation. It required voluntary, unanimous consent of all 13 states in order to make every decision. By 1787 the delegates in the Philadelphia Convention realized that there needed to be a change. They achieved this in the establishment of a form of national union that is unique in the world today-- **Federalism.**

Federalism is the principle that **most** powers should be decentralized among state and local governments, but that a few defined powers are delegated to a national government. James Madison described a federation when he said: "The powers delegated by the ...Constitution to the federal government are few and defined. Those which are to remain in the State governments are numerous and indefinite."[5]

Jefferson said that "the way to have good and safe government is not to trust it all to one, but to divide it among the many..."[6]

The Constitution does not make the states merely administrative arms of the national government. It establishes, in effect, a dual form of government -- both the national government and the state governments having supreme authority over their defined areas of jurisdiction. This means that every American citizen has actually two law-making bodies to which he must submit. He must obey Federal laws as well as state laws equally. But what if one conflicts with the other? The answer is they don't and never will (if they both act according to the Constitution), because they make laws dealing with completely different areas of life. The national government can only make laws dealing with such items as the regulation of

*James Madison, the chief architect of the Constitution, received much of his training from Rev. John Witherspoon.*

interstate and foreign commerce, coining money, the postal services, copyrights, citizenship laws, and the armed forces. The state governments can only make laws dealing with such things as public education, voting procedures, marriage and divorce, corporations and traffic. Neither can interfere in the area of the other without being unconstitutional and thus subject to indictment. Each sovereign government is held in check from encroaching on the other by the higher law of the Constitution, declared supreme in Article 6, paragraph 2.

The Constitution establishes only 18 powers in the national government in Article 1, Section 8. Then it declares these powers off-limits to the states in Section 10. But then it reserves every other undefined power to the states in the 10th Amendment:

"The powers not delegated to the United States by the Constitution, nor prohibited by it to the states, are reserved to the states respectively, or to the people."

These 18 powers delegated to the national government were permanently surrendered. They could not be altered except by amendment to the Constitution. This makes the federation a **permanent** union, unlike the uncertainty of a confederation. The Civil War was precipitated by the secession of the "Confederate" states from the Union. Our Founders established a permanent union of states by a national covenant -- the Constitution. The Latin word for Covenant is "Foedus" (from which we get our word "federal"). The bottom line of any covenant, whether in marriage or in church or in civil government, is that there should be no divorce. All problems and conflicts must therefore be patiently discussed and debated until they are resolved. This requires Christian character and virtue in order to work.

The idea of an unbreakable union was rooted in the federal theology of the colonial churches. A sermon by Ezra Stiles in 1760 entitled *Christian Union* was one of the most widely published and distributed pamphlets of the Founders' Era.

The idea of an unbreakable covenant was not the only idea the Founding Fathers borrowed from the churches. They also borrowed the idea of dual sovereignty. Federalism means dual government. The only model in history to which our founders could refer was in the primitive churches of the first century. No civil government in history had ever attempted such a scheme, but in the New Testament church our founders saw evidence of dual government to which every Christian was submitted. Each local church was governed by its only local presbytery of elders (1 Timothy 3:1-5, 4:14, 5:17). Yet there was a measure of authority exercised by apostles and prophets in the mother church at Jerusalem that was also binding on the church at large (Acts 15:2,6;16:4). These dual governments were also operating in the denominational arrangements of the Colonial churches. A Presbyterian in Virginia was loyal to his local church leadership, but also to the Presbyterian denominational leadership at large. Separatist leader Rev. John Robinson, pastor of the Pilgrims, emphasized loyalty to the local congregation (or the principle of self-government). Puritan clergyman William Ames emphasized loyalty to the Church of England at large (or the principle of union). They debated their points equally well and many of the colonial churches achieved a balance of both.

One of the delegates in the Constitutional Convention was James Wilson of Pennsylvania, who later was named as a justice of the first

Supreme Court. He said that a free republic is best symbolized by a pyramid with a majority of powers decentralized among the people and only a few granted to the national government.[7] (This is why our founders put a pyramid on our national seal, which can be found on the dollar bill.) This is federalism, based on the Christian doctrine of the sin nature of man.

## Separation of Powers

In contrast to these men who want to centralize the authority in our nation, our Founders, after they had apportioned most of the powers of government to the states, went even further, due to their mistrust of sinful men, and separated the few and limited powers of the national government into three branches that would check each other. James Madison wrote that: "The accumulation of all powers, legislative, executive, and judiciary, in the same hands whether of one, a few, or many... may justly be pronounced the very definition of tyranny."[8] He went on to say in the *Federalist* No. 47 that "...the three great departments of power should be separate and distinct. The oracle who is always consulted and cited on this subject is the celebrated Montesquieu..."

*Montesquieu*

Montesquieu and our Founders broke the powers of government into these three divisions because that is how the Bible defined God's government of the universe in Isaiah 33:22 -- "For the Lord is our judge (Chief Justice), the Lord is our lawgiver (Legislature), the Lord is our King (Chief Executive); He will save us." Since God is perfect and infallible, He can possess all three powers and still be just and fair, but not sinful men.

The manner in which these three elements were balanced so well in our government is interesting. In the same way that federalism was an idea rooted in church government, so also are the three branches of government. The Protestant Reformation produced three distinct movements of Christians who emphasized three different patterns of church government. The **Episcopalians** emphasized the rule of one from the top down. The **Presbyterians**, emphasized the rule of a few elders. **Congregationalists**, emphasized the rule of many. Each of these groups colonized America, by the design of Providence, into major geographical groupings and formed their colonial civil governments in patterns similar to their churches. The northern colonies, settled predominantly by Congregationalists, established a form of democracy. The southern colonies, being mostly Episcopalian, established "Royal Provinces" which were a form of monarchy. The middle colonies were proprietary, and being influenced greatly by Reformed Presbyterianism, established more aristocratic governments.

191

God allowed these isolated geographical groupings to taste the strengths and weaknesses of their particular form of government for 150 years before bringing them all together through the American Revolution. When delegates arrived in Philadelphia in 1787, they were experienced experts on all three forms and blended them together beautifully. They decided (in the words of James Madison) that "the essential qualities of a monarchy -- unity of council, vigor, secrecy... -- will enable the President to execute the laws with energy and dispatch."[9] They established an unelected Supreme Court and U.S. Senate in order to give "to this part of the system all the advantages of an aristocracy -- wisdom, experience, and a consistency of measures."[10] Finally, elements of democracy were established in the House of Representatives which would be elected directly by the people every two years (these three elements are also seen on the State level in governors, judges and state legislators).

Our federal government therefore -- specifically the first three Articles of the Constitution -- is a reflection of church government. The Episcopalian form of church government alone is not the Biblical model found in the New Testament, neither is the Presbyterian or Congregational. It is only when all three are blended together that you have balanced Biblical Christian church government. It follows in civil government as well. If our founders had all been Congregationalists, then our Constitution would probably have established more of a pure democracy in America. But that alone would not be the Biblical model of civil government. God providentially shaped the colonization of America in such a way that democracy, aristocracy and monarchy would be blended together into a balanced Christian Republic-- the first in history!

**Representative government** is also an aspect of our Constitution that is Biblical. It will be dealt with in chapter 18.

The Declaration of Independence and the Constitution were clearly founded upon Christian ideas of man and government. Our Founders were the first men to "hold these truths" and establish a nation upon them. Without Christianity, there never would have been a Constitution. As Noah Webster, the father of the dictionary and a key Federalist in the passage of the Constitution, said:

> "The religion which has introduced civil liberty, is the religion of Christ and his apostles, which enjoins humility, piety, and benevolence; which acknowledges in every person a brother, or a sister, and a citizen with equal rights. This is genuine Christianity, and to this we owe our free constitutions of government."[11]

---
# Chapter 14
---

# Principles of Christian Economics

Much of the material in this chapter was adapted from an article on "The Principle Approach to American Christian Economics" by Charles Hull Wolfe in the book, *A Guide to American Christian Education for the Home and School, the Principle Approach,* by James B. Rose. After much study on Christian Economics, we found Mr. Wolfe's approach to be the most clear, complete, and easily understood. We are deeply indebted to him to allow us to borrow so freely of his ideas.

## Defining Christian Economics

Since economics is the science that deals with production, distribution, and consumption of goods and services, Christian Economics is the "discipline that studies the application of Biblical principles or laws to the production, distribution, and consumption of goods and services." It entails "how men use God-given natural resources, ideas, and energy to meet their human needs and glorify Him."[1]

## A Christian Economy will Flow from the Heart of Man Outward

Christianity produces internal liberty in man, which is the foundation for a Christian economy. The internal change of heart that Christ brings produces Christian character and self-government which is necessary for an economy to be prosperous. Christian character and self-government produce:

- People who will not steal. Billions of dollars are lost each year by American businesses to theft by their employees. This theft is much greater than that by non-employees.

- People with a strong work ethic who will labor hard and be productive. This will cause an economy to grow.

- People who will save and invest to acquire greater return later.

- People who have concern for their posterity and will seek to pass on a greater estate than they received.

The truth of the gospel also imparts new ideas and creativity to man which assists him in increasing his material welfare. This occurs as man creates new and better tools. In addition, man gains the understanding that God has given him an abundance to rule the earth and if he seeks His supply, he will find it.

Besides bringing internal liberty to man, the introduction of Christianity in a nation will also manifest itself externally in political freedom. A government acting on Biblical principles is needed for a Christian economy. As Verna Hall stated, "government is the house in which the economy lives." Its policies must promote and protect economic freedom.

Economic freedom will then flow from personal and governmental freedom. Charles Wolfe states that this freedom includes "a people's freedom to own their own property...to choose their own occupation...to keep the fruits of their labors...to buy and sell in a free market, where wages and prices are determined not by government mandate but by voluntary exchanges of free men and women."[2]

## Factors of Production in a Society

Stated in a simple manner, man's material welfare is a product of natural resources mixed with human energy and coupled with the use of tools. Mr. Wolfe represents this by the following formula:

*N.R. + H.E. × T. = M.M.W.*

*Natural Resources + Human Energy × Tools = Man's Material Welfare*

If Natural Resources increase, so does Man's Material Welfare. If Human Energy is exerted, Man's Material Welfare increases. If better tools are created, Man's Material Welfare will also increase.

This equation for Man's Material Welfare is applicable for every nation in the world, yet there is a great difference in how men in a Christian society view the world and apply their physical and mental energies as compared to those men in a secular society. We will examine the factors of production in both a Christian and secular society.

## In a Christian Society with Great Economic Freedom

### Natural Resources

God created man and knew that he would have certain basic needs, such as food, clothing, and shelter. God created everything that was needed to meet those needs. One, God created natural resources. Those men with a Christian worldview believe that God has provided all that they need and, consequently, they have faith to seek, find, and process abundant natural resources. As the Natural Resources available to man increase, his material welfare increases as well.

### Human Energy

God not only created natural resources, but He also created man with human energy. God told him to "have dominion" or rule over the earth (Genesis 1:26). Man was placed in the garden to cultivate and keep it (Genesis 2:15), which required labor. After the fall, cultivating the ground required an additional "sweat of [man's] face" (Gen. 3:19).

In a Christian society, men will be inspired by God to work. In addition,in a nation of economic freedom, men will be able to partake of the fruit of their labors which will encourage them to exert more energy. As man works harder and exerts more human energy, his material welfare (and that of the nation) will increase.

### Tools

From the beginning, man was unable to cultivate the ground and rule over the earth, or even meet his basic needs well, with his bare hands alone. Mr. Wolfe writes that "to take the natural resources God (had) created and turn them into... food, clothing, and shelter" to meet man's needs, tools were needed to help him "till the soil, to cut down trees and saw timber, to mine and refine minerals, and to tend sheep and weave wool."[3] Knowing this, God gave man "ideas for inventing and making tools." Man was given "intelligence and physical strength," that is "mental and muscular energy," to take the Natural Resources and create tools to meet his needs.[4]

Man has used tools from the beginning. Adam and Cain were farmers and likely used simple tools (possibly a digging stick or simple plow) and some kind of sickle or cutting tool to harvest grain. Abel was a shepherd and likely had a rod and staff.

The Bible has many references to tools. Wolfe states these include "hammers, axes,...plows drawn by oxen, millstones for grinding meal,...furnaces for refining silver and gold, ovens, and baking and frying pans."[5]

Wolfe writes: "The usefulness of each tool is measured by the amount of time and energy it saves; by the increase in the quantity and (or) quality of the goods and services that can be produced through its use."[6]

The following chart reveals how advancements in agricultural tools have produced economic progress:[7]

| Time Period | Tool | Production by one man |
|---|---|---|
| Adam | Simple Tools | Probably enough food for Eve and himself |
| Abraham | Wooden Plow drawn by oxen | Food for large family |
| 18th Century | Horse drawn iron plow | Food for 3 families |
| 1940's | Tractor | Food for 14 families |
| Today | Advanced Tractors & tools | Food for 60 families |

Development of better tools has primarily occurred in nations where people have had access to the truth of the Bible (and hence the mind of Christ) which has enabled them to receive many ideas for inventing new and better tools. As we have seen, these advancements in tools have caused man's material welfare to improve.

We should remember that man's productivity is a result, not only of better, but also of better use of those tools. That is why we must be diligent in our work. God has given man all he needs for his human welfare -- natural resources, human energy, and ideas for creating tools -- but man must labor to take what God has given and transform it into the food, clothing, shelter, and other things that meet his human needs. Labor is the title deed to property.

## In a Secular Society with Limited Economic Freedom

The factors of production in the equation, N.R. + H.E. x T. = M.M.W., are viewed differently in a secular society by those with a nonchristian world-view, than those in a Christian society.

### Natural Resources

A secular society will lack faith in God's providence and consequently men will find fewer natural resources. The secular or socialist has a limited resource mentality and views the world as a pie (there is only so much) that needs to be cut up so that everyone can get a piece. In contrast, the Christian knows that the potential in God is unlimited and that there is no shortage of resources in God's earth. The resources are waiting to be tapped.

We do not live in a resource-short world. Known reserves of minerals and energy resources are greater today than in 1950 despite increasing consumption. Ideas allowing us to tap into unused natural resources are limitless. For example, about 100 years ago, the American Indians wiped oil on their faces. Today, new uses of that natural resource have transformed our economy and brought a higher standard of living for everyone. In recent years, the computer world has been revolutionized by the silicon chip, which is made from the same material as sand.

While many secularists view the world as over-populated, Christians know that God has made the earth sufficiently large, with plenty of resources to accommodate all the people He knew would come into existence. There is plenty of room and food for the entire world population today. All the five billion people on the earth could live in the state of Texas in single family homes with front and back yards and be fed by production in the rest of the United States. Present world agricultural areas, if developed by present technology, could feed 31 billion people. Our earth has plenty of room and plenty of natural resources.

### Human Energy

Those with a secular world-view will lack a God-inspired strength and work ethic. Such strength and character would cause them to be more productive through hard labor, honesty, investment in the future, etc. In addition, the lack of incentives of freedom found in secular nations with limited economic freedom cause men to exert less energy since they cannot eat of the fruit of their labor. The net result is that man's material welfare suffers.

## Tools

Secularists are cut off from the Bible and the mind of Christ (the chief source of creativity), and so they get fewer ideas for inventing new and better tools. Lack of new and better tools keeps production and man's material welfare from increasing.

Comparing the factors of production in Christian and secular societies reveals why some countries prosper and some do not. Mr. Wolfe writes: "While men and women in every country try to multiply their human energies with the help of tools in order to transform natural resources into useful goods and services, Christian free societies generally do it more efficiently than others."[8]

A study by Dr. Browning of incomes of different nations and people groups confirms this observation. He found that "between protestant and catholic groups it was noted consistently that the protestant countries had higher per capita income than the catholic countries. But those that were not Christian had no income or low incomes or were starving to death."[9]

There are a few exceptions to this finding. The most notable is the nation of Japan. However, the reason that Japan has prospered is that "they have simply imitated the principles and techniques on which America's original prosperity was built"[10] -- principles that grew out of our Christian society (and which have in part been abandoned today).

As Mr. Wolfe reveals, the Japanese have imitated our Puritan work ethic, Yankee ingenuity, the idea that "a penny saved is a penny earned," individual responsibility for quality of work, giving workers a voice in the decision making process of businesses, and encouraging workers and managers to come together in a kind of voluntary union.

While application of these principles have caused the material welfare of the Japanese to increase greatly, this increase has come at the expense of greater life and liberty in other areas. Material welfare is not the only aspect of a Christian economy. The pressure to succeed is so great upon many Japanese youth today, that many are not holding up under the stress. Many are also "sold out" to their jobs and work so much they have no time for anything else.

In a Christian economy people will earn more with less work which means:

- People will have more free time for worship of God, instruction, recreation, and service to others.
- People will have more money to give to Churches, charities, and foreign missionary efforts.
- People can acquire more luxuries.

## The Real Wealth of a Nation

While America has in recent years abandoned some of the principles that produced our prosperity, we are still the most prosperous nation in the world. Wolfe writes that "the best way to compare the real wealth of the people of one country with the wealth of the people of another is how many hours of work it takes a factory worker to earn the money needed to buy the same basic commodities in retail stores in that country."[11]

To purchase a kilogram of bread, a factory worker must work 18 minutes in Moscow, 12 minutes in London, and 8 minutes in Washington. To purchase a car (Volga, Ford), that work time is 35 months in Moscow, 8.5 months in London, and 4.1 months in Washington.[12]

If you visit the Philippines, you will find that clothes are 1/3 to 1/4 the price of those in the United States. While this may be of benefit to the American traveler, this price reflects a much greater percentage of the average Filipino income than Americans spend on clothes. An American worker's average income is about 10 times that of the average worker in Manila. So the average Filipino spends more of his income on clothes and food than the average American, even though these items are less expensive in Manila than the United States. Filipinos spend much more on other items because appliances, cars, and other things not made in the Philippines, cost more than they do in the States.

## Why Are Some Nations in Poverty?

As we have seen, the equation, N.R. + H.E. x T. = M.M.W., applies to every country in the world. Those societies built on Christian principles will have a proper view of natural resources, the character to exert human energy, and access to the creativity of God leading to better tools, all of which cause man's material welfare to increase. While any nation adhering to this truth will see the material welfare of it's citizens increase, most people and nations are quite poor. In fact, 46% of the world lives in poverty today. Why? Some claim that it is because many nations lack natural resources. Yet, some nations, such as Japan, with few natural resources are quite prosperous. There are also many nations with abundant natural resources that are much less prosperous than other nations with fewer natural resources.

The primary reason that nations are in poverty is lack of spiritual resources and truth. A secularist world-view keeps each element of the factors of production from increasing, which stifles man's material welfare. India is a good example of how a people's religion directly affects it's economic prosperity. Today, India has widespread hunger problems, yet these are not due to a lack of food, but are a result of the people's religious beliefs. The majority of Indians are Hindus. The Hindu religion teaches that people who die are reincarnated as animals; therefore, their laws and religion prohibit the people from killing rats, mice, cows, or other animals.

There are 200 million "sacred cows" in India. Each cow eats enough food to feed seven people. The feed from these cows alone would feed 1.4 billion people, which is over 1/4 the world's population. The mice and rats, which they will not kill, eat much of their grain as well. This grain, not to mention the meat from the cows, would supply plenty of food for all the starving people of India.[13]

The economic state of a nation depends upon it's religion.

## Profit Motive

We have seen that man's material welfare increases in a Christian Society because Christian faith and character help "enlarge, vitalize, and improve" the three factors of production. But, as Charles Wolfe writes:

> "The economic incentives of freedom are also important. To find and process natural resources such as oil and minerals is extremely costly. So is the protracted process of researching, developing and producing new and more efficient power tools. The profit motive provides individuals with the needed incentive in a Christian free economy based on individual enterprise."

> "History shows that in a Christian free economy. . .men tend to invent more and better tools, invest more in producing those tools, and use those tools more efficiently than in a secular society with limited economic freedom."[14]

In recent years many nations that have operated on communistic economic principles, which eliminate the profit motive, have been allowing more individual enterprise because it causes the people to be much more productive. Two such nations are Russia and China.

Russia has allowed "each farming family 2-3 acres of ground to operate privately and sell its produce in the local market. These tiny private farm plots produce more meat, vegetables and fruit than all of the huge government farms combined."[15]

Communal farming with no individual incentive does not even work with Christians who have common vision, goals, and purposes. The Pilgrims gave us this example in their first two years in America. Compelled by the contract with their financial backers, the Pilgrims farmed the land communally. The lack of incentive to work resulted in such a poor crop that the Pilgrims almost starved during the first two winters. To alleviate this problem, the leaders shifted to an individual enterprise system where every family farmed their own parcel of land, and ate the fruit of their own labor. Governor Bradford wrote that "this had very good success; for it made all hands very industrious. . .The women now went willingly into the field, and took their little ones with them to set corn, which before would aledge weakness, and inability; whom to have compelled would have been thought great tyranny and oppression."[16] They produced an abundant crop and never lacked for food again. Their example shows that "the taking away of property, and bringing in community into a common wealth,"[17] does not make people happy or cause them to flourish, as many ancients, such as Plato, or modern men, such as Marx, have espoused.

*In 1623, when the Pilgrims instituted an individual farming system, much more corn was planted than in the previous two years. However, a drought threatened all their crops. In response, Governor Bradford wrote, "they set apart a solemn day of humiliation, to seek the Lord by humble and fervent prayer...And He was pleased to give them a gracious and speedy answer."*

## *The Wheel of Progress in a Christian Economy*

The diagram of the "Wheel of Progress in a Christian Economy," as given by Charles Wolfe, is an excellent depiction of the necessary elements of a growing and prospering economy. We will look at the individual parts of the wheel.

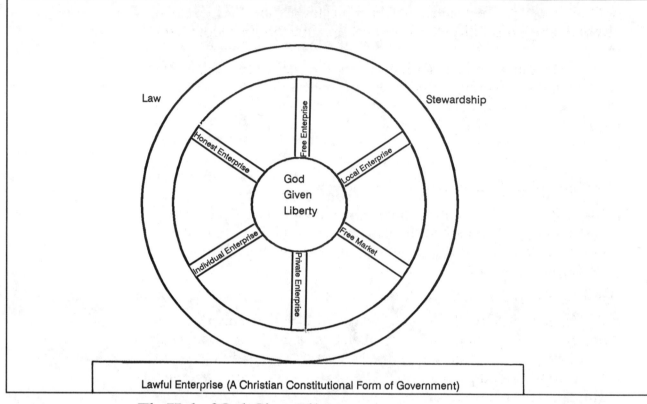

### *The Hub of God-Given Liberty*

We saw earlier how a Christian Economy revolves around or flows out of the heart of man -- from the internal liberty that Christ brings. This God-given liberty, which begins internally but is manifested externally, is the hub of the wheel of progress in a Christian economy.

It is important to recognize that this liberty or freedom is granted by God and not by man or the state. Mr. Wolfe writes that "if the hub of the wheel is seen as freedom granted by man or the state, rather than by God Himself, then that freedom can readily be taken away, in whole or in part, and there is no reliable basis for a continuing, consistent free economy."[18]

The hub, seen as God-given liberty, has a reliable core "to which the various spokes -- the Biblical principles of economics -- can be securely attached." In fact, only a hub of God-given liberty can give rise to the various spokes, for it is only in an economy of liberty that men are allowed to practice individual enterprise, economic self-government, and manifest each aspect of the spokes.[19]

## Rim of Stewardship and Law

The spokes in the wheel of progress in a Christian Economy will be held together, and the wheel will run smoothly, by the discipline of God's law and the practice of Christian stewardship. These make up a rim of responsibility which keep economic freedom under God's control.

In an economy -- as in all society -- the great challenge is not merely to maintain freedom, but to maintain freedom with order. To do this, people must be disciplined from within so they do not infringe upon the rights of others. Therefore, men must understand and obey God's law in order to have a Christian economy, for as they do, the following will result:

- Men will respect each other's property.

In many nations today, people must have a half dozen locks on their cars, and walls, fences, and guards protecting their houses and business to keep other citizens from stealing their property. Growth of the economy will be hindered greatly in this environment.

- They will not steal or cheat one another.

A recent visitor to the United States from Latin America was amazed at many things he witnessed in this country. One thing that he especially took note of were newspaper stands. He marveled that people would put in a quarter and take only one newspaper. He said that this would never happen in his country, because the first person to get their in the morning would put in his quarter, take all the newspapers, and go and sell them on the street. This is a small example of how dishonesty hinders economic freedom. We mentioned before how businesses lose more money by theft from their employees than outside forces. For a nation's economy to grow, the people must be honest.

- They will abide by contracts.
- When citizens are elected or appointed to positions in government, they will not use their power to secretly erode the value of the people's money through inflation, nor will they gradually restrict the people's economic freedom through excessive regulation.

A Christian businessman in a developing country needed to get some raw materials through customs so that he could fill large orders for various customers. Before these materials could be released he needed to get 46 different signatures of government officials. Most of these officials wanted a bribe before they gave their signature, and when the businessman refused, there was such a delay in getting his materials released that he was unable to fill his orders in time, and he lost hundreds of thousands of dollars. Excessive regulation and dishonesty stifle economic growth.

To maintain economic freedom, individuals must also practice Christian stewardship. Wolfe says that they must:

- Be industrious in earning money
- Be disciplined in saving money
- Be wise in investing money
- Be obedient to God's law in how they share it with their church and with those in need
- Practice "the self-denial necessary to restrain themselves from buying many things that would bring immediate gratification, in order to save and invest enough to provide for emergencies and their later years, without having to turn to government for assistance."[20]

In other words, people must work all they can, earn all they can, save all they can, and give all they can.

### The Title Deed to Property is Labor.

*John Locke*

John Locke writes:

"Though the Earth, and all inferior Creatures be common to all Men, yet every Man has a Property in his own Person: This no Body has any right to but himself. The Labour of his Body, and the Work of his Hands, we may say, are properly his. Whatsoever then he removes out of the State that Nature hath provided, and left in it, he hath mixed his Labour with, and joyned to it something that is his own, and thereby makes it his Property. It being by him removed from the Common State Nature hath placed it in, it hath by this Labour something annexed to it, that excludes the common Right of other Men."[21]

All property you possess was acquired by labor--either your labor or someone else's. You take possession or title to property in proportion to your labor or individual enterprise. This is not only true of external property but also internal property.

Rosalie Slater writes:

"We might use the example of learning of a subject in school as an illustration of this principle which Locke is setting forth. God has given the knowledge contained in this subject to all of us--you might say it's our common possession. Yet no one actually has title to it--can prove that he owns it. If any student makes the effort to learn the subject--he acquires title to what he learns. This effort on his part hasn't in the least diminished the amount of the subject which we all still have in common. It's still there. But the student who made the effort to learn the subject does have a title to something which no-one can take from him and which he would not have had if he had not added or invested his own effort. He has property rights in the subject."[22]

### The Measure of Property

If through labor people acquire more property, what is to be the measure of how much one accumulates? John Locke tells us that the measure of property is not how much one wants, but how much one needs--that is what is sufficient for an individual to fulfill God's will in his life.

### The Title to Internal Property is Obtained by Consent.

Miss Slater explains this idea well:

"Just as the Christian values the talents which God has placed in trust with him, and just as he works for their productive fruition in our Lord's service, so he carefully guards the use and disposal of his property. Today much concern is expressed about "property rights" and the infringement upon individual or private enterprise. But the first invasion of property rights occurs internally when the individual consents to the disposal or use or misuse of his opinions, his religious convictions, and his faculties. Often this consent is tacit consent. John Locke differentiated between express consent and tacit consent. The word tacit means:

"Tacit: 'Silent; implied, but not expressed. Tacit consent is consent by silence, or by making no objection.

"'So we say, a tacit agreement or covenant of men to live under a particular government, when no objection or opposition is made; a tacit surrender of a part of our natural rights.'

"Thus the surrender of an individual or a nation can occur by *silence*, or by making *no objection*. Christianity, unlike any other religion, requires an *active confession* of faith, an *active acceptance* of Jesus Christ as Lord and Saviour. So a Christian also must refuse, through whatever duly constituted means are at his disposal, to permit his rights of conscience, his convictions, or, indeed, his very faculties, and talents, to be used contrary to what he knows to be good and true, and in accord with the laws of God.

*Consent* is one's title to the property of conscience. And as John Locke reminds us only *express consent* makes one a "member of any Commonwealth". So only *express refusal* to have one's property used for purposes which do not support righteous government can make one truly faithful to the stewardship of conscience."[23]

## The Spokes

### 1. Individual Enterprise

The idea of individual enterprise, which we spoke of before, follows from God's Principle of Individuality. Every person on earth is distinct, unique, and important in an economic sense. It follows that:

* Each person has "special God-given talents as a producer." This leads to specialization and division of labor (which leads to greater wealth in a nation).

* Each person has "individual desires as a customer."

* Each person has "individual rights, such as the right to enter an occupation of one's choice" (which promotes greater productivity), "the right to start one's own business, and the right to buy the goods one prefers."

* Each person has "individual economic responsibilities." Each citizen should provide for themselves and their family rather than rely upon the civil government to meet their needs. They should also voluntarily help the poor and those with genuine need. According to the Bible, providing for the poor is the responsibility of individuals and the church. The state has assumed this responsibility in the United States as the church and individuals gave it up.[24]

### Caring for the Poor

Welfare states are not biblical and do not work. America in recent decades has shown this to be true. While government money spent on welfare has increased dramatically, so has the nation's poverty. Today, only 30 cents of each welfare dollar actually goes to meet the need of the poor. The other 70 cents is consumed by the governmental bureaucracy. Since President Johnson announced his war on poverty in the 1960's, America has spent hundreds of billions of dollars on the fight, yet poverty is increasing. Government money is not the solution to poverty. Compare the following figures:

● In 1950, 1 in 12 Americans lived below the poverty line.

● In 1951, government spent about $4 billion on social welfare programs.

● In 1979, 1 in 9 Americans lived below the poverty line.

● In 1981, government spent $316.6 billion on social welfare programs.[25]

The Bible says that the family and church are the primary institutions of health, education, and welfare. As we reassume our responsibilities, we can eliminate the need for the civil government to spend hundreds of billions of dollars on welfare.

Individual enterprise opposes economic collectivism and its emphasis upon the group and forced common production. Individual enterprise applies the Bible Principle, "as you sow, so shall you also reap," which encourages productivity.

## 2. Economic Self-Government (Free Enterprise)

An individual who governs himself will direct and control his own economic affairs in a responsible manner. He will be:

\* "A self-governed producer" -- "not needing constant supervision...to assure the quality and quantity of his work."

\* "A self-governed customer" -- "buying only what he needs and never spending in excess of his income."

\* "A self-governed saver" -- "regularly saving some of his earnings to assure a strong economic future."

\* "A self-governed manufacturer or retailer" -- "producing and selling quality goods and services, with due concern for the rights and needs of employees and customers."[26]

A nation of self-governed people will cause the economy to grow and remain free.

## 3. Christian Character (Honest Enterprise)

We have already seen how Christian character is the foundation for a free and prosperous society. A few specific character qualities that effect the economy of a nation include:

\* Diligence and industry -- hard work increases productivity which brings about increased prosperity.

\* Faith in God's Providence -- hard work alone does not guarantee prosperity; we must also trust and obey the Lord to experience His blessings (Matthew 6:33; Deuteronomy 28). Individuals and the nation must put their faith in God to experience His blessings.

* Love for our neighbor -- As we express Christian love, we will care for the needy in the land.

* Honesty -- Honest employees will not steal from their employers; an honest civil government will not steal from its citizens by use of fiat money.

### Honest Money

A biblical economy will have an honest money system. Leviticus 19:35-37 states:

> "You shall do no wrong in judgment, in measurement of weight, or capacity. You shall have just balances, just weights, a just ephah, and a just hin: I am the Lord your God, who brought you out from the land of Egypt. You shall thus observe all My statutes, and all My ordinances, and do them: I am the Lord."

Money is a commodity. It is something of genuine value in the marketplace, whether cattle, coconuts, shells, silver or gold -- all of

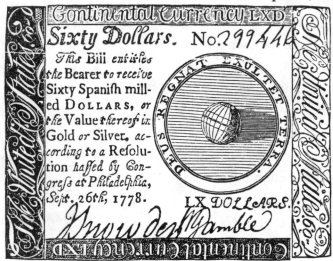

*The worthlessness of "Continental Money" motivated our founders to establish a currency consisting of the precious metals.*

which have been used as money. Historically, exchange began with barter. Money makes exchange much easier, because people can trade their goods for money and use the money to buy other things they want. In the Bible money was silver or gold, a precious metal. This is money based on principle.

"Paper money initially is not money. It is a substitute for money, and is useful because it is difficult to fold coins into a wallet. But if paper money is honest, it will always be backed by a specific amount of real, 'hard' money and redeemable at any time."[27]

America was on a gold standard throughout most of her history. In 1933 we shifted to a silver standard. In 1968 our silver certificates were replaced with Federal Reserve Notes thus eliminating honest money from our nation. When we had honest money there was never any prolonged inflation in this nation. Today's paper money is not backed by anything except the government's promise that it is good. Compared to a 1932 dollar, the dollar today is worth about 5 cents. It is interesting to note that an ounce of gold today will purchase about the same amount of goods that an ounce of gold bought 60 years ago.

Money with no precious metal backing, fiat money, allows the central government to spend more than it collects in taxes, because the FED (Federal Reserve Board) can print new "money" (increase the money supply) anytime there is a need. This is inflationary.

## Inflation

Greg Anthony writes that "one of the Biblical signs of a nation backsliding is the condition of its currency and the degree of honesty in its weights and measures. When nations began backsliding in history, dross (common-based metal) began to appear in their coinage."[28] In rebuking Israel from turning from God, Isaiah points out how "your silver has become dross" (Isa. 1:22).

To many people today, inflation means an increase in prices. This, however, is simply the symptom of the national government increasing the money supply to pay for their budget deficits. When the money supply is increased, either through printing more money or credit-expansion, the purchasing power of each dollar falls, and businesses must increase the prices they charge to keep up with their own higher costs.

Anthony says, "the only one to benefit from inflation is the first one to spend money, (i.e. the government). It is a hidden form of tyrannical taxation because as the government spends more and more money created from thin air, the purchasing power of the citizen's bank account goes down and down. Inflation is theft! Remember the Bible declares, 'thou shalt not steal' (Ex. 20:15). If a private citizen decides to set up a printing press and make some money, he is called a criminal (counterfeiting); if the government does the same thing it is called 'monetizing the debt' or 'stimulating the economy'. What is the difference?"[29]

**Inflation** discourages savings by promoting a "spend now" attitude. It encourages debt, deceives people about pay increases and future wealth accumulations, is a hidden theft tax, and decreases capital available for investment.

**To get rid of inflation we should** abolish the central bank (Federal Reserve), repeal all tender laws, and return to a gold warehouse receipt standard. In addition, we must also end fractional reserve banking.

## Basics of Banking

Banks were places for the safe keeping of money. People who used this service paid a fee for it. Gradually, banks began to act not only as warehouses to store money, but as intermediaries between savers who were willing to lend, and other who wanted to borrow. Banks could only loan out what they had in reserve. If a bank was lending your money for you, you could not get it back until the borrower repaid it. You earned interest for your investment.

Today, American banks, international banks, and most banks in other nations have a fractional reserve banking system. Banks only need to keep a small percentage of "cash" in their vaults (around

10%), and can loan the rest. This is inflationary because "money" is created through the loaning process.

### 4. Private Property (Private Enterprise)

A person's property is whatever he has exclusive right to possess and control. Property is first internal. A person's conscience is his most precious aspect of property because it tells him what is right and wrong in his actions. Each person in a free government must be a good steward of his conscience and keep it clear. By doing so, he will know what is right and wrong from within and, therefore, he will be able to live his life in a right manner.

How one takes care of his internal property will determine how he takes care of his external property. The following chart reveals various aspects of internal and external property:

| Internal Property | External Property |
| --- | --- |
| Thoughts | Land/Estate |
| Opinions | Money |
| Talents | Freedom of Speech |
| Conscience | Freedom of Assembly |
| Ideas | Bodily Health |
| Mind | Possessions |
| Affections | Freedom of Worship |

Governments exist to protect property of every sort, most importantly, liberty of conscience. Tyrannical governments will usually invade rights of conscience before invading external property rights. The power that can invade liberty of conscience can also usurp civil liberty. Internal property rights must, therefore, be guarded at all costs, for as they are diminished, every inalienable right of man is jeopardized.

Private property rights are a basic necessity for any society that desires to be free and prosperous. Noah Webster wrote:

"The liberty of the press, trial by jury, the Habeas Corpus writ, even Magna Charta itself, though justly deemed the palladia of freedom, are all inferior considerations, when compared with a general distribution of real property among every class of people...Let the people have property and they will have power - - a power that will forever be exerted to prevent a restriction of the press, and abolition of trial by jury, or the abridgement of any other privilege. The liberties of America, therefore, and her forms of government, stand on the broadest basis."[30]

A Christian nation will "let the people have property" and hence power.

The famous British political scientist, John Locke, wrote in his treatise *Of Civil Government:*

"For Men being the Workmanship of one Omnipotent, and infinitely wise Maker: All the Servants of one Sovereign Master, sent into the World by His Order, and about His Business, they are His Property, whose Workmanship they are, made to last during His, not one anothers Pleasure..."[31]

Locke goes on to state that while we are God's property, God has given us the responsibility to be good stewards over our persons. He wrote that "every man has a Property in his own Person."[32] It follows we have a God-given right to everything necessary to preserve our persons, to internal and external property.

Before any property can be taken from us, we must give our consent. If our property can be taken without our consent, then we really have no property. This is why any taxes imposed by a government on its citizens must be done by elected representatives. We give our consent to taxes or laws affecting our property rights through our representatives. If they do not represent our views, we should work to replace them in a lawful manner.

A people standing on the principle of property will take action to prohibit government or other citizens from taking anyone's personal property without their consent, or from violating anyone's conscience and rights. Lack of this principle in the lives of citizens will lead to unjust taxation, a government controlled economy, and usurpation of both internal and external property rights.

### 5. *Local Business (Local Enterprise)*

Economic growth occurs as small businesses (that may grow into large businesses) are started locally by responsible individuals who have prepared themselves -- people who do not depend on someone else to employ them, but who save their money, get an idea for serving others, become self-employed, win customers, and then employ others. This is how new jobs are created. This is how our economy grows.

Christian education will produce such knowledgeable and motivated individuals in our nation. These people will not look to the government to create jobs but will be entrepreneurs and assume that responsibility themselves.

### 6. *Voluntary Union (Free Market)*

A voluntary working together of all peoples and regions of a nation will encourage economic growth. This would prohibit any tariff barriers within a nation and create a nationwide "common market." This would allow each person in each region or district of a nation to do what he could do best (and working with the natural resources in his locality), and exchange it for the production of others, using honest money as the medium of exchange. Each person is free to sell or not to sell at whatever price they want to offer, but they cannot force anyone to buy. Exchange of goods and services is voluntary and will occur as all involved believe they benefit from the exchange.

The prices of goods and services will be determined by "supply and demand." In a free market the supply of goods and services will balance out the demand for those goods and services at a price buyers are willing to buy and sellers are willing to sell. The greater the supply of any particular kind of good or service, the more the price will tend to go down. The greater the demand for any kind of good or service, the more the price will tend to go up.

## The Road Bed: A Christian Constitutional Form of Government (Constitutional/Lawful Enterprise)

A civil government built on Biblical principles provides the road on which the wheel of economic progress can turn with great efficiency. Such a government, rooted in the Law and the Gospel and based on the Christian idea of man and government will assist economic progress by providing an environment of freedom with order in which production and exchange can flourish, protecting private property, punishing theft and fraud, and not providing for the people's economic needs.

Such a government will be "limited in its functions and cost -- to have just enough power to guard the citizen's rights, but not the power to interfere with honest economic activities."[33]

### The Constitution and Money

Most of the powers of Congress, according to the Constitution, deal either with money or the military. Our Constitution declared in Article 1, Section 8, Paragraph 1, that all taxation would "be uniform throughout the United States," yet today we have a graduated income tax system, not uniform at all. Those who labor more diligently so as to earn more money are penalized by a higher tax bracket. Congress was given power to borrow money, but our Founders believed it should be as sparingly as possible. Jefferson said: "We shall all consider ourselves unauthorized to saddle posterity with our debts, and morally bound to pay them ourselves." Deficit spending and graduated taxation were virtually unheard of until the passage of the

16th Amendment establishing a federal income tax in 1913. Income taxes began to be automatically withheld from wages by employers in 1943. Over the years our taxes have grown dramatically, where the total tax rate today averages over 40% of each individual's income.

Congress refuses to balance its budget as a routine practice. There has been only one budget balanced in the last 27 years. How do they get away with what every state government and private business and individual would be put in jail for? The answer is that they just print up more money!

The Constitution says in Article 1, Section 8, paragraph 5 that Congress only has power "to coin money." This means that they are not allowed to print paper money. In James Madison's notes of the Constitutional Convention he says that originally the delegates considered allowing the Congress to "emit bills of credit" (or paper money), but Madison records that the phrase was struck out in order "to shut and bar the door against paper money." Later in Section 10, Paragraph 1, it states that only "gold and silver coin" would be legal "tender in payment of debts." Andrew Jackson said: "It is apparent from the whole context of the Constitution as well as the history of the time which gave birth to it, that it was the purpose of the Convention to establish a currency consisting of the precious metals."[34]

For about 80 years we had just that. But during the emergency of the Civil War, we began using paper money and never stopped. At least it was redeemable in gold or silver upon demand until 1933 when Franklin Delano Roosevelt used economic "emergency" powers to abolish the gold standard. Then, in 1968, the silver standard was suspended and our currency became completely unredeemable-- merely "fiat" money. Now every time Congress wishes to pay off some of its excessive spending, instead of facing the public with higher taxes, it simply orders more money to be printed and then borrows it. When this happens everyone's money is automatically devalued in its purchasing power. It is a hidden tax; a form of theft.

*Andrew Jackson*

## Taxation

"Render unto Caesar the things that are Caesar's and unto God the things that are God's."

Civil governments need money to accomplish their responsibilities of providing defense, punishing evildoers, and keeping the peace, Gary DeMar writes:

"In the United States the Constitution is our 'Caesar.' We are bound to pay what it stipulates is our due. But, neither citizens nor civil representatives must assume that Jesus gave rulers a blank check in the area of taxation...Paul informs citizens to pay taxes due to civil authorities (Romans 13:7). Notice that Paul does not say 'What they want.' The state must limit taxing authority to those areas specified by God's word. For the most part, our original Federal Constitution (prior to the 1913 passage of the 16th Amendment) has been faithful to the biblical mandate of limited taxation for a specific limited function...The tax limiting effects of the Constitution (Article I, Section 8), seemingly were nullified with the passage of the 16th Amendment in 1913. This amendment effectively gave the Federal Government unlimited taxing power."[35]

This amendment also gave us the progressive income tax, which is an nonbiblical means of taxation that destroys personal property rights. These oppressive forms of taxation have come upon our nation as we have refused to govern and provide for ourselves as God intended us to. When Israel stopped wanting to be self-governed and asked for a king to rule over them, they got a king with greater centralization of power. One consequence of this was the confiscation of their property through taxes (see 1 Samuel 8).

### Types of Taxes

**1. Income tax** - "Another word for taxes is tribute. If God requires only 10% (tithe), to give civil government more would indicate the giving of greater allegiance. This is idolatry."[36]

**2. Property tax** - "Civil government in the United States, in direct violation of biblical law, owns all the land in the country, and rents some of it to its citizens. If you do not pay the property tax (rent), you will be evicted. This is theft: The government has no right whatsoever to tax property, and the principle of eminent domain is a claim to deity. It is specifically forbidden in Scripture (I Sam. 8:14; I Kings 21; Ezk. 46:18)."[37]

**3. Inheritance taxes** - "Nowhere does the Bible allow the fruit of a man's labor to be taken from him after he dies and before his children receive it. This is one way that the kingdom is continued and built. Godly children should not have to start at the bottom when they begin. This increases the wealth in the kingdom of God."[38]

In a Christian economy the children will be wealthier than their parents because the estate will continue to grow and be built up with each generation.

### Biblical Taxes

The Bible mentions two kinds of taxes:

**1. Head Tax or Poll Tax (Ex. 30:11-16)** -- This tax supported the state in it's duties. It was an uniform tax that each male over 20 paid. It was of necessity small so the poor would not be oppressed in paying it.

**2. Tithe** -- A tenth of each person's increase was given to the priests and Levites for them to meet the necessary ecclesiastical and social functions of society. It supports the church and aspects of welfare, education, and other godly social needs. We could say the tithe is a "tax" on people's income. If citizens would tithe, the amount of money the civil government would need to collect would be drastically less.

*Hugo Grotius (1583-1645) was a Dutch lawyer, theologian, statesman, and poet who wrote <u>The Rights of War and Peace</u> in 1625. James Madison called him "the father of the modern code of nations." He, along with the German thinkers Pufendorf and Vattel, developed the concept of a God-given "Law of Nations" that is mentioned in Article 1, Section 8 of the Constitution.*

---

# Chapter 15

---

# Christian Principles of Foreign Affairs

### Freedom and Peace through Strength

The example of Israel, as well as nations throughout history, reveal that a nation can only have liberty and peace through strength. America's Founders agreed. They recognized that a free and prosperous society would face continual threats from outside forces who were no friends of liberty. Consequently, to secure their liberty and peace, the United States Constitution empowered the Congress to "provide for the common Defense [and] promote the general Welfare... [of] the United States."

Consider the following quotes of some of the Founders of America:

### George Washington

"There is a rank due to the United States among nations, which will be withheld, if not absolutely lost, by the reputation of weakness. If we desire to avoid insult, we must be able to repel it; if we desire peace... it must be known that we are at all times ready for war."

"To be prepared for war is one of the most effectual means of preserving peace."[1]

### Benjamin Franklin

"Let us... beware of being lulled into a dangerous security...of neglect in military exercises and discipline, and in providing stores of arms and munitions of war to be ready on occasion; for all these are circumstances that give confidence to enemies, and diffidence to friends; and the expenses required to prevent a war are much lighter than those that will, if not prevented, be absolutely necessary to maintain it."

"...There is much truth in the Italian saying, 'make yourselves sheep and the wolves will eat you.'"[2]

### Thomas Jefferson

"Whatever enables us to go to war, secures our peace."[3]

## A Christian Foreign Policy

A Christian nation should relate to foreign nations in much the same way a Christian should relate to an unbeliever. We are to be peacemakers, mercy-givers, teachers, and defenders of the helpless and the oppressed. We should not try to impose our will upon other nations, but we should sow the truth within the heart of the people in a nation, knowing that this internal change will affect the public affairs of a nation.

### Washington's Farewell Address

In George Washington's *Farewell Address* in 1796, he set forth some basic principles of a proper foreign policy. These include:

### 1. Cultivate peace with all nations and maintain impartiality

"Observe good faith and justice towards all nations; cultivate peace and harmony with all. Religion and morality enjoin this conduct....It will be worthy of a free, enlightened, and...great nation to give to mankind the...novel example of a people always guided by an exalted justice and benevolence....

"Harmony, liberal intercourse with all nations, are recommended by policy, humanity, and interest."

"In the execution of such a plan nothing is more essential than that permanent, inveterate antipathies against particular nations, and passionate attachments for others, should be excluded; and that, in place of them, just and amicable feelings towards all should be cultivated. The nation which indulges towards another an habitual hatred, or an habitual fondness, is in some degree a slave. It is a slave to its animosity or to its affection, either of which is sufficient to lead it astray from its duty and its interest. Antipathy in one nation against another disposes each more readily to offer insult and injury, to lay hold of slight causes of umbrage, and to be haughty and intractable, when accidental or trifling occasions of dispute occur. Hence, frequent collisions, obstinate, envenomed and bloody contests. The nation, prompted by ill will and resentment, sometimes impels to war the government, contrary to the best calculations of policy. The government sometimes participates in the national propensity, and adopts through passion what reason would reject; at other times, it makes the animosity of the nation subservient to projects of hostility instigated by pride, ambition, and other sinister and pernicious motives. The peace often, sometimes perhaps the liberty, of nations has been the victim.

"So, likewise, a passionate attachment of one nation for another produces a variety of evils. Sympathy for the favorite nation, facilitating the illusion of an imaginary common interest, in cases where no real common interest exists, and infusing into one the enmities of the other, betrays the former into a participation in the quarrels and wars of the latter without adequate inducement or justification. It leads, also, to concessions to the favorite nation of privileges denied to others, which is apt doubly to injure the nation making the concessions; by unnecessarily parting with what ought to have been retained; and by exciting jealousy, ill will, and a disposition to retaliate in the parties from whom equal privileges are withheld."

*Washington stressed impartiality in relating to other nations.*

### 2. With trading, keep political connections to a minimum.

"The great rule of conduct for us, in regard to foreign nations, is, in extending our commercial relations, to have with them as little political connections as possible.... But, even our commercial policy should hold an equal and impartial hand; neither seeking nor granting exclusive favors or preferences; consulting the natural course of things...constantly keeping in view, that it is folly in one nation to look for disinterested favors from another; that it must pay with a portion of its independence for whatever it may accept under that character..."

It should be left entirely to the private sector to decide who to trade with, not the government. However, if our national security is threatened, trade can and should be limited.

### 3. No long-term entangling alliances.

> "It is our true policy to steer clear of permanent alliances with any portion of the foreign world.... taking care always to keep ourselves by suitable establishments, on a respectable defensive posture, we may safely trust to temporary alliances for extraordinary emergencies."

Gary North defines these "permanent alliances" that Washington warned against as "the creation of international treaties that would bind together the United States and other nations to perform certain military actions under specified future circumstances."[4] The U.S. did not enter into such a treaty until well into the twentieth century.

The main points were summarized by **Jefferson** in his First Inaugural Address:

> "Peace, Commerce, and Honest Friendship with all nations, entangling alliances with none."

America's impartiality toward all nations and her non-engagement in long-term entangling alliances would allow her to be an example to other nations and in this way positively affect them. If we treat nations equally, and not act as the policemen of the world, then they will more readily seek our advice and judgement, allowing us to sow Christian truth within them.

*Thomas Jefferson*

## The Monroe Doctrine

America's foreign policy was further defined by James Monroe in 1823. In a message delivered to Congress on December 2 Monroe stated:

> "...The American continents by the free and independent condition which they have assumed and maintain, are henceforth not to be considered as subjects for future colonization by any European powers...The political system of the allied powers is essentially different...from that of America...We owe it, therefore, to candor and to the amicable relations existing between the United States and those powers to declare that we should consider any attempt...to extend their system to any portion of this hemisphere as dangerous to our peace and safety. With the existing colonies or dependencies of any European power we have not interfered and shall not interfere. But with the Governments who have declared their independence...we could not view any interposition for the purpose of oppressing them...by any European power in any other light than as the manifestation of an unfriendly disposition toward the United States."

*James Monroe*

## Intervention Should Be Based on Just Principles

The cause of those nations which seek intervention by us should be based on just principles (on the Christian idea of man and government). We must realize that no nation perfectly adheres to these principles, but that should be the desire.

Therefore, the basis for one nation becoming involved in the affairs of another nation includes: 1) Legitimate officials ask for help. 2) A nation's own security is threatened by action in another. 3) Their cause is based on just principles. If it is determined that it is legitimate to give assistance, then the type of aid must be decided, whether money, goods, weapons, troops, etc.

## Perversion of Our Foreign Policy in the Twentieth Century

Until this century, we largely maintained a foreign policy based on the above principles, but we began to act on other ideas beginning this century. Formerly, we were respected in the eyes of the whole world. However, since we have compromised these principles, we are found supporting oppressive regimes and have lost much respect.

Congress wisely rejected Woodrow Wilson's treaty setting up a League of Nations in 1919, but capitulated to the U.N. Charter after World War II. We thus entered into a long-term entangling alliance that George Washington warned against.

The President of the United States is not only our Commander-in-Chief, but also our Chief Diplomat. He establishes foreign policy and proposes treaties, but they must be approved by the Senate. However, in 1945 F.D.R. negotiated a secret treaty at Yalta with Churchill and Stalin that was never submitted to Congress. In it we consented to allow the Soviet Union to take control of Eastern Europe and enslave millions of people under the yoke of communism.

## The Law of Nations

Nations cannot do whatever they want to, even if their law permits it. Everyone is subject to the higher law of God, and as a Christian nation we must not allow other nations to violate our God-given rights.

The United States Constitution gives Congress the right "to declare war" and "to define and punish Piracies and Felonies committed on the high Seas, and Offences against the Law of Nations."

John Eidsmoe writes:

"The United States established war tribunals to bring foreign officials to trial for atrocities committed in violation of the Law of Nations or international law, based on this clause of the Constitution. The fact that such officials could be held to a higher standard of conduct and that simple 'obedience to orders' was not considered an absolute defense to charges of violating international law, indicates further recognition that the laws of man are subject to the law of God."[5]

## *A Christian nation will be an exporter of Christian ideas.*

Marshall Foster writes of how the United States as a Christian nation should relate to other nations:

"As we repair our nation and put it in order, we shall then be in a position to do what we were meant to do originally -- to 'colonize ideas,' specifically, the Christian idea of man and government so that it does not stop on these shores, but goes on to cover the globe. Our historians used to believe that it was part of our mission to colonize America's unique political ideas, but as we have forgotten what our Founding Fathers achieved -- forgotten the source of our freedom and affluence -- we have failed to do this.

"This does not mean that we can export our structure and system of government to other countries and expect it to make sense to them without an understanding of the Christian principles of self-government that underlie the structure. We have learned that self-government begins first with the individual aligning himself with the will of God, then caring for himself and others and applying biblical principles to all areas of his life until he produces a civil government that reflects his godly self-government. All merely external forms of democratic structure which we may attempt to promote in other lands are doomed to failure and will inevitably bring cries of 'American imperialism' or cries of an attempt to exercise external control over other nations.

"Attempts to throw money at the acute problems in Africa and Latin America, when there is little understanding of Christian self-government in these lands, is a tragic waste of resources. If a fraction of the resources now spent on military hardware was spent on colonizing the ideas of our Founders, a proper foundation would be laid for the development of liberty and self-government in these lands.

"The communists know the values of ideas and have for years been colonizing theirs which lead only to chaos and bondage. On the other hand, our political ideas, under the Providence of God, have achieved more civil and religious liberty and more self-government and genuine prosperity than the world has ever known before."[6]

***Missionaries and Christian businessmen should be the ambassadors of Christian nations.***

In his article on *Can We Make a Deal for Peace?*, Lee Grady writes:

"To the humanist, peace is really pacifism. My dictionary accurately defines pacifism as 'opposition to war or to the use of military force for any purpose; an attitude of mind opposing all war and advocating settlement of international disputes entirely by arbitration.' I agree with Dean London of New York University: people majoring in the current 'Peace studies' programs in U.S. colleges should be called pacifism majors. No professor in any of these universities is offering any way to achieve peace according to the true definition.

"Gary North, in *Healer of the Nations*, powerfully refutes this notion by reminding us of the history of U.S. foreign policy. When the Department of State was created in 1789 by President Washington, the staff consisted of six persons. In 1870, slightly less that 100 years later, the entire personnel consisted of only 53 persons -- in spite of the great expansion of our borders and growth in population. By 1909 it grew to 202 persons, and rapid expansion ensued after the World Wars. By 1980, the figure had climbed to 23,497. This included over 3,500 Foreign Service Officers, the elite corps of specialists who staff our embassies and consulates.

"How, you may ask, could the U.S. function as a world power with such a tiny State Department for so many years of its history? Who was conducting the summits? Who was drawing up the treaties and doing all the research? Who was hammering out the peace plans?

"Answer: No one. The United States had made one treaty with France in 1778, which it abrogated in 1800. We made absolutely no entangling alliances with any nations during the 19th century. Dexter Perkins, a specialist in U.S. foreign policy, writes in his History of the Monroe Doctrine that 'nothing is more characteristic of American diplomacy than its general aversion to contractual agreements.' On the contrary, nothing could be more characteristic of our present foreign policy than our infatuation over contractual agreements, as well as summits, treaties, alliances, pacts, and deals between world powers. We also have a recent fixation over meddling in disagreements between other nations.

"Gary North writes: 'This centralization came at the expense of private activities and responsibilities. In the field of international relations, no one before this era had perceived a need for the United States government to send official representatives to every nation or to seek alliances, agreements, and arrangements with every nation. People assumed that private interests would be the basis of the vast bulk of international relations.'

"This is the heart of the problem in foreign policy, according to Dr. North. 'Voters in the West have passively turned over the conduct of foreign policy to professional diplomats.' Now, you may ask: If professional diplomats aren't supposed to be conducting foreign policy, then who is? That brings us to Dr. North's most important theme in his book.

"Practically, foreign policy in this Christian world order will be conducted by missionaries and members of the Christian business and trade community who know how to represent the cause of Christ abroad. Their business as ambassadors of Christ is not to work out terms of compromise; it is to persuade men and governments to surrender to the government of Christ."[7]

Take the example of American businesses in South Africa: they were one of the greatest influences in ending apartheid in that country through their business policies and employment practices. When many began leaving that country for various unfounded reasons, change slowed to a minimum. They no longer exerted their positive influence. (Their leaving also financially hurt those they wished to help.)

Lee Grady continues:

"The prophet Isaiah spoke of a progressive, worldwide surrender to the gospel when he wrote: 'The law will go forth from Zion... and He [God] will judge between the nations, and will render decisions for many peoples; and they will hammer their swords into plowshares, and their spears into pruning hooks. Nation will not lift up sword against nation, and never again will they learn war'(Isaiah 2:4).

"It is important to note that the act of transforming swords into plowshares takes place after the peoples of the earth voluntarily confess, 'Come and let us go unto the mountain of the Lord, that He may teach us His ways' (v. 3). God is waiting for knees to bow in submission before He resolves international conflict. That is His condition for peace.

"North summarizes this idea: 'There can never be peace in history outside of Christ. There can be temporary cease-fire agreements, but never a lasting peace. What Christians must understand is that peace is attained through the preaching of the gospel and the discipling of the nations. There is no other way. God will not permit peace on any other terms.'"[8]

224

# Chapter 16

# The War for the Union

Every American ought to master three basic documents: The Declaration of Independence, The Constitution, and George Washington's Farewell Address. When our eminent first President was leaving office in 1796, he delivered one of the most insightful orations in history. He already perceived some trends in the national life that were dangerous to our union. This was heavy upon his heart. He writes:

"...You should properly estimate the immense value of your national Union to your collective and individual happiness;... indignantly frowning upon the first dawning of every attempt to alienate any portion of our country from the rest. ...Your Union ought to be considered as a main prop of your liberty, and the love of one ought to endear to you the preservation of the other."

Washington then begins to identify some things which may "disturb our Union":

## (1) The Spirit of Party

"...Men may endeavor to excite a belief, that there is a real difference of local interests and views. One of the expedients of party [in order] to acquire influence within particular districts is to misrepresent the opinions and aims of other districts;...The alternate dominion of one faction over another, sharpened by the spirit of revenge ...will gradually incline the minds of men to seek security and repose in the absolute power of an individual;...(also) it opens the door to foreign influence and corruption, which find a facilitated access to the government itself through the channels of party passions."

## (2) The Spirit of Encroachment

*Confederate Troops*

Washington urged each branch or individual official to ..."confine themselves within their respective constitutional spheres, avoiding in the exercise of the powers of one department to encroach upon another. The spirit of encroachment tends to consolidate the powers of all the departments in one, and this to create, whatever the form of government, a real despotism;...Let there be no change by usurpation; for, though this, in one instance, may be the instrument of good, it is the customary weapon by which free governments are destroyed."[1]

Washington then goes on to emphasize the real protection against these dangers: Religion, morality and knowledge. In other words, the "letter" of the Constitution will never work perfectly if the "spirit" of the Constitution departs. It doesn't work for a people without Christian character.

In this light we can begin to understand the events leading to the *War Between the States*.

## The Issue of Slavery

At the founding of our country, every one of our Founding Fathers believed that involuntary slavery was an evil institution that needed to be abolished. But slavery had been around since time began; present in every nation in history, thus they believed such an entrenched social problem must be overcome gradually. Many of them had slaves and yet were leaders in antislavery organizations which were working to educate and prepare them for independence, and change the laws.

During the drafting of the Declaration of Independence in 1776 Jefferson wanted to condemn slavery outright, but many others thought it potentially too divisive to deal with while they were trying to present a united front. They also avoided it in their Articles of Confederation in 1777. Ten years later, however, during the Constitutional Convention, they began to deal with it.

The Constitution did not completely abolish slavery but it did make two major steps forward: (1) The southern states agreed to acknowledge that blacks were persons in the eyes of the law for the first time. Although they only were counted as 3/5's of a person, it was a major concession nonetheless, (2) The southern states also agreed to abolish the slave trade nationally by 1808. The north wanted it immediately, but the economics of the southern states were too dependent upon it, and so they begged for time. The northern states actually had the votes to abolish it immediately but Georgia and South Carolina threatened to pull out of the union completely if that was required. George Mason, a Christian statesman from Virginia rose and sternly warned his follow delegates:

"Every master of slaves is born a petty tyrant. They bring the judgement of heaven upon a country. As nations cannot be rewarded or punished in the next world, they must be in this. By an inevitable chain of causes and effects, Providence punishes national sins by national calamities."[2]

## National Sins

Our Founders went further, and that same year passed the Northwest Ordinance, which prohibited slavery in the new states. In 1788, they abolished slave trade between states. All intentions of that generation were united in their goal to abolish slavery. God wanted to show the world how a Christian nation would deal with such a major social problem. England abolished slavery in a lawful, peaceful manner in 1834, but America failed to deal with slavery as God had intended. One reason for this failure was greed.

In 1783, Eli Whitney invented the cotton gin. This made profits even greater if one had slaves. Thus, as a new generation of Americans arose with less convictions on the matter than their fathers, we began to compromise. The trend towards emancipation came to a halt in the South, and even churches began to justify slavery for the first time around 1810. By then all slave trading had been made illegal, yet slave owning became more entrenched.

Southern statesmen arose who began to argue that each state was free to decide if it wanted to allow slavery or not. They appealed to the fact that our Founders left it this way in the Constitution, yet by so doing, they were holding to the "letter" of the law, but rejecting the "spirit" or intentions behind it. This principle of self-government (or states' rights or popular sovereignty) was championed eloquently by John C. Calhoun in the U.S. Senate in the 1840's. His arguments by the "letter" were absolutely right and often unanswerable, yet were being used to defend something wrong.

A number of years later in 1858, a popular candidate, Stephen O. Douglas was speaking for 'popular sovereignty' in his debates with Abraham Lincoln. Lincoln agreed that his opponent's doctrine was "absolutely and eternally right. But it has no just application as here attempted... whether a negro is not or is a man". He said when self-government is used to oppress another man then it is "despotism".

"Slavery is wrong," Lincoln stated, "and ought to be dealt with as wrong".[3]

The anti-slavery movement became well-organized in 1834 with one-third of its leaders being clergyman. Daniel Dorchester writes:

*"Slavery is wrong and ought to be dealt with as wrong."*
*-Abraham Lincoln*

"The prime impulse [of the anti-slavery movement] was Christian and... many eminent divines acted... the leading part in the abolition movement. The first anti-slavery convention stated:

"'We also maintain that there are at the present time the highest obligations resting upon the people of the free states to remove slavery by moral and political action, as prescribed in the Constitution of the U.S.

"'These are our views and principles--these our designs and measures. With entire confidence in the overruling justice of God, we plant ourselves upon the Declaration of Independence and the truths of divine revelation as upon the everlasting rock.

"'We shall organize anti-slavery societies, if possible, in every city, town and village in our land.

"'We shall send forth agents to lift up the voice of remonstrance, of warning, of entreaty and rebuke.

"'We shall circulate unsparingly and extensively anti-slavery tracts and periodicals.

"'We shall enlist the pulpit and the press in the cause of the suffering and the dumb.

"'We shall aim at a purification of the churches from all participation in the guilt of slavery.

"'We shall encourage the labor of freemen over that of the slaves by giving a preference to their productions...

"'We shall spare no exertions nor means to bring the whole nation to speed repentance...'"[4]

These evangelical "abolition societies", (as opposed to some which were anti-religious and anti-constitutional) eventually helped birth the Republican party in 1854.

As new states were entering the Union, there was a great struggle over which ones would allow slavery or forbid it. Senator Henry Clay of Kentucky was a great Christian statesman who worked to preserve our union by compromise. The Congress determined that all states south of a certain line could have slavery, but those north of it could not. This measure was overturned, however, in 1857, when the Supreme Court declared that blacks were not persons, but mere "property". The Court said the Constitutional right to property made it illegal for any state to forbid slavery. Abraham Lincoln criticized this decision as fundamentally wrong.

John Brown had been working for years against slavery by politics, but after the Court's Dred Scott decision he felt that the issue could never be resolved by mere legal action. He, therefore, devised a plan of flight for the slaves, which, if it succeeded, would "destroy the money-value of slave property" by rendering it insecure in the eyes of slaveholders. His plan was to use the Appalachian mountain range (running through most of the slave states) as his base of operations from which five man squads would go down to the fields and induce the slaves to flee with them to the mountains.

He never planned an insurrection and slaughter of slave masters, but he did plan to supply the runaway slaves with arms and ammunition in case they needed to defend themselves in the mountains from attack.

His plans, however, without sanction of any legitimate civil authorities were illegitimate, and quickly turned lawless. He was cap-

*John Brown after his capture.*

tured at Harper's Ferry and eventually hung for treason and murder. He was trying to do a good thing, but in an unbiblical way. Before his death he stated:

> "I have no regret for the transaction for which I am condemned. I went against the laws of men, it is true, but 'whether it be right to obey God or men, judge ye.' Christ told me to remember them that were in bonds as bound with them, to do toward them as I would wish them to do towards me in similar circumstances. My conscience bade me do that. I tried to do it, but failed."

> "I, John Brown, am now quite certain that the crimes of this guilty land will never be purged away but with blood. I had, as I now think vainly, flattered myself that without very much bloodshed it might be done."[5]

*Daniel Webster*

## The Principle of Union

As the principle of self-government was being championed by Calhoun, the principle of Union was articulated best by Daniel Webster. The speeches of Webster, Clay and Calhoun -- all Christian statesmen -- took place in the "golden-era" of the Congress.

We pointed out earlier that self-government and Union are two principles which must be kept in tension or balance such as was established by our Founders or there results either centralism or disintegration. Though the Civil War focused on the issue of slavery, the principle at stake was Union. Our founders had rejected the loose-knit Confederation for a permanent Federation when they drafted the Constitution. This is likened to a marriage covenant - if there are problems, you must patiently work through it, divorce is not an option.

*Henry Clay*

We cannot break our Federal union for any reason (as long as there are Constitutional avenues for redress), thus secession of the Southern states over slavery became legitimate grounds for President Lincoln to go to war. It would be inaccurate to think that the North was more godly or Christian than the south. In reality, the South had become the center of true revival and the bastion of Calvinism and Christian character, while the North had drifted into Unitarianism and dead formalism.

## The Almighty Has His Own Purpose

*John C. Calhoun*

The Civil War is unique in all history. America was a Christian nation in both north and south but it had compromised in dealing with slavery. God could not allow it to continue and hinder his long-term

230

destiny on America in the eyes of the world. He used the war to judge us and yet deliver us at the same time.

A history of the individuals involved, however, is intriguing, for some of the greatest Christian generals and statesmen existed on both sides. Abraham Lincoln described it best in his Second Inaugural Address:

"Both read the same Bible and pray to the same God, and each invokes His aid against the other. It may seem strange that any men should dare to ask a just God's assistance in wringing their

*General Stonewall Jackson and his men at prayer.*

bread from the sweat of other men's faces, but let us judge not that we be not judged. The prayer of both could not be answered. That of neither has been answered fully. The almighty has His own purposes. Woe unto the world because of offences, for it must needs be that offences come, but woe to that man by whom the offence cometh. If we shall suppose that American slavery is one of those offences which, in the providence of God, must needs come, but which having continued through His appointed time, He now wills to remove, and that He gives to both North and South this terrible war as the woe due to those by whom the offence came, shall we discern there any departure from those divine attributes which the believers in a living God always ascribe to Him? Fondly do we hope, fervently do we pray, that this mighty scourge of war may speedily pass away. Yet if God wills that it continue until all the wealth piled by the bondsman's two hundred and fifty years of unrequited toil shall be sunk, and until every drop of blood drawn with the lash shall be paid by another drawn with the sword, as was said three thousand years ago, so still it must be said, that the judgements of the Lord are true and righteous altogether."[6]

God accomplished two things in this time period: He eradicated slavery and preserved the union. How He did it is fascinating.

When Lincoln was elected President he never intended to emancipate the slaves. In fact, he could not legally, but he did eventually under the authority of emergency war powers. But he did not do so until 1863, motivated by the North losing almost every major battle. Lincoln wrote shortly before his assassination:

"On many a defeated field there was a voice louder than the thundering of a cannon. It was the voice of God, crying, 'Let My people go'. We were all very slow in realizing it was God's voice, but after many humiliating defeats the nation came to believe it as a great and solemn command. Great multitudes begged and prayed that I might answer God's voice by signing the Emancipation Proclamation, and I did it, believing we never should be successful in the great struggle unless the God of Battles has been on our side."[7]

Between 1861 and 1863, associations of clergymen representing Methodists, Baptists, Episcopalians, Lutherans, Quakers, Congregationalists, United Brethren, missions boards and YMCA groups, all over the North sent 79 official condemnations of slavery to President Lincoln, thanking him for his stand, and urging him to further action.

Within a few months' time, 125 remonstrances signed by New England clergymen alone poured into Congress. One memorable protest concerning the extension of slavery in the territories, signed by 3050 New England clergymen, was 200 feet long.

Senator Charles Sumner thanked ministers, saying, "In the days of the Revolution, John Adams, yearning for Independence, said, 'Let the pulpits thunder against oppression, and the pulpits thundered. The time has come for them to thunder again.'"[8]

A religious periodical of the day reports:

"It became the general [consensus] that we were passing through an ordeal of purification rather than destruction. A profound moral feeling began to pervade the sorrow-stricken mind of the country. Good men betook themselves to importunate prayer. Public fasts were observed; religious assemblies were held in behalf of the country. Almost every pulpit discussed public affairs from a religious standpoint; . . . and millions of devout men and women mourned in their closets of devotion over the national sins and perils. . .

"The religious spirit of the nation, instead of decaying, is daily making men's hearts more reverent, more humble, more courageous, and more worthy of our first national heritage of liberty, which God is now a second time purifying by fire!"[9]

But it wasn't without cost. An awesome example of God's explicit judgement for all of those who compromise is revealed by the aftermath of the war. One state had its cities and land devastated more than any other: Georgia. For every wound laid on the back of a slave, God used General Sherman to lay a stripe down the middle of the state. Another result of the war was major division in religious bodies. The three denominations who suffered the worst splits were those held the most slaves: the Presbyterians, the Methodists, and the Baptists. Such is the curse of compromise.

Why was the North losing all the battles? Because God induced the greatest generals to fight for the South.

## The Christian Character of the Generals

Robert E. Lee of Virginia was offered command of the Union Army by President Lincoln at the beginning of the war. After much prayer, he declined saying: "I look upon secession as anarchy. If I owned the four millions of slaves in the South, I would sacrifice them all to the Union -- but how can I draw my sword upon Virginia, my native state?"[10]

Lee later accepted the command of the Army of Virginia. This may have not been the best decision, yet it seems that Providence had willed it, so that the two greatest generals would lead the Confederate army to victory until the slaves were emancipated.

In a conversation with a minister shortly after the start of the war, Lee was asked: "Is it your expectation that the issue of this war will be to perpetuate the institution of slavery?" Lee replied: "The future is in the hands of Providence, but if the slaves of the South were mine, I would surrender them all without a struggle to avert the war." The minister then tells us:

> "I asked him next upon what his calculations were based in so unequal a contest, and how he expected to win success; was he looking to divided counsels in the North, or to foreign interposition? His answer showed how little he was affected by the hopes and fears which agitated ordinary minds.
>
> 'My reliance is in the help of God.'
>
> 'Are you sanguine of the result?' I ventured to inquire.
>
> 'At present I am not concerned with results. God's will ought to be our aim, and I am contented that His designs should be accomplished and not mine.'"[11]

*Robert Edward Lee*

Lee did much to promote revival in his army and saw every soldier as a soul to be saved. So concerned was Lee for the spiritual welfare of his soldiers that one of his biographers says, "One almost feels as if he cared more for winning souls than battles, and for supplying his army with Bibles than with bullets and powder."[12]

The same was true of another Christian General, Thomas Jonathan "Stonewall" Jackson. Jackson was one of the best (if not best) military leaders in our nation's history. The confederate troops under his command (for the first few years of the war) obtained victory after victory over the Union Army. In a majority of these battles, the Union forces greatly outnumbered Jackson's men. Jackson's fearlessness in battle earned him the name "Stonewall". Mark Grimsley writes:

"He displayed extraordinary calm under fire, a calm too deep and masterful to be mere pretence. His apparent obliviousness to danger attracted notice, and after First Manassas someone asked him how he managed it.

"'Captain, my religious belief teaches me to feel as safe in battle as in bed,' Jackson explained. 'God has fixed the time for my death. I do not concern myself about that, but to be always ready, no matter when it may overtake me.' He added pointedly, 'Captain that is the way all men should live, and then all would be equally brave.'

"As a field commander, Jackson's religion came into play in various ways. During military operations he prayed frequently, lived simply, and in his reports habitually gave God all credit for the slightest success. 'Without God's blessing,' Jackson declared, 'I look to no success, and for every success my prayer is, that all the glory may be given to Him to whom it is properly due.' Whenever possible he also avoided marching or fighting on the Sabbath.

"Jackson considered his army to be, among other things, an enormous opportunity to further the gospel. In prayer he pleaded with God to 'baptize the whole army with His Holy Spirit.' In practice he worked ceaselessly to sharpen the spiritual devotion of his men. Orders that religious services be conducted frequently found their way into his military correspondence, and although he stopped short of declaring them mandatory, Jackson had a way of seeing to it the services were well-attended. Riding through the camps one Sunday to make sure his men were at worship, Jackson came upon a captain, indolently smoking a pipe. The captain greeted him uneasily. Without returning the 'good morning,' Jackson went straight to the point: 'Captain, is divine service going on in your camp?' 'I don't know, sir.' 'Where is your Colonel's headquarters' The captain pointed them out and inquired, 'Shall I take you to them, sir' 'Yes,' Jackson clipped, and as they neared the headquarters tent, added, 'I see service is going on...Captain, the next time I order divine service, won't you promise me to attend?' The captain made the only safe response -- 'Yes, sir' -- and joined the assemblage.

"During the winter of 1862 and 1863, while the Confederate army bivouacked along the Rappahannock, a religious revival swept the entire command. Jackson, of course, enthusiastic, bent his energies toward facilitating the tide of Christian sentiment that bathed the army. He also strove to better organize the chaplains of the army, arguing they should meet together and

*Jackson pleaded with God to "baptize the whole army with His Holy Spirit."*

'through God's blessing devise successful plans for spiritual conquests.'"[13]

*The Emancipation Proclamation*

While the Confederate Army was enjoying revival (up to 150,000 Southern troops were saved during the war), it also enjoyed phenomenal success in almost every major battle. This induced Abraham Lincoln to seek God for the reasons why. He concluded that the nation's chief sins were slavery and pride. On September 22, 1862, he issued the Emancipation Proclamation which declared all slaves free in states that were still in rebellion as of January 1, 1863. Then he called for a national Day of Humiliation, Fasting and Prayer throughout the North on April 30th of 1863. He stated in part:

"...It is the duty of nations as well as of men to own their dependence upon the overruling power of God; to confess their sins and transgressions in humble sorrow, yet with assured hope that genuine repentance will lead to mercy and pardon; and to recognize the sublime truth, announced in the Holy Scriptures and proven by all history, that those nations only are blessed whose God is the Lord;

"And insomuch as we know that by His divine law nations, like individuals, are subject to punishments and chastisements in this world, may we not justly fear that the awful calamity of civil war which now desolates the land may be but a punishment inflicted upon us for our presumptuous sins, to the needful end of our national reformation as a whole people? We have been the recipients of the choicest bounties of Heaven. We have been preserved these many years in peace and prosperity. We have grown in numbers, wealth, and power as no other nation has ever grown; but we have forgotten God. We have forgotten the gracious hand which preserved us in peace, and multiplied and enriched and strengthened us; and we have vainly imagined, in the deceitfulness of our hearts, that all these blessings were produced by some superior wisdom and virtue of our own. Intoxicated with unbroken success, we have become too self-sufficient to feel the necessity of redeeming and preserving grace, too proud to pray to the God who made us;

"It behooves us, then, to humble ourselves before the offended Power, and confess our national sins, and to pray for clemency and forgiveness."[14]

Interestingly, within two days, one of the most crucial Providential occurrences of the entire war occurred. God had removed the stigma of slavery from this nation and gave Lincoln and others in the North a measure of repentance. Providence now turned to a new objective: preserve the Union of the United States as one whole people. Within just two days of this Day of Prayer, General Stonewall Jackson, who had never lost a battle, was Providentially removed from the scene.

"In an accident of war, Stonewall Jackson was shot by his own men. Anguished staff officers brought him to a battlefield operating table; a surgeon chloroformed him and amputated his left arm.

"Upon learning of Jackson's fate the next morning, General Robert E. Lee lamented, 'He lost his left arm, but I have lost my right.'"[15]

*"Stonewall" Jackson*

Shortly after this on May 10, 1863, Jackson died. However, even in his odd death (previously, Jackson had many times lead his men into battle and exposed himself to enemy fire, yet he remained unharmed, protected, as he believed, by God), he believed God was fulfilling His purposes and causing "all things to work together for good to those that love God." Had God not removed him the outcome of the war may have been different.

Just around the corner was the Battle that marked the turning point of the war -- Gettysburg. This was a major offensive for the South but without Jackson and Providential assistance, they would never succeed. Immediately following the battle, William Johnson records how Union General Sickles asked President Lincoln whether or not he had been anxious about the battle at Gettysburg.

"Lincoln gravely said, "No, I was not; some of my Cabinet and many others in Washington were, but I had no fears." General Sickles inquired how this was, and seemed curious about it. Mr. Lincoln hesitated, but finally replied: "Well, I will tell you how it was. In the pinch of your campaign up there, when everybody seemed panic-stricken, and nobody could tell what was going to happen, oppressed by the gravity of our affairs, I went to my room one day, and I locked the door, and got down on my knees before Almighty God, and prayed to Him mightily for victory at Gettysburg. I told Him that this was His war, and our cause His cause, but we couldn't stand another Fredericksburg or Chancellorsville. And I then and there made a solemn vow to Almighty God, that if He would stand by you boys at Gettysburg, I would

*Pickett's charge at Gettysburg.*

stand by Him. And after that (I don't know how it was, and I can't explain it), soon a sweet comfort crept into my soul that God almighty had taken the whole business into his own hands and that things would go alright at Gettysburg. And that is why I had no fears about you."[16]

As General Lee was retreating from this major defeat, that he probably knew sealed the doom of the Confederacy, an encounter with a wounded Union soldier revealed his great Christian character. The Northern soldier wrote afterwards:

"I had been a most bitter anti-South man, and fought and cursed the Confederates desperately. I could see nothing good in any of them. The last day of the fight I was badly wounded. A ball shattered my left leg. I lay on the ground not far from Cemetery Ridge, and as General Lee ordered his retreat, he and his officers rode near me.

"As they came along I recognized him, and, though faint from exposure and loss of blood, I raised my hands, and looked Lee in the face, and shouted as loud as I could--'Hurrah for the Union!'

"The General heard me, looked, stopped his horse, dismounted, and came toward me. I confessed I at first thought he meant to kill me. But, as he came up, he looked down at me with such a sad expression upon his face that all fear left me, and I wondered what he was about. He extended his hand to me, grasping mine firmly, and looking right into my eyes, said, 'My son, I hope you will soon be well.'

"If I live a thousand years, I shall never forget the expression on General Lee's face. There he was, defeated, retiring from a field that had cost him and his cause almost their last hope, and yet he stopped to say words like these to a wounded soldier of the opposition who had taunted him as he passed by! As soon as the General had left me, I cried myself to sleep there on the bloody ground."[17]

After such a defeat, Lee saw the opportunity to continue to promote revival. General Lee often issued orders for his

*General Robert E. Lee*

239

troops to observe days of fasting and prayer, and attend services. In one such order on Thursday, August 13, 1863, Lee told his army to cry out to God for forgiveness of their sins and humble themselves before Him. He asked God to save their enemies as well as their own troops, and declared that "God is our only refuge and our strength."[18]

Chaplain Jones relates the effect this order had:

"I can never forget the effect produced by the reading of this order at the solemn services of that memorable fast-day. A revival was already in progress in many of the commands -- the day was almost universally observed -- the attendance upon preaching and other services was very large. The solemn attention and starting tear attested the deep interest felt, and the work of grace among the troops widened and deepened and went gloriously on until over fifteen thousand of the soldiers of Lee's army professed repentance toward God and faith in Jesus as a personal Saviour. How far these results were due to this fast-day, or to the quiet influence and fervent prayers of the commanding general, eternity alone shall reveal."[19]

Lee would personally pray with his men:

"While the Army of Northern Virginia confronted General Meade at Mine Run, near the end of November, 1863, and a battle was momentarily expected, General Lee, with a number of general and staff officers, was riding down his line of battle,

*Lee at the soldiers' prayer meeting.*

when...[they] came upon a party of soldiers held on the eve of battle. An attack from the enemy seemed imminent--already the sharpshooting along the skirmishline had begun--the artillery was belching forth its hoarse thunder, and the mind and heart of the great chieftain was full of the expected combat. Yet, as he saw those ragged veterans bowed in prayer, he instantly dismounted, uncovered his head and devoutly joined in the simple worship. The rest of the party at once followed his example, and those humble privates found themselves leading the devotions of their loved and honored chieftain."[20]

On almost the same date in November, Lincoln returned to the field where Gettysburg was fought to dedicate it as a national cemetery. In only four minutes, perhaps the greatest speech in history was delivered:

"Fourscore and seven years ago our fathers brought forth upon this continent a new nation, conceived in liberty, and dedicated to the proposition that all men are created equal. Now we are engaged in a great civil war, testing whether that nation, or any nation so conceived and so dedicated, can long endure. We are met on a great battlefield of that war. We have come to dedicate a portion of that field as a final resting-place for those who here gave their lives that that nation might live. It is altogether fitting and proper that we should do this. But in a larger sense we cannot dedicate, we cannot consecrate, we cannot hallow this ground. The brave men, living and dead, who struggled here, have consecrated it far above our power to add or detract. The world will little note, nor long remember, what we say here, but it can never forget what they did here. It is for us, the living, rather to be dedicated here to the unfinished work which they who fought here have thus far so nobly advanced. It is rather for us to be here dedicated to the great task remaining before us, that from these honored dead we take increased devotion to that cause for which they gave the last full measure of devotion; that we here highly resolve that these dead shall not have died in vain; that this nation, under God, shall have a new birth of freedom, and that the government of the people, by the people, and for the people, shall not perish from the earth."[21]

Shortly before his death an Illinois clergyman asked Lincoln, "Do you love Jesus?" Mr. Lincoln solemnly replied: "When I left Springfield I asked the people to pray for me. I was not a Christian. When I buried my son, the severest trial of my life, I was not a Christian. But when I went to Gettysburg and saw the graves of thousands of our soldiers, I then and there consecrated myself to Christ. Yes, I do love Jesus."[22]

*Lincoln delivering his Gettysburg address. While at Gettysburg Lincoln said, "I then and there consecrated myself to Christ."*

A year and a half later, General Robert E. Lee surrendered to Ulysses S. Grant at Appomattox.

"On the day of the receipt of the news of the capitulation of Lee, the Cabinet meeting was held an hour earlier than usual. Neither the President nor any member was able, for a time, to give utterance to his feelings. At the suggestion of Mr. Lincoln all dropped on their knees, and offered, in silence and in tears, their humble and heartfelt acknowledgments to the Almighty for the triumph He had granted to the national cause."[23]

Later that year, slavery was abolished by Constitutional amendment. Lincoln was assassinated, and Lee became president of what is now Washington and Lee University where men were being trained for the ministry. There he is buried, while thousands of other American soldiers have been buried around his former home which still stands at Arlington National Cemetery.

# Effects of the War Between the States

As we have seen, two Providential results of the war were the abolition of slavery and the preservation of the Union. While these were great benefits, many negative results occurred due to the war and the following decades of the Reconstruction of the South. A summary of these effects follows:

**Positive Aspects of the War**
1. Abolition of Slavery -- Not only was slavery ended in America, but our struggle helped to pave the way for the worldwide eradication of an institution which had plagued the world for thousands of years.
2. Preservation of the Union -- The United States of America remained one nation under God, which would allow her to exert a much stronger positive role in various future events, as well as remain in a more unified position to fulfill her God-given destiny.

**Negatives Aspects of the War**
Due to the sin of the nation, that brought about the War in the first place, and the rise of an ungodly element in America, which exerted a great influence in the Reconstruction Period, a number of negative things followed the War between the States.

After the war an ungodly, radical Republican element gained control of the Congress. They wanted to centralize power and shape the nation according to their philosophy. In order to do this, they had to remove the force of Calvinism in America, which was centered in the South at this time, and rid the South, which was opposed to centralization, of its political power. They used their post-war control of Congress to reconstruct the South, pass the Fourteenth Amendment, and in many ways accomplish their goals. This explains the strong bias against the Republican Party in the South up to recent times.

Another aspect of reconstruction was that the bias against blacks in the South became more bitter and entrenched than ever before.

It has taken over a hundred years for the scars, devastations, and biases to be healed. While these negative effects have in many ways been overcome, the increase in the power of the National Government, which followed the war, has not been abated but continues to grow and reach far beyond it's Constitutional authority.

*Samuel, the prophet/statesman, was an example of God's people being active in public affairs. Like Israel, America's decline began when God's people neglected their political responsibilities.*

# Chapter 17

# The American Apostasy and Decline

## *Finding The Cause of America's Problems*

Only if we correctly identify and diagnose the true cause of America's problems, can we begin to really solve them. Most Christians today place the blame on various conspiracies of men: the humanists, the ACLU, the big bankers, the Trilateral Commission, the New Age Movement, the World Council of Churches, the Homosexuals, the Feminists, the Communists, the Democrats, the Pope, etc. Information regarding such groups and their activities can be useful, yet must never be regarded as the source of our problems. God forbid it in Isaiah 8, verse 12 and 13:

"You are not to say, 'It is a conspiracy!', in regard to all that this people call a conspiracy. And you are not to fear what they fear or be in dread of it. It is the Lord of hosts whom you should regard as holy. And He shall be your fear, and He shall be your dread."

Most Christians today seem to fear these groups more than they do God. This is wrong, for it diminishes the true Biblical understanding that God is Sovereign over the earth. God sees human conspiracies and laughs at them for He knows what He has planned will prevail. This should be our perspective toward conspiracies. Psalm two says:

"Why are the nations in an uproar, and the people devising a vain thing? The kings of the earth take their stand, and the rulers take counsel together against the Lord and against His Anointed: 'Let us tear their fetters apart, and cast away their cords from us!' He who sits in the heavens laughs; the Lord scoffs at them. Then He will speak to them in His anger and terrify them in His furry: 'But as for Me, I have installed My King upon Zion, My holy mountain.' I will surely tell of the decree of the Lord: He said to me, 'Thou art My Son, today I have begotten Thee. Ask of Me, and I will surely give the nations as Thine inheritance...' Now therefore, O kings, show discernment; take warning, O judges of the earth. ...Do homage to the Son, lest He become angry, and you perish in the way..."

This prophecy was, of course, describing the first coming of Christ, when He died, rose again, and was given absolute authority to reign. Just prior to His ascension, Jesus delegated this responsibility and authority to His church. Matthew 28:18-19 says:

"And Jesus came up and spoke to them, saying, 'All authority has been given to Me in heaven and on earth. Go therefore and make disciples of all nations."

## Christians are Responsible

The church has been given authority to shape history. If our nation is in an awful condition, God holds us responsible. In 2 Chronicles 7:14 He says:

"If...My people who are called by My name humble themselves and pray, and seek My face and turn from their wicked ways, then I will hear from heaven, will forgive their sin, and will heal their land."

### The power for healing our land rests with God's people.

America's decline has not occurred because the ideas and leadership of various organizations have overcome Biblical ideas. Rather, it is because we abdicated our responsibility to lead and left a void or vacuum in the public realm that has been surrendered by default. Rosalie Slater says it well:

"For one hundred and fifty years and more, up to the time of our Revolution, the seven years of that long struggle, and through the ratification of our Constitution--even through the perilous years of the French Revolution--we maintained our Christian character as a nation. Then began our period of 'falling away' when we worshipped the 'effect' of our great success--and forgot the 'cause'. This vacuum was readily filled with man-centered philosophies which replaced the internal battles of conscience with the social, economic and political struggles of society.

"Thus we veered from a period when, even our governmental proclamations were filled with the language of salvation and the recognition that Christ alone could change the hearts of men, to a pre-occupation with educational, social, economic, and eventually political arrangements, which claimed to insure progress and improvement for society and hence for man."[1]

*"If...My people...humble themselves and pray..I will heal their land."* 2Chron.7:14

America has repeated the folly of Israel. God warned them of the danger of apostasy once they entered the promised land and began to enjoy prosperity and peace. Within a short time a generation arose in Israel as well as America that was unfaithful to the God and traditions of their freedom in their fathers. They began to neglect the things that produced their freedom in the first place. We lost our virtue and our self-government and became prey to what Samuel Adams called "internal invaders":

"A general Dissolution of Principles and Manners will more surely overthrow the Liberties of America than the whole Force of the Common Enemy. While the People are virtuous they cannot be subdued; but when once they lose their Virtue they will be ready to surrender their Liberties to the first external or internal Invader. . . If Virtue and Knowledge are diffused among the People, they will never be enslaved. This will be their great Security."[2]

*Samuel Adams*

The only way that "tares" can be sown is when the church is "asleep" i.e. neglecting her role in society (Matthew 13:24 and Proverbs 24:30-34).

Today, the American Christian Republic still stands by the grace of God, yet its foundations have seriously eroded away.

If our nation's problems were the result of some conspiracy of men, the solution would be beyond the reach of most of us, and thus fatalism, apathy and despair would prevail. However, since God says the real problem began with our neglect, then the solution is within the grasp of the church. If we accept our responsibility and do our duty, we have grounds for hope.

## Why The Influence of Christianity Has Eroded

The Father of American Geography, Dr. Jedidiah Morse, was a clergyman. He preached an insightful Election Sermon in 1799 from Biblical text: "If the foundations be destroyed, what can the righteous do?" (Psalm 11:3). He said:

"To the kindly influence of Christianity we owe that degree of civil freedom, and political and social happiness which mankind now enjoys. In proportion as the genuine effects of Christianity are diminished in any nation, either through unbelief or the corruption of its doctrine, or the neglect of its institutions; in the same proportion will the people of that nation recede from the blessings of genuine freedom, and approximate the miseries of complete despotism. I hold this to be a truth confirmed by experience. If so, it follows, that all efforts made to destroy the foundations of our holy religion, ultimately tend to the subversion also of our political freedom and happiness. Whenever the pillars of Christianity shall be overthrown, our present republican forms of government, and all the blessings which flow from them, must fall with them."[3]

He said that the "genuine effects of Christianity are diminished in any nation" through (1) unbelief, (2) corruption of its doctrines, and (3) neglect of its institutions. Let us examine each more carefully.

## Unbelief

"And how shall they believe in Him whom they have not heard? And how shall they hear without a preacher?" (Romans 10:14).

"...The church of the living God, (is) the pillar and support of the truth." (1 Timothy 3:15).

Christianity cannot prevail in society without strong vibrant churches. These cannot exist without dedicated godly preachers. This by no means requires a majority of the population to be converted to be a godly nation. Throughout the Revolution, less than a majority of the population were *official* members of a church (although a definite majority attended church and almost everyone had a Biblical view of life). God never requires a "moral majority" to affect a nation only a "righteous remnant" who really understand their duties in all of life. The American Revolution would never have occurred without the Great Awakening. **Revival** and awakening of the lost is, therefore, the remedy to unbelief.

## Corruption of Doctrine

The doctrine that this refers to has nothing to do with your typical "statement of faith" that most Christians hold to as essential fundamentals. Those doctrines are generally confined to religious questions concerning the Godhead, salvation, etc.

The doctrines that, when corrupted or neglected results eventually in the decline of Christianity in society, were understood well by the apostles and even our Founding Fathers generation. These are articulated well in a sermon by Paul the apostle in Acts 17:24-28:

> "The God who made the world and all things in it since He is Lord of heaven and earth does not dwell in temples made with hands; neither is He served by human hands, as though He needed anything, since He Himself gives to all life and breath and all things; and He made from one, every nation of mankind to live on all the face of the earth, having determined their appointed times, and the boundaries of their habitation, that they should seek God, if perhaps they might grope for Him and find Him, though He is not far from each one of us; for in Him we live and move and exist."

Four primary doctrines, that have practical implications on how we view the world, as mentioned here:

(1) **Creation - "God made the world."** It didn't just happen by chance. This doctrine began to be neglected in our public schools in the late 1800's. It was no longer being taught in a reasonable way, for Christians began to neglect the field of science. Therefore, it became an irrelevant "religious" dogma, taught in the schools. This neglect left a void for a competing idealogy - Evolution. Darwin wrote his book in 1859, but it never really became predominant in public education until after the Scopes trial in 1925. Evolution forces lost this trial but won the war of ideas, by exposing a lack of Biblical Scientific reasoning. Today, the tables are being turned, as Creation Scien-

*Charles Darwin*

tists are restoring solid reasoning for Christians to articulate rather than simply saying "The Lord made the earth."

**(2) Lordship - "He is Lord of Heaven and earth."** This means He is absolute Master and final authority to whom all must give allegiance. As this doctrine has been neglected, so another competing ideology has gained ascendancy humanism. Humanism says that man is the measure of all things and the one who determines right and wrong for himself. Since 1961 when the Supreme Court recognized humanism as a religion, it has been systematically replacing Christianity as the United States' unofficially established or recognized religion.

**(3) Providence - "He Himself gives to all life and breath and all things; ...For in Him we live and move and exist."** Truly God is the source of every man's provisions, to Whom each man and woman must look. As this doctrine has been neglected, so the competing idealogy of socialism has prospered. Karl Marx's book, written in 1844, never had much influence in America until we had backslid from Christian principles of economics and greed and materialism grew. As monopolies grew, wealth was accumulated instead of compassionately employed to meet the needs of the poor and society. Individual interests replaced the common good of the community. These needs were then exploited by Marxist and Socialist leaders beginning in 1905. Marshall Foster writes that "in the loft above Peck's restaurant at 140 Fulton Street in lower Manhattan, a group of young men met to plan the overthrow of the predominantly Christian world-view that still pervaded America. At this first meeting five men were present: Upton Sinclair, 27, a writer and a socialist; Jack London, writer; Thomas Wentworth Higginson, a unitarian minister; J.G Phelps Stokes, husband of a socialist leader; and Clarence Darrow, a lawyer. Their organization was called the Intercollegiate Socialist Society. Their purpose was 'promote an intelligent interest in socialism among college men and women.' These men were ready to become the exponents of an idea passed on to them by an obscure writer named Karl Marx -- a man who never tried to be self-supporting but was supported by a wealthy industrialist who, inexplicably, believed in his theory of 'the dictatorship of the proletariat.' Although a small group in the beginning, these adherents of socialism more than succeeded in their task."[4]

"By using the proven method of gradualism, taken from the Roman general, Quintus Fabius Maximus, these men and others who joined with them slowly infiltrated" the public schools of our nation. By 1912 there were chapters in 44 colleges. By 1917 there were 61 chapters of student study groups of the League of Industrial Democracy. "At that time John Dewey, the godfather of progressive education, was the vice-president of the league. By 1941 Dewey had become president and Reinhold Niebuhr, the liberal socialist theologian, was the treasurer."[5]

In 1907, Charles and Mary Beard began to popularize Marx's ideas in their revisionist history books.

The loss of Christian character and responsibility led to the failure of many state banks in the early 1900's. In an effort to remedy this situation, power was granted to a centralized Federal Reserve Board in 1913. But this unbiblical economic structure and lack of character produced even greater problems. Within 20 years the Stock Market had crashed and America was in the midst of the Great Depression. With the propagation of socialism, people were ready for the "New Deal" of Franklin Roosevelt. Programs such as Social Security, and other welfare agencies, set up the State as provider rather than God.

Another corrupting event occurred in 1913. In that year a federal income tax amendment was passed which paved the way for deficit spending, inflation and financing of ungodly nations and causes.

**(4) Sovereignty- "He made... every nation... having determined their appointed times and the boundaries of their habitation."** Our Founder's and all preceding generations of Americans were unified and motivated by this basic truth, but it was neglected in our schools little by little until replaced by a new idealogy-Existentialism. Existentialists believe history is meaningless and the future unpredictable and therefore to plan and work for goals is hopeless. Instead their philosophy is "Eat, drink, and be merry for tomorrow we die." It is totally present-oriented and hedonistic. Marshall Foster warns that:

"Many Christians have subconsciously adopted the existential view of history. They de-emphasize their importance in a God-ordained historical chain of Christianity and see themselves simply as individuals God has plucked out of an evil world who are now just awaiting heaven. Their sense of responsibility for the past and their hope and planning for the building of the future are lost in the "now generation" where they are called to focus on self-improvement. This attitude covers the burden of guilt that lays heavily on the head of American Christians, but it does not alleviate their responsibility for our nations crisis....Until the Christian comes to grips with his historical duties denouncing his existential perspective and reaffirming the providential view of history, the renewal of our nation will be impossible."[6]

"In colonial America the God of the Bible was seen as sovereign over men and their property, reflecting the "Biblical worldview" of the Reformation. But in the past 100 years a disarming doctrine, which sees Satan as the sovereign of this world, has been accepted by many in Christian circles. Many bible teachers today see Jesus as an absentee king who is concerned exclusively with building and maintaining His church until He returns to earth. They see Jesus as having the authority and right to rule, but as having given over powers to subjugate the world temporarily to Satan."

"The world-view of the reformers was diametrically opposite to this view. Jesus Christ is the ruler of the earth (1 Timothy 6:16; Hebrews 2:14) and Satan, a defeated foe (John 12:3, Colossians 2:15)."

"One's attitude toward the sovereignty issue is of paramount importance, because it affects what is done in every area of life. Here is the contrast:

### "*If you see God ruling the earth:*

"1. Your commission is to subdue the earth and build godly nations through evangelizing and discipleship.

"2. You see Christian culture as leavening all areas of life, replenishing the earth, and blessing all mankind.

"3. All of God's world is His and every activity, to be seen as a spiritual work of God.

"4. Reformation is expected if a nation is obedient to God's word.

### "*If you see Satan ruling the earth:*

"1. Your commission is just to concentrate on saving souls from this evil world.

"2. You see Christian culture as a counter-culture, an isolated, persecuted minority in an evil world.

"3. Church activity is primary and spiritual, while worldly pursuits are secular and to be dealt with only as a necessity.

"4. Reformation is impossible since things must get worse because Satan is in control.

"The above contrasts illustrate the importance of ideas in determining consequences, because to the degree Christians have abdicated their leadership role and denied the 'crown rights to Jesus Christ,' to that degree the humanists have filled the void."[7]

What is the remedy for the corruption and neglect of these vital doctrines? It is the **Restoration of the New Testament Church** in its practical theology and Biblical reasoning and world-view. After the Civil War "liberal" churchmen of the North continued emphasizing social reform but without the Bible as the basis. This is sometimes called the "Social Gospel" today. The more "Fundamental" or Bible-based churchmen of the South, after the military defeat of the South, became fatalistic. They retreated to emphasizing only religious or church concerns and viewed most social movements with suspicion. Two new "Christian" positions developed among these "fundamentalists": (1) an eschatology of defeat and escape, and (2) a "separation of church and state" concept that sanctioned their non-involvement in society.

## Neglect of Our Institutions

Our corruption in government is largely a result of the church neglecting our educational institutions. In the early 1800's the clergy and church began to gradually cease providing leadership in our public universities and schools. Thus Harvard was taken over by the Unitarians, and as the quality of public education declined, Horace Mann convinced Massachusetts that the answer was to let civil government take charge of it instead of the private sector (families and churches). Rosalie Slater writes that:

"In the years 1837-1848 Horace Mann, whom John Dewey designated as 'the father of progressive education', made a series of Annual Reports to the Massachusetts Board of Education of which he was Secretary. These reports paved the way for a state financed, state directed, and ultimately a state controlled education program superseding local control through the demand for "standardization: of school structures, textbooks, curriculum, and teacher training and certification. But even this might not have proved so effective in the "secularization" of education had we not deliberately removed the

*Horace Mann*

Bible as the basis of our Christian character and substituted for salvation and regeneration of heart a psychological atheism which found man innately "good" and society "bad".

"There were many alert clergymen of the time of Horace Mann who were aware of this "condition" for the drive to achieve 'universal public education'. This 'condition' was that Christianity be neutralized for the larger goal of building, not Christian character and conscience, but humanitarians with benevolent inclinations toward mankind. And for those individuals who wished the schools to teach a patriotism which indicated how great was 'the faith of our fathers' there was substituted a bland form of non-controversial democracy and 'citizenship in the state'. Thus the public school was able to accomplish that which the hired European mercenaries of England never could -- namely to separate our patriotism from our Christian conviction."[8]

The clergy, who began to neglect the preaching of political sermons in weekday classes and in Election Sermons, had also neglected the Sabbath. Deuteronomy 5:15 reveals that the purpose of the Sabbath was to remember God's hand in history. This once was a regular practice in Sunday Schools as well as Sabbath day traditions in the home. The parents and grandparents would tell stories to their children on Sunday about how God's hand was seen in their home, church and nation. This is in serious neglect today in America.

Economic institutions are also in neglect. Marshall Foster says:

"In the early days of our nation, the tithe supported not only churches, but church schools and colleges, and provided for a variety of other social needs. In Rushdoony's 'Revolt Against Maturity' he discusses how one New England town coped with radical population changes wholly by the use of the tithe. Salem, Massachusetts, saw a population boom between 1795 and 1845, doubling its population several times over until it had grown from a village into a city. There was a flood of foreign immigrants and one would think that the town's character would have been completely changed and that the burden of such an influx of people would have caused a complete dislocation of its social fabric. But, as a matter of fact, the needs of the immigrants-as well as of the town's own citizens-were met through a variety of tithing agencies that cared for the poor, provided education, job-training, children's education, Bible courses, and taught the immigrants English. Salem shows what conscientious tithing Christians can accomplish in the field of social welfare. As Powell and Rushdoony point out: 'Conscientious and intelligently administered tithing by even a small minority can do much to reconstruct a land.'"[9]

In the Bible, God commanded Israel to provide for the poor through their tithe (Deut. 14:27-29). The use of the tithe (and charitable organizations) was how every social need was met in America for 300 years before the "New Deal" turned it over to the civil government just 50 years ago. If Christians today would tithe and give special offerings for the poor, to distribute individually or pool together with other Christians in their church, great things could happen. This must be done if we are ever going to disestablish the unbiblical welfare system today. Church-going Christians only give about 2% of their income to the church. In 1983, only 32% of Christians in America tithed. No wonder there is a problem. If every church in America took responsibility for just 3 families, there would be no need for welfare!

So the remedy for our neglect of Christian institutions is the **Reformation of Society**. As Christians commit themselves once again to being the "salt of the earth", corruption shall subside, "the righteous will be in authority," and "the people will rejoice" (Proverbs 29:2). "Righteousness exalts a nation." (Proverbs 14:34).

*Then conquer we must,*
*for our cause it is just,*
*And this be our motto:*
*"In God is our Trust!"*

*"Star-spangled Banner,"*
*1814*

*Francis Scott Key,*
*author of "The Star-spangled*
*Banner"*

# We the People

of the United States, in order to form a more perfect Union, establish Justice, insure domestic Tranquility, provide for the common defence, promote the general Welfare, and secure the Blessings of Liberty to ourselves and our Posterity, do ordain and establish this Constitution for the United States of America.

## Article. I.

Section. 1. All legislative Powers herein granted shall be vested in a Congress of the United States, which shall consist of a Senate and House of Representatives.

Section. 2. The House of Representatives shall be composed of Members chosen every second Year by the People of the several States, and the Electors in each State shall have the Qualifications requisite for Electors of the most numerous Branch of the State Legislature.

No Person shall be a Representative who shall not have attained to the Age of twenty five Years, and been seven Years a Citizen of the United States, and who shall not, when elected, be an Inhabitant of that State in which he shall be chosen.

Representatives and direct Taxes shall be apportioned among the several States which may be included within this Union, according to their respective Numbers, which shall be determined by adding to the whole Number of free Persons, including those bound to Service for a Term of Years, and excluding Indians not taxed, three fifths of all other Persons. The actual Enumeration shall be made within three Years after the first Meeting of the Congress of the United States, and within every subsequent Term of ten Years, in such Manner as they shall by Law direct. The Number of Representatives shall not exceed one for every thirty Thousand, but each State shall have at Least one Representative; and until such enumeration shall be made, the State of New Hampshire shall be entitled to chuse three, Massachusetts eight, Rhode-Island and Providence Plantations one, Connecticut five, New-York six, New Jersey four, Pennsylvania eight, Delaware one, Maryland six, Virginia ten, North Carolina five, South Carolina five, and Georgia three.

When vacancies happen in the Representation from any State, the Executive Authority thereof shall issue Writs of Election to fill such Vacancies.

The House of Representatives shall chuse their Speaker and other Officers; and shall have the sole Power of Impeachment.

Section. 3. The Senate of the United States shall be composed of two Senators from each State, chosen by the Legislature thereof, for six Years; and each Senator shall have one Vote.

Immediately after they shall be assembled in Consequence of the first Election, they shall be divided as equally as may be into three Classes. The Seats of the Senators of the first Class shall be vacated at the Expiration of the second Year, of the second Class at the Expiration of the fourth Year, and of the third Class at the Expiration of the sixth Year, so that one third may be chosen every second Year; and if Vacancies happen by Resignation, or otherwise, during the Recess of the Legislature of any State, the Executive thereof may make temporary Appointments until the next Meeting of the Legislature, which shall then fill such Vacancies.

No Person shall be a Senator who shall not have attained to the Age of thirty Years, and been nine Years a Citizen of the United States, and who shall not, when elected, be an Inhabitant of that State for which he shall be chosen.

The Vice President of the United States shall be President of the Senate, but shall have no Vote, unless they be equally divided.

The Senate shall chuse their other Officers, and also a President pro tempore, in the Absence of the Vice President, or when he shall exercise the Office of President of the United States.

The Senate shall have the sole Power to try all Impeachments. When sitting for that Purpose, they shall be on Oath or Affirmation. When the President of the United States is tried, the Chief Justice shall preside: And no Person shall be convicted without the Concurrence of two thirds of the Members present.

Judgment in Cases of Impeachment shall not extend further than to removal from Office, and disqualification to hold and enjoy any Office of honor, Trust or Profit under the United States: but the Party convicted shall nevertheless be liable and subject to Indictment, Trial, Judgment and Punishment, according to Law.

Section. 4. The Times, Places and Manner of holding Elections for Senators and Representatives, shall be prescribed in each State by the Legislature thereof; but the Congress may at any time by Law make or alter such Regulations, except as to the Places of chusing Senators.

The Congress shall assemble at least once in every Year, and such Meeting shall be on the first Monday in December, unless they shall by Law appoint a different Day.

Section. 5. Each House shall be the Judge of the Elections, Returns and Qualifications of its own Members, and a Majority of each shall constitute a Quorum to do Business; but a smaller Number may adjourn from day to day, and may be authorized to compel the Attendance of absent Members, in such Manner, and under such Penalties as each House may provide.

Each House may determine the Rules of its Proceedings, punish its Members for disorderly Behaviour, and, with the Concurrence of two thirds, expel a Member.

Each House shall keep a Journal of its Proceedings, and from time to time publish the same, excepting such Parts as may in their Judgment require Secrecy; and the Yeas and Nays of the Members of either House on any question shall, at the Desire of one fifth of those Present, be entered on the Journal.

Neither House, during the Session of Congress, shall, without the Consent of the other, adjourn for more than three days, nor to any other Place than that in which the two Houses shall be sitting.

Section. 6. The Senators and Representatives shall receive a Compensation for their Services, to be ascertained by Law, and paid out of the Treasury of the United States. They shall in all Cases, except Treason, Felony and Breach of the Peace, be privileged from Arrest during their Attendance at the Session of their respective Houses, and in going to and returning from the same; and for any Speech or Debate in either House, they shall not be questioned in any other Place.

No Senator or Representative shall, during the Time for which he was elected, be appointed to any civil Office under the Authority of the United States, which shall have been created, or the Emoluments whereof shall have been encreased during such time; and no Person holding any Office under the United States, shall be a Member of either House during his Continuance in Office.

Section. 7. All Bills for raising Revenue shall originate in the House of Representatives; but the Senate may propose or concur with Amendments as on other Bills.

Every Bill which shall have passed the House of Representatives and the Senate, shall, before it become a Law, be presented to the President

---

## Chapter 18

---

# The Power for Reforming America

## *Our Problems Today*

In Chapter 13 we saw the importance of keeping the government as close to the people as possible. This is why our founders limited the power of the national government by keeping most power in the hands of the States and the people.

Today, unfortunately, federalism and a limited or small national government has largely passed away. The pyramid is now inverted. The states have become in many ways mere administrative extensions of Washington, D.C. How has this happened?

The primary cause of the problem is rooted in the 14th Amendment to the Constitution. After the Civil War, Congress desired to prevent the encroachment of such an evil as slavery ever again. Though this was well-intentioned, the method of solving the problem was flawed. It stated in paragraph 1 that no state shall "deprive any person of life, liberty, or property, without due process of law." This was the guilt of the South before the war-- they refused to recognize and protect the inalienable rights of the blacks. Their state legislatures and state courts were immoral because they rebelled against God's higher law. But why could the legislatures and courts get away with it? Because of the backslidden, materialistic character of the people who had elected them. Many of the churches had compromised and the minority of those with moral integrity were too apathetic or lazy to try and change their legislatures by political action.

The problem was with the loss of the "Spirit" of the Constitution: religion, morality and knowledge. The "letter" of the Constitution had left the power of solving social problems with the states; the national government would be too distant from the people to handle such problems. The "Spirit" of the Constitution was strong enough in the northern states so that slavery was abolished there. As soon as the Civil War was over, the Congress, being controlled by the northern states, proposed two amendments-- the 13th was to abolish slavery. It was ratified by three-quarters of the state legislatures in late 1865. Six months later the 14th Amendment was proposed by Congress to protect the rights of all citizens. When it was examined by the state legislatures, many of them (even some in the North) rejected it on the grounds that it would undermine the Founders' idea of federalism on dual government. The problem was in paragraph 5: "The Congress shall have power to enforce, by appropriate legislation, the provisions of this article." The southern states in particular were champions of the idea of strong state government and most therefore refused to ratify this amendment. The radical Reconstruction Congress made a serious mistake at this point. Instead of listening to the serious objections to the wording of the Amendment, they declared the southern legislatures to be illegal governments due to their involvement in the Civil War and placed them under martial law. (If they were truly illegal, then the 13th Amendment ratified by them just six months earlier would also be not legal). Once new legislatures were elected that would ratify the 14th Amendment, then they would enjoy their freedom once again. The 14th Amendment, then, was passed at the point of a gun and has become a very significant cause in the growth of the national government today. The courts have increasingly struck down numerous state laws and the powers of the states have been greatly usurped. In almost every amendment that followed this one, problem-solving or over-riding powers have been granted to the national government. The whole intention of the Bill of Rights, especially Amendment 10, has been completely undermined. The national government can now overrule **any** law passed by any state and is usually done by Executive Orders from the President, or by the federal courts.

Two other amendments have also destroyed state powers, and enlarged the national government. The 16th Amendment in 1913 gave the Congress power to "collect taxes on incomes... without apportionment among the several States." Prior to this, the federal budget was entirely provided by import and federal sales taxes collected by the states and turned over to Congress. Now the national govern-

*United States Capitol, Washington, D.C.*

ment could bypass any accountability to the states as to their spending. History shows that since this was passed the federal deficit has soared and the federal bureaucracy grown to enormous proportions. Now the states get much of their money from the national government but with strict guidelines as to its use, thus becoming administrative agents of the national government.

The 17th Amendment, also passed in 1913, made it so that U.S. Senators would no longer be appointed by the state legislatures to represent their interests as a whole, but would now be "elected by the people thereof." Now, no one in Congress represents only their state. Both Senators and Congressmen represent many different special-interest groups who will help in their re-election. The day of the statesman, moved only by principle, has been eclipsed by the day of the mere politician.

And thus has been the fate of federalism. Thomas Jefferson warned long ago that "the true theory of our Constitution is surely the wisest and best... [for] when all government... shall be drawn to Washington as the centre of all power, it will render powerless the checks provided of one government on another, and will become as... oppressive as the government from which we separated."[1]

Unfortunately, the executive branch has grown in size and power unconstitutionally in many ways since the 14th Amendment. Now, the President makes more laws than Congress through what are known as "Executive Orders." They were originally only administrative instructions or policies that affected federal departments and agencies. Over time, however, the federal courts began to uphold these as legally binding as legislation by Congress. Before Teddy Roosevelt, no President would issue more than 70 executive orders in their term of office, but Roosevelt felt he could do anything not specifically prohibited by the Constitution. Thus in his term, he issued over 1000 orders! This trend continued, and in 1935 Congress began requiring that these be published in the Federal Register. Today there are over 12,500 Executive Orders on the books! The Executive branch has usurped the power of Congress to make laws.

The branch responsible for guarding the Constitutional separation of powers is the nine member Supreme Court, 11 Circuit Courts of Appeals and 144 other federal courts. The Judicial branch has as its primary purpose the interpretation of the laws of Congress in light of the Constitution and higher law. The Court has failed to check the President and the Congress in many of the areas mentioned previously, but, even worse, it has itself acted unconstitutionally. Our Founders never imagined that the Courts would become as powerful as they have. The Constitution reflects this: 255 lines of copy deal with the powers of Congress, 114 with the powers of the President, and only 44 with the Courts. They never imagined that the court needed extensive restraints. An exception to this was Thomas Jefferson who said:

> "The germ of dissolution of our Federal government is in the constitution of the federal judiciary; an irresponsible body working like gravity by night and by day, gaining a little today and a little tomorrow, and advancing its noiseless step like a thief, over the field of jurisdiction, until all shall be usurped from the states, and the judges as the ultimate arbiters of all constitutional questions is a very dangerous doctrine indeed, and one which would place us under the despotism of an oligarchy.... The Constitution has erected no such tribunal."[2]

*Thomas Jefferson*

The Court has evolved to this very state today. Edwin S. Corwin in *The Constitution of the United States* describes four distinct stages in the history of the Supreme Court. From 1800 to 1835, he calls the era of "National supremacy," then from 1835 to 1895 the era of "Constitutional supremacy." These were generally good. But then from 1895 to 1950 was the era of "Judicial supremacy" in which the decisions of the Court were no longer just the interpretation of the laws, but now considered "the law of the land," in place of the Constitution itself. In the words of Chief Justice Charles Evans Hughes in 1907: "the Constitution is what the judges say it is."[3] Finally, Corwin describes our present era as one of "Judicial Activism" or "Judicial Legislation." Today the Court no longer limits itself to settling disputes between parties; it strikes down laws in all fifty states, issues restraining orders, and the like that usurps both legislative and executive powers. The Warren Court that struck down prayer and Bible reading in the early 1960's did not have any judges with any prior substantive judicial experience.[4] Today, lawyers and judges who come out of our law schools never really study the Constitution, which is the very document they are supposed to defend.

Law not founded on absolutes is very dangerous. Without absolutes, the Supreme Court has reversed itself over 100 times. In 1973, the Court invented a new Constitutional right to abortion and has thereby denied the inalienable right to life to over 20 million unborn children to this date. A similar mistake was made in the Dred Scott decision of 1857, when the Supreme Court denied the personhood of blacks. This was finally overturned by the 13th Amendment as a result of the Civil War. Abraham Lincoln criticized the Supreme Court for its denial of the Law of God, which asserts the inalienable liberty of every individual. Lincoln believed that if this Court decision was now the absolute law of the land, then "... the people will have ceased to be their own rulers, having to that extent practically resigned their government into the hands of that eminent tribunal."

## *The Real Problem*

Today, in America, only 50% of registered voters go to the polls, but no more than about 5% participate in the precinct level of politics where the selection or nomination of candidates actually takes place (no more than 1/2 of 1% attend caucuses or conventions). This is really the only place where the divine command for selecting godly leaders is able to be discharged, and it is where your vote and participation is 1000 times more significant than on election day. A political party is simply an organization through which the people choose their representatives. If Christians wait until November to make their choices, they more often than not are forced to choose between "the lesser of two evils," of which really neither fulfill the Biblical requirements in rulers.

This explains more than any other reason why our government has violated the rights of blacks in the past, the unborn in the present, and generally exhibited corruption in every branch over the past 200 years. "The Constitution," to repeat John Adams, "was made only for a moral and religious people. It is wholly inadequate for the government of any other." In a Christian nation, the people make the laws, but the church makes the people. When the church fails to bring the necessary moral influence -- the "Spirit" of the Constitution -- then the "letter" of the law will not work. A brief history of Latin America provides an example. Many of those nations have had a revolution or military coup and then written a piece of paper very similar to our Constitution. Then within a few years, a whole new revolution occurs to overthrow the oppression of the most recent regime. Another "Constitution" is written and the process is repeated. The "letter" is the same as ours but the "spirit" is not there to make it work.

Stop signs are at intersections there, just like in America, but people often do not stop. One international visitor to this country once remarked that little things like our newspaper stands would never work in his country, for the first person to put a coin in the stand would take the whole stack of papers and sell them on the street.

In America, the problem with slavery was not in the letter of the Constitution. The northern states were proof of that. The problem between 1830 to 1860 was a moral one and unfortunately led to corrupt legislatures and corrupt courts in the South that denied the rights of black citizens. If the problem was a moral one, then working for amendments to the "letter" of the Constitution which simply give power to a higher legal body to correct it, really is a dangerous mistake. Though another centralized body of men may have a right moral stance at that time, what do you do when it too is morally wrong on an issue? If the problem was a lack of virtue in some of the states, is it not possible for the same lack of virtue to occur in the national government?

Not only is this probable, but it is history. Today the rights of 20 million unborn children have been disregarded by rulers in the national government who are not "men of truth who rule in the fear of God." The problem, here again, is not with the Constitution, but it is with the men in public office.

Therefore to put the focus of our efforts on amendments to change the Constitution is a mistake. The solution is in changing the men in office. But this will never occur as long as few godly Americans are involved in party politics on the local level.

Changing the letter of the Constitution never solves a problem rooted in the spirit. This is not to say that the letter of the law is useless-- only that it must have the spirit of the law to sustain it. This was the mistake of the liquor prohibition amendment in 1919. A lack of the spirit to sustain prohibition began creating more problems than it solved, and public reaction led to an amendment to repeal it in 1933. This unfortunately convinced those conservative Christians, who had worked for years to pass this mistaken amendment, that Christian involvement in politics was vain, and so they retreated into the four walls of their churches never to come out again until recently.

The same thing would happen with a pro-life amendment if passed immediately unless virtue among the people was restored soon. The immoral lifestyle of the people and millions of unwanted pregnancies would lead to some undesired reaction against it. When the south was forced to outlaw slavery the result was an entrenchment of bitterness and prejudice against the blacks that took longer to eradicate than if it had operated originally from the internal to the external. As awful as slavery was, and as grotesque as the slaughter of the unborn is today, the only lasting and permanent solutions to such social problems must come from the influence of the church on local politics and in building a Godly conscience in the nation.

## The Scriptural Duty of Every American Christian

James Madison articulated clearly that the real power for preserving a republic such as ours was placed in the hands of the people. He said:

"We have staked the whole future of American civilization, not upon the power of government, far from it. We have staked the future of all of our political institutions upon the capacity of mankind for self-government; upon the capacity of each and all of us to govern ourselves, to control oursel-

*James Madison*

ves, to sustain ourselves according to the Ten Commandments of God."

In the book of Exodus, Chapter 18, verses 19-23, Moses is advised by his father-in-law to be "the people's representative before God" but to also command the people themselves to "select out of all the people able men who fear God, men of truth, those who hate dishonest gain; and you shall place these over them, as leaders of thousands, of hundreds, of fifties and of tens...If you do this thing and **God so commands you,** then you will be able to endure..." In a later version of Deuteronomy 1:13, it said the people were to "choose wise and discerning and experienced men..."

The freedom to choose one's representative is not an American invention, but a Divine plan for godly government. John Jay, one of the authors of the *Federalist Papers* and first Chief Justice of the Supreme Court, said:

*John Jay*

"Providence has given to our people the choice of their rulers, and it is the duty, as well as the privilege and interest, of a Christian nation to select and prefer Christians for their rulers."[5]

Noah Webster wrote:

"...let it be impressed on your mind that God commands you to choose for yourselves rulers, 'just men who rule in the fear of God.' The preservation of a republican government depends on the faithful discharge of this duty; if the citizens neglect their duty and place unprincipled men in office, the government will soon be corrupted; laws will be made, not for the public good, so much as for selfish or local purposes; corrupt or incompetent men will be appointed to execute the laws; the public revenues will be squandered on unworthy men; and the rights of the citizens will be violated or disregarded. If a republican government fails to secure public prosperity and happiness, it must be because the citizens neglect the divine commands, and elect bad men to make and administer the laws."[6]

For most Americans, to neglect consistent involvement in local politics is to neglect a great privilege. But for Christians to do so is far worse. It is a failure to keep a Biblical command. Scripture makes it clear that Christians who fail to use what God has given them will not only suffer in this life, but also give an account in the one to come (Matthew 25:14-30).

The qualifications of a candidate should not be issue-oriented as much as character-oriented. They should be "able" and "experienced" men of course for the position which they seek. Beyond that, Scripture says they should be men who "fear God," that is, they should be Christians, as affirmed by John Jay. They should also be "men of truth" and "wise and discerning" men. This means that they should be Christians with a Biblical worldview-- men who reason from absolute truth, not human wisdom. Many candidates may claim to be "Christians," but do not hold to a Biblical worldview. Former President Jimmy Carter was an example of a Christian whose mind was unrenewed by Scripture and thus reasoned and governed from a "humanistic" worldview. Finally, Scripture says that our representatives must "hate dishonest gain." This means that beyond a correct worldview, they must have Christian character, a godly home life, and pure motives.

Only when you are involved in local politics on a consistent basis, going to meetings with the party members regularly, is it possible to know if a candidate meets these criteria. When a vacancy occurs in a public office, candidates are frequently chosen from among the regular members of the party whom you work with and know personally. Over the course of various debates and party activities, you generally gain a feel for each person's worldview and character. Therefore, you can faithfully discharge your Biblical duty and help to nominate a godly representative. If none is available to meet those qualifications, then you should be willing to run yourself.

The nomination of a candidate by a political party is usually determined by a very small percentage of Americans. Consequently, your vote is most influential on this level. If your candidate, whom you have known personally and worked with his campaign, eventually wins at the polls in November and goes to Congress or the state legislature, you automatically have access to him for future issues. People who never are involved in local party politics but then desire to communicate with their Congressman on an issue rarely get to do so. A letter or a phone call is usually received by an assistant who records your views and compiles it with others and passes it on to the Congressman. The Congressman really only sees numbers: so many for and against a certain piece of legislation. Even if Christians manage to outnumber others on an issue and we sway our Congressman by sheer numbers, we end up in the dangerous promotion of democracy. We really do not want representatives who are swayed by majorities, but rather by correct principles. The education of our representative is only possible when we have been faithful to work with him on the local level in consistent party politics.

## "We The People" -- The Power for Changing America

If every godly person who is presently involved in various special interest political groups would focus their time, energy and money into consistent local participation in the political party of their choice, then the very issues that they are interested in would be solved and much more! Two out of three of the political precincts (or neighborhoods of approximately 1000 homes) in this country are continually lacking leadership. If godly people would simply call the headquarters of any political party and ask how to get involved they would be welcomed. Experience has shown that when godly people go consistently to the party meetings and seek to serve and contribute, they can become influential, if not official leaders of that party within two years. The apathy of other Americans can become a blessing and advantage to Christians who choose to get involved and fill the void of leadership.

It must be added here that Christians need to be involved in both of the major political parties. Regardless of whether one party is more resistant to your ideas or not, you need to be there. If one party tends to think that all Christians will be blindly loyal to it, then the Christians will lose their prophetic voice and influence. The ultimate goal should be for enough Christians to become involved in both major parties so that eventually the candidates on the ballot in November are both of the type that fit into Biblical qualifications.

There are only approximately 2.5 million people involved in each political party on the local level today in America. If the Christians get involved nationwide, only 3 million in each party would be necessary to change them dramatically. This is probably less than 10% of all Christians in America who claim to be "born again"! If just 10% of all Christians in America today woke up and realized how easy it is, got involved consistently for the long haul, it would not take long to reform America completely. How long? believe it or not, it could be done within ten years. Here's how:

If Christians in every locality became a controlling influence in a political party after two years of serving there consistently, then every godly representative in the state legislatures and the Congress could be replaced within six years to work with a godly president. New judicial appointments would begin radically changing the unconstitutional influence of the courts within a few years following. Many pro-life activists do not realize that even if *Roe v._Wade* was overturned by the Supreme Court today abortion would still be legal until each state legislature passed new pro-life laws. If a Human Life Amendment was passed by Congress today, it would have to be ratified by 3/4 of the state legislatures. So why wait? Get involved on the local level to change your state legislature today! If we work for more godly representatives in 2/3 of the state legislatures then we can bypass Congress and call a new Constitutional Convention to clean up all of the mess we have made of it in the past 200 years! Then with godly state legislatures, the odds are good that delegates appointed by them to a new Convention will be godly and wise as well.

## The Price of Liberty

Consistent Party Politics. This is the price of liberty for us today. Our Founders paid a higher price with their "lives, liberty and sacred honor." Of the fifty-six signers of the Declaration of Independence, nine died in war, five died from torture, two lost their sons, and twelve lost their homes. But Thomas Jefferson said that the price of maintaining that liberty is "eternal vigilance." James Monroe said:

> "The establishment of our institutions forms the most important epoch that history hath recorded.... To preserve and hand them down in their utmost purity to the remotest ages will require the existence and practice of the virtues and talents equal to those which were displayed in acquiring them."[7]

The power of our republic is on the local level with "We the People." If we are virtuous then it is a good power; if not, then it is dangerous. The trend toward secularism today is making the possibility of virtuous people and rulers even more remote. Charles Finney said the following:

> "The Church must take right ground in regard to politics.... The time has come that Christians must vote for honest men, and take consistent ground in politics, or the Lord will curse them.... God cannot sustain this free and blessed country, which we love and pray for, unless the Church will take right ground. Politics are a part of a religion in such a country as this, and Christians must do their duty to the country as a part of their duty to God .... He [God] will bless or curse this nation, according to the course they [Christians] take [in politics]."[8]

Hopefully, you have been inspired to do many things as a result of this book. One thing of great importance is for you to fulfill your Biblical duty to choose a godly representative by getting involved in local party politics for the rest of your life. Edmund Burke once said,

*Rev. Charles G. Finney*

"All that is necessary for evil to triumph is for good men to do nothing."[9]

# Conclusion

# The Seven Principles of Liberty

In this book we have learned 7 basic principles that produce liberty when applied by individuals or nations. Miss Rosalie Slater identified those principles and recorded them in *Teaching & Learning America's Christian History.* As a summary we will examine each of these principles. While Miss Slater stated them historically, we will state them in general terms since they are applicable to all areas of life.

## 1) The Principle of Power and Form

External forms always result from an internal power. This is true for civil governments, churches, homes, businesses, or associations. The power, which is internal, precedes the form, which is external.

Both a power and a form are needed for anything to function properly. The Bible speaks of certain men who hold to a form of godliness yet deny its power (2 Tim 3:5). Those that do are dead in their faith. The internal power, or Spirit, is the life or energizing force and is essential for any form to work as it should; yet, a form is absolutely necessary to channel the power properly.

For an analogy revealing the need for both power and form, let's consider a fireman fighting a fire. If he rushed to a fire with his hose (the form), but had not turned on the fire hydrant and, therefore, did not have water (the power) flowing through it, the fire would rage on. Similarly, if he just went and opened the hydrant without a hose attached, he would do little, if any, good in extinguishing the flames. Both a power and form are necessary.

We not only need power and form, but we also need a balance between the two. Too much form causes all involved to dry up, while too much power causes them to "blow up." Communism, for example, produces a form of civil government that relies almost totally on external pressure to keep everyone "in line." The internal creativity, life, and motivation of each individual is suppressed by these external constraints.

An over-emphasis on power with little form leads to anarchy and eventually bondage. Historically, this can be seen after many national revolutions, the French being an excellent example.

## 2) *God's Principle of Individuality*

This principle is stated by Rosalie Slater in *Teaching and Learning America's Christian History* as follows:

"Everything in God's universe is revelational of God's infinity, God's diversity, God's individuality. God creates distinct individualities. God maintains the identity and individuality of everything which He created."

God does not create carbon-copy molds of anything - be they humans, animals, trees, minerals, mountains, rivers, planets, or stars. Everything He creates is unique and distinct, yet there is a unity among all things for God created them all.

God's Principle of Individuality reveals a unity with diversity for all creation. Take snowflakes for example. All snowflakes are alike in their material composition (frozen $H_2O$) and their structure (all have $60°$ between their axes), yet no two snowflakes are alike in their crystal growth pattern. William Bentley, affectionately called "Snowflake" Bentley, was the first person to photograph and study snowflakes in depth. Around the turn of the century, this farmer, with his wooden box camera, photographed over 5000 different snowflakes. No two of them were alike.

This individuality is seen in all creation for God Himself is a picture of individuality. God is One (a unity), yet He is also a triune Being (a diversity) - He is three in one.

## 3) *The Christian Principle of Self-Government*

A quote by Hugo Grotius in 1654 summarizes this principle well:

"He knows not how to rule a kingdom, that cannot manage a Province; nor can he wield a Province, that cannot order a City; nor he order a City, that knows not how to regulate a Village; nor he a Village, that cannot guide a Family; nor can that man Govern well a Family that knows not how to Govern himself; neither can any Govern himself unless his reason be Lord, Will and Appetite her Vassals; nor can Reason rule unless herself be ruled by God, and (wholly) be obedient to Him." (T & L, page 119)

Stated another way, you must rule yourself before you can rule others. The Bible says that a man who does not know how to manage his own household, cannot manage the church of God (1Tim.3:5) or any other area.

Today we have many civil government leaders who are attempting to govern our nation whose own lives and families are a mess. It's no wonder that our nation is becoming more of a mess in many ways when we consider who is providing direction for it.

Effective government begins by an individual learning to govern himself. The more internal self-government a person possesses, the less external government he needs. Consequently, the more rules and laws required to keep people acting rightly is a revelation of a diminishing amount of self-government.

As Americans have become less self-governed, our civil government (especially the national government) has grown and grown, making more and more laws and spending more and more money. Lack of self-government leads to greater centralized external government.

## 4) The Principle of Christian Character

"Character" literally means" to stamp and engrave through pressure." This sums up nicely what God is doing in our lives.

God's plan is to make each person like Him. Romans 8:29 tells us that God has predestined that we are to be conformed into the image of Christ. He is building His character within us, or you might say, He is stamping and engraving upon us His image. In so doing, He often uses pressure.

The fifteenth chapter of the gospel of John tells us that Jesus is the vine, and we are the branches, and the Father is the vine-dresser. What happens to every branch that does not bear fruit? It is cut away, then dries up and is finally burned. What happens to every branch that bears fruit? He prunes it. Therefore, no matter what we do we are going to get cut.

Why are branches pruned? To produce fruit of greater quantity and quality. While much of God's pruning hurts, we should greatly rejoice in the pruning process as we understand He is building His character within us.

Character has been defined as a convictional belief that results in consistent behavior. We can see that character begins internally (a convictional belief) and is expressed externally (consistent behavior).Our internal character will be seen in our external lifestyle.

God is stamping His image upon us so that we might be examples of him to the world, and be able to fulfill his purpose for our lives. We saw how the Pilgrims exemplified this principle so very well.

## 5) *The Principle of Christian Union*

Only an internal unity of ideas and principles produces an external union among people. This is the basis of the Christian Union of the United States of America. About two centuries ago, thirteen independent states were able to join together in a permanent union because they all embraced the Christian idea of man and government. Their motto, E. Pluribus Unum ("From many, one"), expresses this unity with union.

While the United States reveals a Christian Union, the Soviet Union is an example of an unbiblical union. External force and fear is used to hold all the people groups together. It is an involuntary union and, hence, will never last. In America, unity brings union; in Russia, union attempts to force unity.

Stronger internal bonds will produce a stronger union and action. If the original colonies had never formed a union, they would have never individually made the positive impact upon the world that corporately the United States has been able to make. In fact, they might not ever have survived. Similarly, the Church has made the greatest impact upon society as they have moved together in union.

As the internal unity breaks down within a family, church, or civil government, so does the external union. Therefore, in order to keep any union strong, common Biblical ideas and principles must be sown in the hearts of the people. A union can not be maintained long by only external means such as laws or force. Union must voluntarily flow from the hearts of an enlightened people.

## 6) *The Principle of Christian Education*

Christian Education can also be called the Principle of Sowing and Reaping because education "plants seeds" in people which will grow and produce results.

The Bible tells us that we will reap what we sow. In the birth of the United States, the first Christian nation in history, we see the fruit of seeds that had been planted for generations by parents, ministers, statesmen, teachers, and others.

The Bible tells us much about the "seed principle." It is extremely important for us to understand the parable of the sower and the soils (Mark 4), and that the kingdom of God (as well as faith) is like a seed. Although we are instantly converted when we repent and submit ourselves to Christ, the establishment of God's character and kingdom within us is a gradual process. It takes place like the growth of a plant or tree. A seed is planted; nourishment, care, and sunlight is provided; and then a mature plant comes forth bearing fruit (we must remember the pruning process, also).

This same principle applies in establishing God's truth in the nations of the world. It is a gradual process that must occur through Christian Education.

## 7) The Principle of Christian Economics or the Principle of Property

The following statement by James Madison reveals much about the Principle of Property:

"Property...In the former sense, a man's land, or merchandise, or money, is called his property. In the latter sense, a man has a property in his opinions and the free communication of them. He has a property of peculiar value in his religious opinions, and in the profession and practice dictated by them...He has an equal property in the free use of his faculties, and free choice of the objects on which to employ them. In a word, as a man is said to have a right to his property, he may be equally said to have a property in his rights." (CHOC, page 248A)

God has created everything, including us, and given us the right to possess property, both internal (opinions, ideas, talents, etc.) and external (land, merchandise, money, etc.). In the United States this right is acknowledged to be endowed by God and is also secured by the law of the land, the Constitution.

God requires us to be good stewards of everything He puts into our hand, whether that be houses, land, and money or talents, abilities, and knowledge. The idea of stewardship is embodied in the Principle of Property.

How we take care of our external property reflects how we take care of our internal property. If our house is constantly in a disheveled state, we can be assured that our thoughts are just as disorderly.

# A Checklist for Reforming America

Throughout this book we have seen that we must take action to assure that America is re-established on a firm Christian base, and hence, secure our God-given liberties and provide a free and prosperous platform from which we can go and make disciples of all the nations. The following checklist will help remind you of certain areas where you can begin to take action:

*"Christians, America needs you!"*

### Personal and Family

[ ] I will acknowledge the Lordship of Jesus in my life.
[ ] I will remember God and His Providential hand in history.
[ ] I purpose to implant the Principles of Liberty in my heart.
[ ] I purpose to be self-governed in the use of the property God has given me by tithing to my local church and supporting ministries and those in need as God directs.
[ ] I will take responsibility in educating my children in the Biblical principles of liberty, effectively communicating the vision to them.

### Church

[ ] I will continually receive instruction from my pastor on applying God's Word to every aspect of life.

[ ] I will support my church in fulfilling Christ's command to make disciples of all the nations.

### Education

[ ] Since the education of my children is my responsibility, I will carefully choose who I delegate that responsibility to, and to what schools my children go.

[ ] I will become aware of who is on the school board in my community and will work to replace those who do not act in accordance with Godly principles.

[ ] I will work to educate my neighbor in Biblical principles.

[ ] I will work to see that our public schools and universities begin operating on the Biblical base which was their foundation.

[ ] I will work to establish a media with a biblical worldview.

### Civil Government

[ ] I will take responsibility for choosing and instructing those who stand in my place in every area of civil government.

[ ] I will register to vote.

[ ] I will participate regularly in a political party on the local level.

[ ] I will keep informed on political issues affecting myself, my community, my state, and my nation.

# How You Can Get Ongoing Help in Reforming America:

### 1) Join or start a Biblical Reformation Committee in your area

*The Providence Foundation is associated with thousands of people across America who are involved in regular meetings that provide inspiration, encouragement, education, practical training, and planning of coordinated strategies for discipling their communities. Please contact us if you would like to join or start a Biblical Reformation Committee in your community. We will gladly provide speakers, materials, and training to assist you in your effort to bring Godly reform.*

### 2) Join a growing network of Christian reformers and educators nationwide

*By becoming a member of the Providence Foundation you will be participating in spreading His truth throughout the nations and stopping the decline of America. As a member you will receive our monthly journal "Providential Perspective", which provides hard-to-find historical documentation of God's government in the affairs of men. You will also receive a 25-35% discount on all books we distribute, plus discounts on registration to any seminars we conduct across America. To join, we ask that you become a regular contributor of at least $10 per month or $100 per year. If you wish to become a partner with us or to receive more information, please return the following form.*

---

## Yes, I Want to Participate in Equipping Christians to Disciple Nations

☐ I wish to become a member of the Providence Foundation with a regular gift of $_____ month/quarter/year. Enclosed is my first gift of $_____ .

☐ I wish to support the work of the Providence Foundation with a special gift of $_____ .

☐ I am interested in scheduling a presentation or seminar in my area. Please send me more information.

☐ Please send me information on ordering your books and materials.

☐ Please put me on your mailing list to receive your free *Reformation Report*.

☐ I want to attend or help start a Biblical Reformation Committee in my area.

Name_____

Address_____

City/State/Zip_____

Phone_____

Please return to:
**Providence Foundation**
**P.O. Box 6759**
**Charlottesville, Virginia 22906**

Resources Available from:

# The Providence Foundation

## Seminars and Presentations

### America's Providential History

Tracing the hand of God in the birth and development of our nation.

### Principle Approach to Education

Instruction for home-schooling parents and teachers on a biblical approach to education.

### The Spirit of the Constitution

The Christian foundations of our Constitution.

### Principles for the Reformation of the Nations

International students and indigenous Christians learn the principles for reforming their nations.

### Biblical Economics

Introducing principles of sound economics for personal and national prosperity.

### In Search of Democracy

Teaching a Biblical power and form of government.

### America's Freedom: Founded on Faith

An introductory slide presentation showing the Christian history of America and the foundations necessary for a free, just, and prosperous society.

### Christian History Tours

Tours of the nation's historic shrines revealing the hand of God in the founding and establishing of the United States of America.

*For more information contact:*

*Providence Foundation*
*P.O. Box 6759*
*Charlottesville, Virginia 22906*
*(804) 978-4535*

*Summer Institute for Christian Statesmanship*

An intensive school on topics that are covered in all our seminars and more.

## Publications

*America's Providential History*

The America's Providential History Course in book form.

*The Story of America's Liberty (Video)*

Discover the principles that made this nation both strong and free. In those principles and in the lives of courageous men and women who died for them, you will discover what modern history has sought to ignore -- that God Almighty was truly America's Founding Father.

*The Spirit of the Constitution*

A special Bicentennial publication showing how the Constitution is a product of Christianity and why it does not work without it.

*Principles for the Reformation of the Nations*

The principles for reformation of the nations in book form.

*Biblical Economics*

The principles of sound economics for personal and national prosperity in book form.

*"In God We Trust", A Christian History Tour of the United States Capital*

A guide book of the nation's Capital revealing the hand of God in the establishment of the United States of America.

*America, the Game*

This game celebrates our American experience and spiritual heritage. Two to six players start on the Eastern seaboard, and as they answer historical questions correctly, they advance west across the colorful board, strategically planning their route to be the first to reach the Pacific.

*In Search of Democracy*

This tape series and booklet examines the foundations, framework, and historical development of Biblical government and law.

*Reformation Report*

A quarterly update on the work of the Providence Foundation sent to members and anyone desiring to be on our mailing list. Includes news of special events and special offers of interest to Christian reformers.

*Providential Perspective*

A monthly journal made available to our members of some of the hard to find historical documentation of God's government in the affairs of men all over the world.

# Endnotes

## Chapter 1

1. Peter Marshall and David Manuel, *The Light and the Glory* (New Jersey, 1977), p.370.
2. David Barret, *Chaos, Cosmos, and Gospel...*(Birmingham, 1987).
3. Marshall Foster and Mary-Elaine Swanson, *The American Covenant the Untold Story,* (California, 1983) p. 48.
4. Verna M. Hall and Rosalie J. Slater, T*he Bible and the Constitution of the United States of America* (San Francisco, 1983), p. 18. [designated *Bible and Constitution* in future footnotes]
5. *The Christian History of the American Revolution, Consider and Ponder,* compiled by Verna M. Hall (San Francisco, 1976), p. 47. [to be designated *Consider and Ponder* in future references]
6. *The Christian History of the Constitution of the United States of America*, compiled by Verna M. Hall (San Francisco, 1980), p. 186. [designated CHOC]
7. James Madison, *Journal of the Federal Convention,* Albert, Scott & Co., 1893, pp. 259-260.
8. B.F. Morris, *Christian Life and Character of the Civil Institutions of the United States* (Philadelphia, 1864), pp. 327-328.
9. *Consider and Ponder,* p. 46.

## Chapter 2

1. Rosalie J. Slater, *Teaching and Learning America's Christian History* (San Francisco, 1980), p. 142.
2. Slater, p. 149.
3. Slater, pp. 145-146.
4. CHOC, p.4.
5. Slater, p. 148.
6. Slater, p. 149.
7. Slater, p. 147.
8. CHOC, pp. 3-4.
9. Slater, p. 153.
10. Ibid.
11. CHOC, pp. 4-5.

## Chapter 3

1. CHOC, p. 1.
2. CHOC. p. 2.
3. Slater, p. 213.
4. Slater, p. 214.
5. Norman Cousins, *"In God We Trust"* (New York, 1958), p. 368.

## Chapter 4

1. *Eerdmans' Handbook to the Bible,* Edited by David Alexander and Pat Alexander (Grand Rapids, 1973), p. 588.
2. David Chilton, "Alfred the Great", in *Equity,* the newsletter of the Christian Public Policy Council, Jan. 1989, p. 3.
3. W. Cleon Skousen, *The Making of America* (Washington, D.C., 1985), p. 32.
4. Slater, p. 167.
5. Ibid.
6. Slater, p. 168.
7. Charles Carleton Coffin, *The Story of Liberty* (New York, 1878), p.79.
8. The American Vision, 360 Years Later (Cassette Study Guide), 1980, p. 2-3. This quote is an excerpt from his *Book of Prophecies*. The complete work of Christopher Columbus' *Book of Prophecies* has for the first time been translated into English by Kay Brigham and published by CLIE publishers of Barcelona on the occasion of the Quincentenary of Columbus's first voyage to the Americas. This is the only book Columbus wrote and clearly reveals that God and the Bible were the most powerful motivating cause which inspired his vision to sail to the Indies.
9. Daniel Dorchester, *Christianity in the United States* (New York, 1895), p. 24.
10. Morris, pp. 41-42.
11. Slater, p. 169.
12. Slater, p. 171.
13. Slater, pp. 170-171.
14. Slater, p. 171.

## Chapter 5

1. This and preceding quotes on Tyndale from Slater, pp. 334-336.
2. CHOC, p. 183.
3. Glen A. Jaspers and Ruth Jaspers Smith, *Restoring America's Heritage of Pastoral Leadership* (Granger, Indiana, 1982), p. 28.

## Chapter 6

1. Foster and Swanson, p. 71.
2. Foster and Swanson, p. 72.
3. Ibid.
4. Ibid.
5. Ibid.

## Chapter 7

1. *Bible and Constitution,* p.14.
2. Morris, pp. 98-101.
3. Edwin Scott Gaustad, *A Religious History of America* (New York, 1974), p. 104.
4. Morris, pp. 101-104.
5. Foster and Swanson, p. 90.
6. Foster and Swanson, p. 91.
7. Ibid.
8. CHOC, p. 252.
9. Foster and Swanson, p. 95.
10. Morris, p. 69 and Gaustad, pp. 66-67.

11. Hildegarde Dolson, *William Penn, Quaker Hero* (New York, 1961), p. 104.
12. Morris, p. 56.

## Chapter 8

1. Slater, pp. 278-279.
2. Gary Demar, *God and Government,* Vol. 2 (Atlanta, 1984), p. 12.
3. Greg Anthony, *Biblical Economics*, 1988, p. i.
4. Slater, p. 88-89.
5. Slater, p. 88.
6. *Consider and Ponder,* pp. 605-606.
7. CHOC, p. 273.
8. Samuel Blumenfeld, *Is Public Education Necessary?* (Boise, 1985), pp. 19-20.
9. Samuel Blumenfeld, *N.E.A. -- Trojan Horse in American Education* (Boise, 1985).
10. Rosalie Slater, from an essay in the preface to a Facsimile Edition of Noah Webster's 1828 Edition of *An American Dictionary of the English Language* (San Francisco, 1980), p. 12. [designated Webster's 1828 in future footnotes]
11. Webster's 1828, p. 27.
12. John H. Westerhoff III, *McGuffey and His Readers* (Milford Michigan, 1982).
13. Ibid.
14. "America's Universities", an unpublished paper by Mark Beliles.
15. Morris, pp. 74-75.
16. Slater, p. IX.
17. Ibid.
18. Gaustad, p. 45.
19. Morris, pp. 77-78.
20. Beliles
21. Gaustad, p. 90.
22. Morris, p. 72.
23. Webster's 1828, p. 12.
24. CHOC, p. XIV.

## Chapter 9

1. Slater, p. 40.
2. Skousen, p. 678.
3. Skousen, p. 679.
4. Slater, p. 38-39.
5. Slater, p. 48.
6. CHOC, p. 374.
7. Morris, p. 339.
8. Norman V. Pope, "Educator, Minister, Patriot," in *Nation Under God*, ed. Frances Brentano (Great Neck, New York, 1957), pp. 41-42.
9. Slater, p. 249.
10. John Wingate Thornton, *The Pulpit of the American Revolution* (Boston, 1860).
11. Thornton, quoted in *Consider and Ponder*, pp. 191-192.
12. American Political Science Review, Vol. 78, 1984.
13. Morris, pp. 377-380.

## Chapter 10

1. Slater, p. 252.
2. Slater, p. 257.
3. CHOC, p. 322.

4. CHOC, pp. 365-370.
5. CHOC, p. 332.
6. CHOC, p. 337.
7. CHOC, p. 339.
8. Slater, pp. 262-263.
9. Gary Demar, *God and Government,* Vol. 1 (Atlanta, 1982), p. 118.
10. Demar, p. 108.
11. Jedidiah Morse, *Annals of the American Revolution*, first published in 1824, reissued in 1968 by Kennikat Press.
12. *Consider and Ponder,* p. 402.
13. Alice Baldwin, *The New England Clergy and the American Revolution*, Fredick Ungar Pub. Co., 1928.
14. CHOC, p. 343.
15. CHOC, p. Id.
16. Franklin Cole, ed., *They Preached Liberty* (Indianapolis), p. 39.
17. Slater, pp. 256-257.
18. Cole, p. 39.
19. *Consider and Ponder,* p. 407.
20. Quoted in Morris, p. 432.
21. *America,* Vol. III (Chicago, 1925), pp. 184-185.
22. *Consider and Ponder,* p. 510a.
23. *Consider and Ponder,* pp. 536-543.
24. *The Proceedings of the Virginia Convention in the Town of Richmond on the 23rd of March, 1775*, Saint John's Church, 1927, pp. 12-13.
25. Morris, pp. 346-347.
26. Morris, p. 349.
27. Slater, p. 248.
28. CHOC, p. 373.
29. Broadside printed in Salem, Massachusetts-Bay by E. Russell by Order of the Council, R. Derby, President.
30. CHOC, p. 372.

## Chapter 11

1. Robert Flood, *Men Who Shaped America* (Chicago, 1976), p. 43.
2. Flood, p. 45.
3. *The Annals of America,* Vol. 2 (Chicago., 1968), p. 276.
4. George Bancroft, *History of the United States,* Vol. VI (Boston, 1878), p. 355.
5. Peter Marshall and David Manuel, *The Light and the Glory* (Old Tappan, New Jersey, 1977), p. 309.
6. Bancroft, p. 321.
7. Ibid.
8. Foster and Swanson, p. 126.
9. Robert B. Weaver, *Our Flag and Other Symbols of Americanism* (Alexandria, VA, 1972), p. 9.
10. *The Story of the Seal* (Merrimac, Ma.), p. 19.
11. Slater, p. 339.
12. Bancroft, p. 41.
13. *Consider and Ponder,* p. 61.
14. Ibid.
15. Bart McDowell. *The Revolutionary War* (Washington, D.C., 1970), p. 128.
16. William Wilbur, *The Making of George Washington* (Alexandria,VA, 1973), p. 196.
17. *Consider and Ponder,* p. 61.

18. Wilbur, p. 195.
19. Bancroft, p. 50.
20. McDowell, p. 131.
21. Bancroft, p. 41.
22. Bancroft, p. 42.
23. *Consider and Ponder,* p. 66.
24. Ibid., p. 68.
25. William J. Johnson, *George Washington the Christian,* reprinted by Mott Media, 1976, pp. 120-121.
26. Ibid., p. 104.
27. Bruce Lancaster, *The American Revolution* (Garden City, NY, 1957), p. 42.
28. Johnson, p. 113.
29. Johnson
30. The American Vision, 360 Years Later
31. Bancroft, Vol. V, p. 387.
32. Story from Washington Irving, *Life of Washington,* part two (New York), pp. 182-189; and from Foster.
33. Marshall, pp. 317-318.
34. Ibid.
35. B. F. Morris, pp. 530-531.
36. "The Providential Discovery of the Treason of Benedict Arnold -- September 25th, 1780", Foundation for American Christian Education
37. *America,* Vol. III, pp. 284-285.
38. "The Providential Discovery of the Treason of Benedict Arnold"
39. Foster and Swanson, pp. 165-166.
40. William McAuley Hosmer, "Divine Providence -- God Himself in the Battle of Yorktown," Foundation for Christian Self-Government Newsletter, Sept. 1981.
41. Ibid.
42. Ibid.

## Chapter 12

1. John Fiske, *The Critical Period of American History, 1783-1789* (New York, 1894), p. 231.
2. Ibid.
3. Albert Henry Smyth, ed., *Writings of Benjamin Franklin,* Macmillan Co., 1905-7, Vol. 9, p. 702.
4. Robert A. Rutland, ed., *The Papers of James Madison,* University of Chicago Press, 1962, Vol. 10, p. 208.
5. Skousen, p. 5.
6. John C. Fitzpatrick ed., *Writings of George Washington,* United States Government Printing Office, 1930, Vol. 29, p. 525.
7. James Madison's Notes of Debates in the Federal Convention of 1787 (New York, 1987), pp. 209-210.
8. B.F. Morris, *p. 252.*
9. B.F. Morris, p. 253.
10. B.F. Morris, pp. 252-253.
11. *Writings of George Washington.*
12. George Bancroft, *History of the United States of America,* D. Appleton and Co., 1891, Vol. 6, p. 420.
13. Bancroft, p. 414.
14. Morris, p. 271.
15. Morris, p. 273.
16. Morris, p. 274.
17. Morris , p. 275.
18. Morris, p. 328.

19. David Barton, *Myth of Separation* (Aledo, TX, 1989), p. 64.
20. *The Rebirth of America,* Arthur S. DeMoss Foundation, 1986, p. 21.
21. John Adams, *Address to the Officers of the First Brigade of the 3rd Division of the Militia of Massachusetts.*
22. Walker P. Whitman, *A Christian History of the American Republic: A Textbook for Secondary Schools,* (Boston: Green Leaf Press, 1939,1948), p. 91.
23. Robert L. Cord, *Separation of Church and State* (New York, 1982), p. 245.
24. Henry B. Watson, George Washington, *Architect of the Constitution* (Alexandria, VA, 1983), p. 119.
25. Slater, p. 251.
26. Moody Adams, *America is Too Young to Die,* 1976, p.25.
27. Skousen, p. 664.
28. Sol Bloom, *The Story of the Constitution* (Washington, D.C., 1937), p. 43.
29. Morris, p. 326.
30. Morris, p. 234.
31. Morris, p. 235.
32. Morris, p. 231.
33. Morris, p. 239.
34. Cord, p. 12-13.
35. Skousen, p. 681.
36. Saul K. Padover, ed. *The Complete Jefferson,* Tudor Publishing Co. 1943, p. 412.
37. Zorach V. Clauson, 343 U.S. 306 at 313.
38. Lynch V. Donelly, 465 U.S. at 673.

## Chapter 13

1. *CHOC - Self-government with Union,* p. 34.
2. Morris, p. 250.
3. Donald Lutz, "The Relative Influence of European Writers on Late 18th Century American Political Thought," *American Political Science Review,* LXXVIII (1984) 189-197.
4. *Newsweek ,* Dec. 26, 1982.
5. *The Federalist Papers,* p. 236.
6. *Our Ageless Constitution ,* p. 32.
7. Skousen, p. 177.
8. *Our Ageless Constitution,* p. 33.
9. Hamilton, Madison and Jay, *The Federalist Papers* (New York, 1982), p. 244.
10. Hamilton, Madison and Jay.
11. Noah Webster, *History of the United States,* 1833, quoted in *The Christian History of the American Revolution,* by Verna Hall, p. 255.

## Chapter 14

1. Charles Hull Wolfe, "The Principle Approach to American Christian Economics," in *A Guide to American Christian Education for the Home and School, the Principle Approach,* by James B. Rose (Palo Cedro, CA), p. 415.
2. Ibid.
3. Ibid., p. 402.
4. Ibid.
5. Ibid.
6. Ibid.

7. Ibid., pp. 402-403.
8. Ibid., p. 398.
9. Greg Anthony, *Biblical Economics*, 1988, p. 13
10. Wolfe, p. 398.
11. Ibid., p. 403.
12. Ibid.
13. "How to Understand the Purpose behind Humanism" booklet, Institute in Basic Youth Conflicts, 1983, p. 7.
14. Wolfe, p. 403.
15. Cleon Skousen, *Study Guide to the Making of America.*
16. William Bradford, *Of Plimoth Plantation* (Boston, 1901), p. 162.
17. Ibid., p. 163.
18. Wolfe, p. 405.
19. Ibid.
20. Ibid.
21. CHOC, p. 64.
22. Slater, p. 234.
23. Slater, p. 228-229.
24. Wolfe, p. 406.
25. George Grant, *In the Shadow of Plenty* (Fort Worth, Texas, 1986), p. 4.
26. Wolfe, p. 406.
27. David Chilton, *Productive Christians in an Age of Guilt Manipulators: A Biblical Response to Ronald J. Sider*, quoted in Anthony, p. 27.
28. Anthony, p. 28.
29. Ibid., pp. 28-29.
30. Verna Hall and Rosalie Slater, *The Bible and the Constitution of the United States of America* (San Francisco, 1983), p. 35.
31. CHOC, p. 58.
32. Slater, *Teaching and Learning*, p. 231.
33. Wolfe, p. 406.
34. *Our Ageless Constitution*, edited by W. David Stedman and LaVaughn G. Lewis (Asheboro, NC, 1987), p. 37.
35. Gary DeMar, *God and Government, Vol. 2, Issues in Biblical Perspective* (Atlanta, 1984), pp. 131, 121.
36. Anthony, p. 34.
37. Chilton, quoted in Anthony, p. 34.
38. Anthony, p. 34.

## Chapter 15

1. *Our Ageless Constitution*, p. 39.
2. Ibid.
3. Ibid.
4. Gary North, *Healer of the Nations, Biblical Principles for International Relations* (Fort Worth, TX, 1987), p. 11.
5. John Eidsmoe, *Christianity and the Constitution* (Grand Rapids, Michigan, 1987), p. 364.
6. Foster and Swanson, pp. 145-146.
7. Lee Grady, "Can We Make a Deal for Peace?" The Forerunner, Vol. VIII, No. 8, December 1987, pp. 15-17.
8. Ibid.

## Chapter 16

1. David H. Appel, ed. *An Album for Americans* (New York p. 65-66.
2. Foster and Swanson, p. 142.

3. G. Frederick Owen, *Abraham Lincoln: The Man and His Faith* (Wheaton, IL, 1981), p. 86-87, 91.
4. Daniel Dorchester, p. 454.
5. *Old South Leaflets*
6. Appel, p. 120.
7. William J. Johnson, *Abraham Lincoln The Christian*, Mott Media, p. 106.
8. Dorchester, p. 473.
9. Dorchester, p. 460.
10. J. William Jones, *Personal Reminiscences, Anecdotes, and Letters of General Robert E. Lee*, D. Appleton and Co., 1874, p. 138.
11. Gamaliel Bradford, *Lee the American*, Houghton and Mifflin Co., 1913, p. 92.
12. Bradford, p. 242.
13. Mark Grimsley, "Jackson: The Wrath of God," *Civil War Times*, pp. 15-19.
14. Johnson, p. 107, 108.
15. Grimsley, p. 18.
16. Johnson, pp. 112-114.
17. Philip Alexander Bruce, *Robert E. Lee*, W.B. Jacobs and Co., 1907, p.359.
18. Robert E. Lee, Jr. *Recollections and Letters of General Robert E. Lee*, Doubleday, Page and Co., 1904, p. 105.
19. J. William Jones, *Christ in the Camp*, B.F. Johnson and Co, 1897, p. 56.
20. Jones, *Christ in the Camp*, p. 51.
21. Appel, p. 117.
22. Johnson, p. 172.
23. Johnson, pp. 178-179.

## Chapter 17

1. Slater, p. 54.
2. Slater, p. 251.
3. CHOC, p. IV.
4. Foster and Swanson, p. xvii.
5. Foster and Swanson, p. xviii.
6. Foster and Swanson, p. 37.
7. Foster and Swanson. p. 106-107.
8. Slater, pp. 52-53.
9. Foster and Swanson, p. 125.

## Chapter 18

1. Skousen, pp. 576-577.
2. Skousen, p. 588.
3. Skousen, p. 578.
4. Shousen, p. 577.
5. Morris, p. 153.
6. Noah Webster, *History of the United States* (New Haven, 1833), pp. 307-308.
7. Morris
8. Charles G. Finney, *Revivals of Religion* (Virginia Beach, VA, 1978), p. 311.
9. *Rebirth of America*, p. 213.

# Bibliography

Adams, Moody. *America is Too Young to Die.* 1976.

Alexander, David, and Pat Alexander, editors. *Eerdmans' Handbook to the Bible.* Grand Rapids: William B. Eerdmans Publishing Co., 1973.

*America, Great Crises in Our History Told by Its Makers, A Library of Original Sources.* 12 volumes. Issued by Americanization Department, Veterans of Foreign Wars of the United States, Chicago, 1925.

*American Vision, 360 Years Later, The* (Cassette Study Guide). Atlanta: American Vision, 1980.

Amos, Gary T. *Defending the Declaration.* Brentwood, Tennessee: Wolgemuth & Hyatt, 1989.

*Annals of America, The.* Chicago: Encyclopaedia Britannica, 1968.

Anthony, Greg. *Biblical Economics.* Charlottesville, Virginia: Providence Foundation, 1988.

Appel, David H., editor. *An Album for Americans.* New York: Crown Publishers, Inc.

Baldwin, Alice. *The New England Clergy and the American Revolution.* Fredick Ungar Pub. Co., 1928.

Bancroft, George. *History of the United States.* 6 volumes. Boston: Little, Brown, and Co., 1878.

Bancroft, George. *History of the United States of America.* 10 volumes. D. Appleton and Co., 1891.

Barret, David. *Cosmos, Chaos, and Gospel, a Chronology of World Evangelization from Creation to New Creation.* Birmingham, AL: New Hope, 1987.

Barton, David. *Myth of Separation.* Aledo, Texas: Wallbuilder Press, 1989.

Bloom, Sol. *The Story of the Constitution.* Washington, D.C.: United States Constitution Sesquicentennial Commission, 1937.

Blumenfeld, Samuel L. *Is Public Education Necessary?* Boise, Idaho: The Paradigm Company, 1985.

Blumenfeld, Samuel L. *NEA: Trojan Horse in American Education,* Boise, Idaho: The Paradigm Company, 1985.

Bowen, Catherine Drinker. *Miracle at Philadelphia.* Boston: Little, Brown and Co., 1986.

Bradford, Gamaliel. *Lee the American.* Houghton and Mifflin Co., 1913.

Bradford, William. *Of Plimoth Plantation.* Boston: Wright & Potter Printing Co., 1901.

Bruce, Philip Alexander. *Robert E. Lee.* W.B. Jacobs and Co., 1907.

Brutus, Junius. *A Defense of Liberty Against Tyrants (Vindiciae Contra Tyrannos).* Edmonton, AB Canada: Still Waters Revival Books, reprinted from the 1689 translation, 1989.

Chilton, David. *Productive Christians in an Age of Guilt Manipulators: A Biblical Response to Ronald J. Sider.* Tyler, TX: Institute for Christian Economics, 1982.

Chilton, David. "Alfred the Great," *Equity,* the newsletter of the Christian Public Policy Council, January, 1989.

*Christopher Columbus's Book of Prophecies,* Reproduction of the Original Manuscript with English Translation by Kay Brigham. Quincentenary Edition. Barcelona, Spain: CLIE Publishers.

Coffin, Charles Carleton. *The Story of Liberty.* New York: Harper & Brothers, 1878.

Cole, Franklin, editor. *They Preached Liberty.* Indianapolis: Liberty Press.

Cord, Robert L. *Separation of Church State.* New York: Lambeth Press, 1982.

Cousins, Norman. *"In God We Trust,"* The Religious Beliefs and Ideas of the American Founding Fathers. New York: Harper & Brothers, 1958.

Dabney, R.L. *Life and Campaigns of Lieut.-Gen. Thomas J. Jackson.* Original published in 1865. Republished by Sprinkle Publications, Harrisonburg, Virginia, 1983.

D'Aubigne, J.H. Merle. *History of the Reformation of the Sixteenth Century.* Translated by H. White. New York: Hurst & Company.

Demar, Gary. *God and Government, Vol. 1, A Biblical and Historical Study.* Atlanta: American Vision Press, 1982.

Demar, Gary. *God and Government, Vol. 2, Issues in Biblical Perspective.* Atlanta: American Vision Press, 1984.

Dolson, Hildegarde. *William Penn, Quaker Hero.* New York: Random House, 1961.

Dorchester, Daniel. *Christianity in the United States.* New York: Hunt & Eaton, 1895.

Dreisbach, Daniel L. *Real Threat and Mere Shadow, Religious Liberty and the First Amendment.* Westchester, Illinois: Crossway Books, 1987.

Edwards, Brian. *God's Outlaw.* Wheaton, Illinois: Tyndale House Publishers, Inc., 1981.

Eidsmoe, John. *Christianity and the Constitution.* Grand Rapids, Michigan: Baker Book House, 1987.

Findlay, Bruce Allyn, and Esther Blair Findlay. *Your Rugged Constitution.* Stanford, California: Stanford University Press, 1969.

Finney, Charles G. *Revivals of Religion.* Virginia Beach, VA: CBN University Press, 1978.

Fiske, John. *The Beginnings of New England.* New York: Houghton, Mifflin and Co., 1898.

Fiske, John. *The Critical Period of American History, 1783-1789.* New York: Houghton, Mifflin and Company, 1898.

Fitzpatrick, John C., editor. *Writings of George Washington.* United States Government Printing Office, 1930.

Flood, Robert. *Men Who Shaped America.* Chicago: Moody Press, 1976.

Foster, Marshall, and Mary-Elaine Swanson. *The American Covenant the Untold Story.* California: Mayflower Institute, 1983.

*Franklin, Benjamin, The Autobiography of.* Compiled and edited, with notes by John Bigelow. New York: Walter J. Black, Inc., 1932.

Frothingham, Richard. *The Rise of the Republic of the United States.* Boston: Little, Brown, and Co., 1895.

Gaustad, Edwin Scott. *A Religious History of America.* New York: Harper & Row, 1974.

Grady, Lee. "Can We Make a Deal for Peace?" *The Forerunner,* Vol. VIII, No. 8, December 1987.

Grant, George. *In the Shadow of Plenty.* Fort Worth, Texas: Dominion Press, 1986.

Grimsley, Mark. "Jackson: The Wrath of God," *Civil War Times.*

Guyot, Arnold. *The Earth and Man.* Boston: Gould and Lincoln, 1863.

Guyot, Arnold. *Physical Geography.* New York: Ivison, Blakeman and Co., 1885.

Hall, Verna M., and Rosalie J. Slater. *The Bible and the Constitution of the United States of America.* San Francisco: Foundation for American Christian Education, 1983.

Hall, Verna M., compiler. *The Christian History of the American Revolution, Consider and Ponder.* San Francisco: Foundation for American Christian Education, 1976.

Hall, Verna M., compiler. *The Christian History of the Constitution of the United States of America, Christian Self-Government.* San Francisco: Foundation for American Christian Education, 1980.

Hall, Verna M., compiler. *The Christian History of the Constitution of the United States of America, Christian Self-Government with Union.* San Francisco: Foundation for American Christian Education, 1979.

Hamilton, Alexander, James Madison and John Jay. *The Federalist Papers.* First published in 1787-1788. New York: Bantam Books, 1988.

Hardinge, Leslie. *The Celtic Church in Britain.* London: Church Historical Society, 1973.

*Holy Bible, The.* As printed by Robert Aitken and Approved & Recommended by the Congress of the United States of America in 1782. Reprinted, New York: Arno Press, 1968.

Hosmer, William McAuley. "Divine Providence--God Himself in the Battle of Yorktown." Foundation for Christian Self-Government newsletter, Sept. 1981.

"How to Understand the Purpose Behind Humanism." Institute in Basic Youth Conflicts, 1983.

*Inaugural Addresses of the Presidents of the United States.* Washington, D.C.: United States Government Printing Office, 1969.

Irving, Washington. *Life of Washington.* New York: The Cooperative Publication Society, Inc.

Jaspers, Glen A., and Ruth Jaspers Smith. *Restoring America's Heritage of Pastoral Leadership.* Granger, Indiana: Pilgrim Institute, 1982.

Johnson, William J. *George Washington the Christian.* Reprinted by Mott Media, Milford, MI., 1976.

Johnson, William J. *Robert E. Lee the Christian.* Reprinted by Mott Media, 1976.

Johnson, William J. *Abraham Lincoln the Christian.* Reprinted by Mott Media, 1976.

Jones, J. William. *Christ in the Camp.* B.F. Johnson and Co., 1897.

Jones, J. William. *Personal Reminiscences, Anecdotes, and Letters of General Robert E. Lee.* D. Appleton and Co., 1874.

*Journal of the Proceedings of Congress, 1774.* A Facsimile of the Official Edition Printed in 1774. Philadelphia: Printed for the Library Company of Philadelphia, 1974.

Lancaster, Bruce. *The American Revolution.* Garden City, NY: Garden City Books, 1957.

Lossing, Benson J. *Seventeen Hundred and Seventy-Six, or the War of Independence; a History of the Anglo Americans.* New York: Edward Walker, 1847.

Lutz, Donald S. "The Relative Influence of European Writers on Late Eighteenth-Century American Political Thought," *American Political Science Review*, Vol. 78, 1984.

Madison, James. *Journal of the Federal Convention.* Albert, Scott & Co., 1893.

Madison, James. *Notes of Debates in the Federal Convention of 1787 Reported by James Madison.* New York: W.W. Norton & Co., 1987.

Magoon, E.L. *Orators of the American Revolution.* New York: C. Scribner, 1857. Reprinted by Sightext Publications, El Segundo, California, 1969.

Marshall, Peter, and David Manuel. *The Light and the Glory.* Old Tappan, New Jersey: Fleming H. Revell, 1977.

Marshall, Peter, and David Manuel. *From Sea to Shining Sea.* Old Tappan, New Jersey: Fleming H. Revell, 1986.

McDowell, Bart. *The Revolutionary War.* Washington, D.C.: National Geographic Society, 1970.

McLaughlin, Andrew C. *Foundations of American Constitutionalism.* Greenwich, Conn.: Fawcett Publications, Inc., 1966.

Morris, B.F. *Christian Life and Character of the Civil Institutions of the United States.* Philadelphia: George W. Childs, 1864.

Morse, Jedidiah. *Annals of the American Revolution.* First published in 1824. Reissued, Port Washington, N.Y.: Kennikat Press, 1968.

Noll, Mark A., Nathan O. Hatch and George M. Marsden. *The Search for Christian America.* Westchester, Illinois: Crossway Books, 1983.

North, Gary. *Healer of the Nations, Biblical Principles for International Relations.* Fort Worth, Texas: Dominion Press, 1987.

North, Gary. *Honest Money,* Biblical Principles of Money and Banking. Ft. Worth, Texas: Dominion Press, 1986.

*Old South Leaflets.* Published by The Old South Association, Old South Meeting-house, Boston, Mass.

Owen, G. Frederick. *Abraham Lincoln: The Man and His Faith.* Tyndale House Publishers, Inc., 1981.

Padover, Saul K., editor. *The Complete Jefferson.* Tudor Publishing Co., 1943.

Peck, Jesse T. *The History of the Great Republic, Considered from a Christian Standpoint.* New York: Broughton and Wyman, 1868.

Pope, Norman V. "Educator, Minister, Patriot," in *Nation Under God,* Frances Brentano, editor. Great Neck, New York: Channel Press, 1957.

Powell, Edward A., and Rousas John Rushdoony. *Tithing and Dominion.* Vallecito, CA: Ross House Books, 1982.

"Proceedings of the Virginia Convention in the Town of Richmond on the 23rd of March, 1775, The." Richmond: Saint John's Church, original publication copyrighted in 1927.

"Providential Discovery of the Treason of Benedict Arnold--September 25th, 1780, The." San Francisco: Foundation for American Christian Education.

*Rebirth of America, The.* Arthur S. DeMoss Foundation, 1986.

*Remember William Penn, 1644-1944, a Tercentenary Memorial.* Compiled by the William Penn Tercentenary Committee. Harrisburg, PA: Commonwealth of Pennsylvania, 1945.

Rollin, Charles. *The Ancient History of the Egyptians, Carthaginians, Assyrians, Babylonians, Medes and Persians, Grecians, and Macedonians; including a History of the Arts and Sciences of the Ancients.* 2 volumes. New York: George Dearborn, 1836.

Rose, James B. *A Guide to American Christian Education for the Home and School, the Principle Approach.* Palo Cedro, CA: American Christian History Institute.

Rushdoony, Rousas John. *The Institutes of Biblical Law.* The Presbyterian and Reformed Publishing Company, 1973.

Rutherford, Samuel. *Lex Rex, or The Law and the Prince.* First published in 1644. Reprint, Harrisonburg, Va: Sprinkle Publications, 1982.

Rutland, Robert A., editor. *The Papers of James Madison.* University of Chicago Press, 1962.

Sandoz, Ellis, editor. *Political Sermons of the American Founding Era, 1730-1805.* Indianapolis: Liberty Press, 1991.

Schaeffer, Francis A. *How Should We Then Live?* Old Tappan, New Jersey: Fleming H. Revell Company, 1976.

Schaeffer, Francis A. *A Christian Manifesto.* Westchester, Illinois: Crossway Books, 1982.

Sidney, Algernon. *Discourses Concerning Government.* Edited by Thomas G. West. Indianapolis: Liberty Classics, 1990.

Skousen, W. Cleon. *The Making of America.* Washington, D.C.: The National Center for Constitutional Studies, 1985.

Skousen, W. Cleon. *Study Guide to the Making of America.* Washington, D.C.: The National Center for Constitutional Studies.

Slater, Rosalie J. *Teaching and Learning America's Christian History, the Principle Approach.* San Francisco: Foundation for American Christian Education, 1980.

Slater, Rosalie J. An essay on Noah Webster in the preface to a reprint of *An American Dictionary of the English Language* by Noah Webster, 1828. San Francisco: Foundation for American Christian Education, 1980.

Smyth, Albert Henry, editor. *Writings of Benjamin Franklin.* Macmillan Co., 1905-7.

Stedman, W. David, and LaVaughn G. Lewis, editors. *Our Ageless Constitution.* Asheboro, NC: W. David Stedman Associates, 1987.

Stoel, Caroline P., and Ann B. Clarke. *Magna Carta, Liberty Under the Law.* Portland, Oregon: published jointly by Magna Carta in America and Graphic Arts Center Publishing Co., 1986.

*Story of the Seal, The.* Merrimac, MA.: Destiny Publishers.

Thornton, John Wingate. *The Pulpit of the American Revolution.* Boston: Gould & Lincoln, 1860.

Tocqueville, Alexis de. *Democracy in America.* Edited by J.P. Mayer. Garden City, NY: Doubleday & Co., Inc., 1969.

Walton, Rus. *One Nation Under God.* Nashville: Thomas Nelson, 1987.

Walton, Rus. *Biblical Solutions to Contemporary Problems.* Brentwood, Tennessee: Wolgemuth & Hyatt, 1988.

Watson, Henry B. *George Washington, Architect of the Constitution.* Alexandria, Virginia: Patriotic Education, Inc., 1983.

Weaver, Robert B. *Our Flag and Other Symbols of Americanism.* Alexandria, Virginia: Patriotic Education, Inc., 1972.

Webster, Noah. *History of the United States.* New Haven: Durrie & Peck, 1833.

Wells, William V. *The Life and Public Services of Samuel Adams.* 3 volumes. Boston: Little, Brown, and Company, 1865.

Westerhoff III, John H. *McGuffey and His Readers.* Milford, Michigan: Mott Media, 1982.

Whitehead, John W. *The Second American Revolution.* Elgin, Illinois: David C. Cook Publishing Co., 1982.

Wilbur, William. *The Making of George Washington.* Alexandria, Virginia: Patriotic Education, Inc., 1973.

Willard, Emma. *A System of Universal History in Perspective.* Hartford: F.J. Huntington, 1835.

Willard, Emma. *History of the United States, or Republic of America.* New York: A.S. Barnes & Co., 1849.

# Index

## Bible References

## A

**The Foundation for American Christian Education**
P.O. Box 27035
San Francisco, CA 94127
415-661-1775

**Wallbuilders**
P.O. Box 397
Aledo, TX 76008
817-441-6044

**Heritage Institute Ministries**
P.O. Box 1353
Buzzards Bay, MA 02360
508-888-1889

**Plymouth Rock Foundation**
Fiske Mill
Marlborough, NH 03455
603-876-4685

**American Christian History Institute**
P.O. Box 648
Palo Cedro, CA 96073
916-547-3535

**Pilgrim Institute**
52549 Gumwood Road
Granger, IN 46530
219-277-1789

**Mayflower Institute**
P.O. Box 4673
Thousand Oaks, CA 91359

**Strategic Christian Services**
1221 Farmer's Lane, Suite B
Santa Rosa, CA 95405
707-578-2370

**American Vision**
P.O. Box 720515
Atlanta, GA 30328
404-988-0555

**Coalition On Revival**
789 E. El Camino Real
Sunnyvale, CA 94087

**Rutherford Institute**
P.O. Box 4782
Charlottesville, VA 22906-7482
804-978-3888

**Christian Advocates Serving Evangelism**
P.O. Box 450349
Atlanta, GA 30345
404-633-2444

**Family Research Council**
601 Pennsylvania Ave., N.W., Suite 901
Washington, D.C. 20004
202-393-2100

**Concerned Women for America**
370 L'Enfant Promenade S.W., Suite 800
Washington, D.C. 20004
202-488-7000

**Christian Coalition**
Box 1990
Chesapeake, VA 23320
804-424-2630

**Good News Communications**
2876 Mabry Rd., N.E.
Atlanta, GA 30319

# RESOURCE ORDER FORM

## BOOKS

|  | Price | Qty. | Total |
|---|---|---|---|
| **America's Providential History** | $15.95 | _____ | _____ |

How the Lord guided our nation from the very beginning. Proof from history: our nation grew from Christian principles. How to bring them back into the mainstream.

| **Liberating the Nations** | $12.95 | _____ | _____ |
|---|---|---|---|

God's plan, fundamental principles, essential foundations, and structures necessary to build Christian nations.

| **Defending the Declaration** | $11.95 | _____ | _____ |
|---|---|---|---|

How the Bible and Christianity influenced the writing of the Declaration of Independence.

| **Watchmen on the Walls** | $5.95 | _____ | _____ |
|---|---|---|---|

The role of pastors in equipping Christians to fulfill their civil duties.

| **In God We Trust** | $6.95 | _____ | _____ |
|---|---|---|---|

A Christian tour guide for historic sites in Washington D.C., Philadelphia and parts of Virginia.

| **Jefferson's Abridgement** | $5.95 | _____ | _____ |
|---|---|---|---|

An abridgement of the Words of Jesus of Nazareth as compiled by Thomas Jefferson while President. With an introductory essay on Jefferson's religious beliefs.

| **In Search of Democracy** | $4.95 | _____ | _____ |
|---|---|---|---|

The foundations, framework, and historical development of biblical government and law.

## Videos/Game

| **The Story of America's Liberty** | $19.95 | _____ | _____ |
|---|---|---|---|

A 65-minute video that looks at the influence of Christianity in the beginning of America, examining principles and providential occurrences.

| **Dawn's Early Light** | $19.95 | _____ | _____ |
|---|---|---|---|

A 28-minute version of The Story of America's Liberty with up-dated statistics.

| **America: the Game** | $29.95 | _____ | _____ |
|---|---|---|---|

An exciting way to learn about the history of America and God's hand in it. Over 2000 questions.

## Audios

America's Freedom: Founded on Faith; "No Cross, No Crown"; Reforming the Nations – an Example from the Life of Noah Webster; Teaching History from a Providential Perspective; The Principle Approach; God Governs in the Affairs of Men; Biblical Economics; Honest Money and Banking; Biblical Government and Law; Forming a Christian Union; Women: Preservers & Propagators of Liberty as Teachers of the Human Race; Fundamental Principles of Christian Nations; Christ's Teaching of Public Affairs; Biblical Principles of Business, Exemplified by Cyrus Hall McCormick.

List individual tapes:_____

| _____ | $4.95 | _____ | _____ |
|---|---|---|---|
| **In Search of Democracy** | $19.95 | _____ | _____ |

Four-tape series on the foundations, framework, and historical development of biblical government and law.

| **The Principle Approach to Education for Home or Church Schools** | $99.95 | _____ | _____ |
|---|---|---|---|

A biblical approach to teaching the academic subjects. Includes 24 tapes and a 160-page manual.

|  |  |
|---|---|
| Subtotal | _____ |
| Shipping (10% with $2.50 minimum; Game $4.50) | _____ |
| TOTAL | _____ |

Name_____ Address_____

City_____ State_____ Zip_____

Make checks payable to and order from: Providence Foundation, P.O. Box 6759, Charlottesville, VA 22906